PRAISE FOR *LOCAL DOLLARS, LOCAL SENSE*

"There is no task more urgent facing this country than rebuilding local economies, and Michael Shuman knows this inside and out. This book should be required reading for Americans."
— **James Howard Kunstler**, author of *The Long Emergency* and other books

"This long-awaited book is a masterpiece and a field guide to a much-needed journey into creating the kind of economy our children will be happy to inherit. Future generations will praise *Local Dollars, Local Sense* as one of those seminal works that helped transform human societies."
— **John Perkins**, author of *Confessions of an Economic Hitman* and *Hoodwinked*

"Michael Shuman answers a lot of questions I've always wondered about, and in the process paints a practical vision of exactly where we need to be headed in this country. Consider this book an excellent investment!"
— **Bill McKibben**, author of *Eaarth* and *The End of Nature*

"Want something that makes sense amid the increasingly crazy world of global finance? Going local is it and Michael Shuman has been at the forefront of this cutting-edge thinking for more than a decade. He not only maps the emerging process of economic localization, but also gets down to the nitty gritty: the investment strategies and the financial practitioners who are making it real."
— **Woody Tasch**, chairman, Slow Money; chairman emeritus, Investor's Circle; and author of *Inquiries into the Nature of Slow Money*

"Brilliant and perfectly timed, *Local Dollars, Local Sense* enables us to transform worry and confusion about our personal finances, and the nation's, into rewarding action. Shuman shows us—in part with compelling stories—how investment choices are really exciting sources of power to achieve peace of mind for our families as we create thriving, democratic communities. I love this ground-breaking, liberating book!"
— **Frances Moore Lappé**, author of *EcoMind: Changing the Way We Think, to Create the World We Want*

"Where to invest your money in these uncertain times? Bring it home, advises Michael Shuman. But don't put it under the mattress! This smart and thoughtful book explains the many ways we can invest in our local economies to not only receive a more reliable return than the stock market casino can provide, but also to live in more self-reliant and joyful communities. Join the shift toward true prosperity. This book shows you how."
— **Judy Wicks**, cofounder of Business Alliance for Local Living Economies

"Local small businesses employ more people and respond to community needs better than big corporations do—but nearly all our investment dollars support Wall Street banks and huge companies. The path to local investing has been strewn with obstacles. Michael Shuman clears a path for us all, showing how local investing can help solve some of America's biggest social, economic, environmental, and political problems. This is a book many of us have been waiting for."
— **Richard Heinberg**, author of *The End of Growth* and *Peak Everything*

"Prepare to rethink everything you've learned about investing! In this tour de force, Michael Shuman provides an eye-opening look at how local companies can trump market returns, and how legalized crowdfunding might do more for job creation than the failed policies of throwing taxpayer money at big corporations. The book abounds with examples of community investment that are helping to rebuild local economies, and provides a tantalizing glimpse of life beyond corporate capitalism."

—**Amy Cortese**, author of *Locavesting: The Revolution in
Local Investing and How to Profit from It*

"*Local* is the new *green*, because *local* encompasses the wholeness of real places—nature and people and the complex web of relationships among them. Living on an island, I have a special appreciation for local resilience. I know my community is my real security. My bank. The financial system makes it easy to invest in distant corporations and difficult to invest in our own neighbors' start-ups and business expansions. Enter Michael Shuman and this wonderful book, *Local Dollars, Local Sense*. He outlines many practical innovations that can flow money back into the productivity and prosperity of the places we call home. With the growing interest in moving our money out of Wall Street and into Main Street, Michael's book provides a very welcome road map for local investing."

—**Vicki Robin**, author of *Your Money or Your Life*

"Changing the direction our money flows in away from the tax havens and the banks and toward the urgent rebuilding of community resilience at the local scale is one of our most pressing and urgent tasks. Michael Shuman inspires and equips us for this work with great vision and purpose."

—**Rob Hopkins**, author of *The Transition Companion*
and cofounder of the Transition Network

"How can we secure our personal finances while simultaneously helping to rebuild our communities? Read this book and find out. Michael Shuman's advice urgently needs to be heeded. Authoritative yet highly readable, *Local Dollars, Local Sense* illuminates the path toward a very different economy, providing practical advice that is more intensely relevant with every passing day."

—**Helena Norberg-Hodge**, founder of International Society
for Ecology and Culture; producer of *The Economics of Happiness*

"Michael Shuman has done it again. In *Local Dollars, Local Sense*, he answers the central question of the era: How does capital get invested? Whether you are concerned with job creation, environmental destruction, immigration, public health, or education, this book will not only tell you why things are going wrong, it will tell you how we can make things right."

—**Kevin Danaher**, cofounder of Global Exchange and Green Festivals

"In an important and path-breaking work, Michael Shuman shows clearly and persuasively how to transform our nation's financial system from a destructive engine for increasing economic inequality into a positive force for creating human well-being and community resilience. . . . *Local Dollars, Local Sense* must be required reading for every elected official in the country as well as all 'experts' in finance and business from the academic and corporate worlds."

—**H. Thomas Johnson**, professor of sustainability management,
Portland State University, and author of *Profit Beyond Measure*

LOCAL DOLLARS, LOCAL SENSE

LOCAL DOLLARS, LOCAL SENSE

**HOW TO SHIFT YOUR MONEY FROM
WALL STREET TO MAIN STREET
AND ACHIEVE REAL PROSPERITY**

MICHAEL H. SHUMAN

Foreword by PETER BUFFETT

A COMMUNITY RESILIENCE GUIDE

CHELSEA GREEN PUBLISHING
WHITE RIVER JUNCTION, VERMONT

Editor: Joni Praded
Developmental Editor: Daniel Lerch
Copy Editor: Laura Jorstad
Proofreader: Eileen Clawson
Indexer: Margaret Holloway
Designer: Peter Holm, Sterling Hill Productions

Printed in the United States of America
First printing January, 2012
10 9 8 7 6 5 4 3 2 1   12 13 14 15 16

Our Commitment to Green Publishing
Chelsea Green sees publishing as a tool for cultural change and ecological stewardship. We strive to align our book manufacturing practices with our editorial mission and to reduce the impact of our business enterprise in the environment. We print our books and catalogs on chlorine-free recycled paper, using vegetable-based inks whenever possible. This book may cost slightly more because we use recycled paper, and we hope you'll agree that it's worth it. Chelsea Green is a member of the Green Press Initiative (www.greenpressinitiative.org), a nonprofit coalition of publishers, manufacturers, and authors working to protect the world's endangered forests and conserve natural resources. *Local Dollars, Local Sense* was printed on FSC®-certified paper supplied by Thomson-Shore that contains at least 30 percent postconsumer recycled fiber.

Library of Congress Cataloging-in-Publication Data
Shuman, Michael.
  Local dollars, local sense : how to shift your money from Wall Street to Main Street and achieve real prosperity / Michael H. Shuman ; foreword by Peter Buffett.
     p. cm.
  Includes bibliographical references and index.
  ISBN 978-1-60358-343-5 (pbk.) -- ISBN 978-1-60358-344-2 (ebook) 1. Community development. 2. Communities--Economic aspects. 3. Economic development. 4. Regional economics. I. Title.
  HN49.C6S58 2012
  332.6--dc23
                        2011042189

Chelsea Green Publishing Company
85 North Main Street, Suite 120
White River Junction, VT 05001
(802) 295-6300
www.chelseagreen.com

In Memory of Jack Jacob Shuman (1922–2010)

INTRODUCTION TO THE
COMMUNITY RESILIENCE GUIDES

In the twenty-first century, we face a set of interconnected economic, energy, and environmental crises that require all the courage, creativity, and cooperation we can muster. These crises are forcing us to fundamentally rethink some of our most basic assumptions, like where our food and energy come from, and where we invest our savings.

While national and international leadership are key to navigating the bumpy road ahead, that leadership thus far is sadly wanting. And, in any case, many of the best responses to these challenges are inherently local.

Thankfully, a small but growing movement of engaged citizens, community groups, businesses, and local elected officials are leading the way. These early actors have worked to reduce consumption, produce local food and energy, invest in local economies, and preserve local ecosystems. While diverse, the essence of these efforts is the same: a recognition that the world is changing and the old way of doing things no longer works.

Post Carbon Institute has partnered with Chelsea Green Publishing to publish this series of Community Resilience Guides to detail some of the most inspiring and replicable of these efforts. Why community resilience? *Community*, because we believe that the most effective ways to work for the future we want are grounded in local relationships—with our families and neighbors, with the ecological resources that sustain us, and with the public institutions through which we govern ourselves. *Resilience*, because the complex economic, energy, and environmental challenges we face require not solutions that make problems go away but responses that recognize our vulnerabilities, build our capacities, and adapt to unpredictable changes.

These are frightening, challenging times. But they are also full of opportunity. We hope these guides inspire you and help you build resilience in your own community.

Asher Miller
Executive Director
Post Carbon Institute

CONTENTS

What kind of world do we want to live in? One that lasts for our children, their children, children of people we'll never know? Or one that is, as it is now, consumptive beyond its capacities?

Most Americans understand that we're in the midst of a financial crisis, with unemployment stubbornly stuck between 9 and 10 percent and poverty worsening for millions of our fellow citizens. But we're also about to face a deeper crisis still as oil runs out, as climate change and other environmental shocks take hold, and as the American dollar ceases to be the world's reserve currency and weakens our ability to influence global events.

Being my father Warren's son, I've certainly learned that investment matters! And how we prioritize our savings shapes our future. For the last generation or two, many of us have invested our savings in Fortune 500 companies through our stocks, bonds, and retirement accounts. When these companies were embedded in American life, employing Americans and supporting our communities, that investment was sensible. But the road to profitability has taken some treacherous turns. Today, too many of these companies have largely abandoned America and their communities for over-seas manufacturing, markets, and tax havens.

Prioritizing Fortune 500 investments necessarily meant neglecting locally owned businesses. These local businesses comprise more than half the U.S. economy by output and jobs. A growing body of evidence suggests that these businesses are remarkably profitable and competitive (for example, they've maintained their share of U.S. GDP since 1990). Moreover, we know these businesses are the best job producers per dollar of investment or purchasing. They also have the ability to promote local entrepreneurship, smart growth, environmental stewardship, political participation, and social harmony. I do not believe that there is a solution to our current socioeconomic challenges without renewing our support for local business—especially our investment in them.

The values I experienced growing up long emphasized real wealth over phantom wealth and long-term investing over short-term speculation. And I witnessed the power of community and family loyalty over anonymous profit maximization. Increasingly, the investments that meet these values are in local business.

The reality today is that even though local businesses comprise more than half the economy, almost none of our savings support them. Our short-term savings, in banks, have been increasingly consolidated in a small number of multistate banks, which lend less to local business than do local banks and credit unions. And our long-term savings are almost 100 percent invested in nonlocal business. I believe this is a huge market failure.

A key to this failure is that most Americans are not allowed to invest in local businesses. This is partially a consequence of outdated securities laws passed during the Great Depression. These laws make it impossibly difficult and expensive for "unaccredited investors," which 98 percent of Americans are, to put even small investments into small business. The time is right to reform these laws, even as we ratchet up laws on hedge funds, speculation, derivatives, and other risky activities largely done by the 2 percent of the public that's accredited.

This book shows how local investment by unaccredited investors, even without legal reform, is possible: through cooperatives and through loans that members can make to their expansion; through local banks and the creative use of deposits; through community-development financial institutions; through presales, peer-to-peer lending, and community networks of businesses and investors; through direct public offerings within a given state; through local investment clubs and local revolving loan funds; and through emerging local stock market and local mutual funds. While most of these initiatives are still in their early stages of development, the immediate evidence is that smart investing through these methods can deliver at least as good a return as Wall Street's.

You may be surprised to read that the historic returns of Wall Street, once you remove inflation and other accounting tricks, is in the range of 2.5–3.5

percent per year. This is a benchmark that certainly local business can
Indeed, other forms of local investment that one can control—investing in
one's house, energy efficiency, garden, or education—can probably generate
a better annual return than the stock market.

The world is constantly changing. *Revolution* should not be a scary word.
It has three basic definitions: rotation, rebellion, transformation. Great
moments of history are written when what is usually just rotation—cycles
of nature, repetitious—becomes transformative.

The American Revolution did not happen in 1776. It took several decades,
at least, to achieve the transformative qualities that we mark in that year. It
was 100 years between the Civil War and Civil Rights, and we are still on a
march toward greater social justice.

As the saying goes, "when you have a hammer, everything looks like a
nail." Systems define the process. But if the nail changes, the hammer must
eventually change, too.

Ultimately, this is a book about changing nails. Lots of them. Because the
hammer that is our socioeconomic structure (with a large dose of techno-
cultural mash) cannot last. Nothing does. At some point the repetition
becomes too much. And the opportunity for a new (r)evolution emerges.

Evolution: development, growth, advancement.

The fear of the idea of things being different—the end of the world as we
know it—is joined by the accompanying realization that a revolution also
brings certain core principles back around. Not the end of the world as we
know it . . . but a return of fundamental aspects of human nature that have
always existed: community, relationship, connection—connection to the
impact of our investments, to the source of our food, to our footprint on
the planet.

This book provides a clear map that Americans can follow—as individuals,
as communities, and as entrepreneurs—for simultaneously revitalizing their
communities *and* their personal bottom lines.

PETER BUFFETT

ACKNOWLEDGMENTS

My last book, *The Small-Mart Revolution*, thanked several hundred people promoting localization ideas and innovations. I will spare Earth's forests and not repeat all their names here, but I nevertheless wish to tip my hat to the leaders of what is becoming one of the fastest-growing, most powerful movements of our time. You know who you are, and you have my continued appreciation for the inspiring work you do.

The idea of writing this book was originally raised by Asher Miller and Daniel Lerch of the Post Carbon Institute, and they ultimately became my sponsors, partners, and taskmasters. Both were extraordinarily generous in giving me wide latitude to shape this work as I saw fit, and in extending deadlines when it was clear that my dad (to whom I dedicate this book) was entering his final months of life. Funding came in part from the Lydia B. Stokes Foundation, through the trustees Nancy Deren, Tom Willits, and Thalia Venerable.

My partners at Cutting Edge Capital, Jenny Kassan and John Katovich, have been my most important teachers in helping me to understand the bizarre and arcane field of securities law. My colleagues currently involved at the Business Alliance for Local Living Economies (BALLE), who have organized national webinars and workshops around "community capital," deserve special thanks, especially Grant Abert, Baye Adofo-Wilson, Alissa Barron, Matt Bauer, Leslie Christian, Merrian Fuller, Laury Hammel, David Korten, Michelle Long, Derrell Ness, Jamilla Payne, Paul Saginaw, Don Shaffer, Andy Shallal, Ellen Shepard, Elizabeth Ü, Judy Wicks, and Sandy Wiggins.

I'm grateful to the more than three dozen individuals who submitted to interviews for this book. They constitute some of the brightest thinkers and leaders in the emerging field of local investing, and I encourage readers to continue following their work.

Amy Cortese, author of *Locavesting* (2011), which I commend to anyone who enjoys this book, generously shared her manuscript ahead of publication, enabling the two of us to shape our books to be complementary and to highlight different case studies.

To my manuscript readers—Amy Cortese, John J. Dill II, Jeff Mansour, Jenny Kassan, and David Spector—sincere thanks for the many mistakes they caught and great tweaks they suggested.

My biggest thanks—by far—goes to Kate Poole, one of the finest research assistants I have ever had. She conducted interviews for the book with remarkable persistence, enthusiasm, and intelligence.

Finally, I wish to thank those closest to me—my mom, my sister, my children (Adam and Rachel), and my friends—for tolerating my absences over the past year as I wrote on a publication schedule that sometimes felt like the Bataan March.

My dad was a reliable reviewer of all my previous books, and I regret that he will never read this one. Dad died on the same day in December 2010 that Bernie Madoff's son, Mark, committed suicide. As I elaborate in the last chapter of this book, Dad couldn't have been more different from the man who became a billionaire by fraud. Dad lived like a king on a modest budget. He taught my sister and me to value the people around us not by the size of their wallet, but by the depth of their character. Unlike poor Mark Madoff, I am grateful to be able to embrace the memory of my father through this book with the kind of pride that money can't buy.

Throughout most of the day on May 6, 2010, stocks on the major exchanges were faring poorly. Western banks had decided to cut off credit to Greece.

This was a huge turnaround. A decade earlier, a huge opportunity was seen in extending cheap credit to millions of Greeks who were long accustomed to stashing cash in their pillows and loaning exclusively to relatives. Ignoring their own history at Troy—to beware of strangers bearing gifts—the Greeks acceded to Western bankers, and their appetite for credit grew into the same addiction that now afflicts almost every developed economy in the world. Like the millions of Americans whose credit cards are now unpayable, the Greeks, by May 2010, had become "unbankable."

Foreseeing a wave of bankruptcies that could shake up the global economy, investors on May 6 were now moving their money out of corporate stocks and into safer financial instruments like bonds, CDs, and cash. By the early afternoon, the value of the New York Stock Exchange and the NASDAQ had shrunk by 3 percent. Shortly after 2:30 PM Eastern Time, investors noticed that the already slumping curves on their computer screens were suddenly spiking downward. Stocks were down 4 percent—no, 5 percent. Stop orders (in which traders automatically seek to sell securities losing value) submitted hours, days, or even weeks earlier were suddenly executed. But because there weren't enough buyers for the sellers, prices continued to plunge, and panic ensued. Minus 6 percent, minus 7 percent, minus 8 percent.

"On the trading floor of the New York Stock Exchange," *The New York Times* reported the next day, "traders shouted or watched open-mouthed as the screens lighted up with plummeting prices and as phones rang off the hook. 'It was almost like *The Twilight Zone*,' said Theodore R. Aronson of Aronson, Johnson & Ortiz, a money management firm in Philadelphia."[1]

Some traders wondered if their eyes had failed them—maybe the 8 was really a 3. But their vision was perfect. Some stocks suddenly lost nearly all their value. Accenture Corp., which had been trading at $40 per share, was down to a penny in minutes. Where would it end? Investors stared at their monitors with dismay and saw their wealth and their dreams disappear.

Then at around 2:45 PM, as if the finance fairies had finally descended, the markets began to rebound. Minus 7 percent, minus 6 percent. Investors caught their breath, thinking—well, hoping—maybe this *was* a fluke. Minus 5 percent, minus 4 percent. And that's more or less where things stood still until the markets closed at 4:00 PM.

The Securities and Exchange Commission (SEC) hastily called emergency meetings of the exchange leaders to sort out what had caused the meltdown. Were there bugs in the computer programs? Had a few big hedge fund transactions triggered the sudden collapse? Were there appropriate brakes in place to prevent calamities like this from happening again? Should preposterous transactions—like those yielding a 10,000 percent return in three minutes—be undone? What was not on the table—but definitely on the minds of millions of Americans—was whether we should continue to rely on a system where our life savings could vanish in literally seconds.

Over the past three years, investors—ranging from the biggest hedge fund managers like George Soros to modestly investing pensioners—have been on a terrifying roller-coaster ride. For a few months in late 2008 and early 2009, the global economy teetered on the abyss. What started as a modest tempest, with several billion dollars of housing loans going bad, intensified into a Category Five hurricane. Various financial instruments that had leveraged these loans, such as the now infamous credit default swaps (CDSs), became worthless. Investment giant Lehman Brothers went bust, and the insurance titan AIG almost followed. Many other large banks teetered on the brink. Only through the intervention of both the outgoing and incoming presidential administrations, as well as an unusually united Congress, were they saved through what became known as TARP—the Toxic Assets Relief Program. Millions of Americans were not as lucky and lost their homes, and one out of four found themselves "underwater," owing more on their mortgages than their houses were now worth.

By 2010, the crisis appeared to ease a bit. Stock markets regained some of their value, and some regions saw home values stabilize; but the official unemployment rate hovered ominously between 9 and 10 percent despite nearly a trillion dollars of government stimulus. Congress assembled a new package of financial reforms to prevent a repeat. And a consensus emerged that the worst of the crisis was over. Until May 6.

Some financial crises pass quickly. The 1987 stock market crash was like that, and by the late 1990s a new generation of day traders was convincing analysts like James Glassman and Kevin Hassett to title their book *Dow 36,000: The New Strategy for Profiting from the Coming Rise in the Stock Market.* The country also recovered in a few years from the popping of the tech bubble in the late 1990s. But this crisis is different. Millions of Americans are seriously asking whether they can continue to entrust their retirement and their kids' education to such a rickety financial system. They want to put their money to work in the enterprises they know and care about. They want to invest in their own schools, hospitals, factories, and homes. For the first time in generations, they are thinking about how to invest *locally*.

The financial experts running Wall Street insist this is silly. Local businesses—that is, those connected to a particular place and owned by geographically proximate members—are unreliable, the backwater of the old economy, not the places where serious investors should place their money. But what truly has become ridiculous is continuing to pour our hard-earned dollars, month after month, into global businesses and stock market casinos that increasingly bear no relationship to our own prosperity. Real prosperity must begin at home.

The $15 Trillion Shift

America's investment system is broken. Even though roughly half the jobs and the output in the economy come from local small business, almost all our investment dollars go into big corporations on Wall Street. The overall wealth of the country is more than $150 trillion.[2] Some of this wealth is held in the form of land, buildings, and machinery and is considered "illiquid"—not very easy to convert into dollars. The most liquid assets held by households and nonprofits are stocks, bonds, mutual funds, pension funds, and life insurance funds, and at the end of 2010 these totaled about $30 trillion. To put this number in perspective, all the production in the United States each year—the gross domestic product (GDP)—currently totals about $15 trillion. So Americans have double their GDP in long-term savings. *Not even 1 percent of these savings touches local small business.*

Were local businesses uncompetitive, unprofitable, and obsolete for the U.S. economy, this gap would be understandable. But as we will see, local businesses are actually more profitable than larger corporations—and their competitiveness is impressive despite decades of inattention from policymakers and economic developers. This investment gap represents a huge market failure. It means that Americans are systematically overinvesting in Wall Street and underinvesting in Main Street. Were this $30 trillion allocated efficiently, at least $15 trillion would move into locally owned small businesses.

Imagine the kinds of new businesses and economic revitalization that would be possible with a $15 trillion shift. To put this number in perspective, it represents twenty times more money than all the funding the federal government allocated in the first national stimulus program of 2009–2010. It represents about $50,000 for every American man, woman, and child. For even a small town of five thousand, this shift would make $250 million available for starting or expanding local business. For a suburban town of fifty thousand, it would mean $2.5 billion more of capital. For a metro area of half a million, $25 billion more would be available.

What stands in the way of this shift is obsolete institutions and laws that make local investment extremely difficult and expensive. Securities laws from the Great Depression effectively enacted a system of investment apartheid, with "accredited investors" being able to invest in any business they wish and unaccredited investors being essentially told to get lost. Accredited investors make up the richest 2 percent of Americans—those who earn more than $200,000 (or $300,000 with a spouse) or have more than $1 million in assets, excluding their primary residence. As long as entrepreneurs don't lie about their business plans, governance, and numbers, they can easily approach any "accredited" investor for money. The other 98 percent of us are "unaccredited" and presumed too gullible to invest in a company without massive legal paperwork. Before a business can make an investment "offering" to even a single unaccredited investor, it must pay an attorney to produce a private placement memorandum and various regulatory filings and documents; legal, accounting, and government fees could easily run $25,000 to $50,000. If a company wants many unaccredited investors, it must create a public offering that could cost another $50,000 or more, and it then must make ongoing, exhaustive filings to the SEC.

The thick offering documents are frankly worthless to the layperson for whom they were written to protect. They are filled with turgid, legalistic prose that lives on lawyers' hard drives. Often these documents are printed IN A TINY FONT IN ALL CAPITAL LETTERS THAT NO HUMAN BEING HAS EVER BEEN OBSERVED TO READ. Besides ensuring full employment for attorneys, securities law can claim one stunning achievement: It has managed to keep small investors away from small businesses. Again, 98 percent of the American public cannot invest in more than half of the economy.

This exclusion is especially galling given that there's overwhelming evidence that local businesses are the most important sources of new income, wealth, and jobs for communities. At a time when *official* U.S. unemployment is at its highest levels since the Great Depression, the sluggishness with which either political party has sought to fix this problem by reforming securities law and promoting local investment is stunning.

Most Americans, of course, don't really invest in individual companies. They take advantage of tax laws to place small percentages of their paychecks into their individual retirement accounts (IRAs) and 401(k) accounts sheltered from income taxes. But for any investor—accredited or unaccredited—who wishes to put this money into a portfolio of local businesses, the market failure is just as bad. There is not a single mutual fund or investment broker in the country that gives "retail" investors the opportunity to invest in a portfolio of local businesses. The curious investor who presses her broker or financial advisor for some local-investment options is told, condescendingly, that these small businesses are too risky and their profits too insignificant to bother with, even though there's compelling evidence, as we'll see, that they are less risky and more profitable than the Fortune 500.

What about the socially responsible investment movement—the Calverts and the Pax World Funds? Aren't more and more Americans telling their investment brokers to screen their funds so that they are no longer investing in cigarettes, nuclear weapons, or toxic dump? In fact, socially responsible investment, despite laudable intentions, is simply about removing the most offensive global businesses from one's portfolio. When I set up my very first IRA in the mid-1980s, I chose Pax World for exactly this reason. It never dawned on me that despite the screens I was still investing in lots of reprehensible companies. For many years, highly rated companies on SRI lists included Walmart, Home Depot, and Starbucks—the Death Stars for local retailers, hardware stores, and coffeehouses. Not a few SRI investors pumped up portfolios with U.S. federal government bonds, which might cause the morally attentive investor to worry that they were unintentionally propping up their least favorite federal boondoggle. Municipal bonds were also common, even though many of these were financing the corporate attraction and retention policies that were wrecking local businesses. The possibility of investing directly in local businesses was not even on the table.

Our current investment system has utterly failed local companies, irrespective of their value, performance, and profitability. It all but requires that we invest in the global, publicly traded corporations. And it all but forces a successful local entrepreneur looking for more capital—whether it's to grow the company, to cash out and retire, or to move on and start another venture—to go public or sell out to a big nonlocal company. The absence of local exit mechanisms explains, for example, why a great local business like Tom's of Maine, known for its natural toothpastes, was willing to be bought by Colgate. Had robust local-investment markets been in place, perhaps Ben & Jerry's would never have been gobbled up by Unilever, or the Body Shop by L'Oréal, or Stonyfield Yogurt by Dannon, or Odwalla Juices by Coke.

Elizabeth Ü, a rising star in the local-investment field and author of a forthcoming how-to guide called *Finance for Food: A Sustainable Food Entrepreneur's Guide to Raising Mission-Aligned Capital*, observes, "For those companies that would prefer to stay small or stay in their communities, that do not want to become the next organic behemoth in some big box stores around the country, what kinds of financing models can we create that will serve their needs? Today, we run the risk of matching up our best entrepreneurs with investors who don't necessarily share their values. When we look at capital markets for, say, local food businesses, there are insufficient capital tools available to serve the needs of the vast majority of entrepreneurs, much less the investors who would like to support them."

From Wall Street to Vall Street

Another approach to investment can be found in rural Sweden. Exasperated by mainstream financial institutions that had been sucking up the savings of businesses and residents in Åres Gröna Dalar for investments thousands of miles away, an organization called Fjällbete organized some simple ways to invest in local food production. Everyone from modest farmers to wealthy venture capitalists in the region can now invest in sheep, their sheds, their grazing land, and machinery for processing their wool and meat. People can buy shares of these capital assets and then trade them with one another. Because a land embankment defining the edge of a sheep-grazing area is called a *vallen* in Swedish, the locals joke that this is their Vall Street.

This book is about how every community in America can replace Wall Street with Vall Street. It describes dozens of practical ways people are already investing their money in local enterprises they know and trust. These innovations involve investment instruments that are simple and transparent, which means that the risks can be easily evaluated and the chances of fraud can be minimized.

We need Vall Streets to correct a market failure that exists not only in the United States but throughout the world. Even though the majority of the Earth's nearly seven billion inhabitants live at or near poverty levels, their national governments—irrespective of size, wealth, and politics—have historically focused their economic-development investments on big business. A global consensus is emerging, however, that a key to ending poverty in the most distressed corners of the planet is to seed and spread small and microenterprises. Traditional public-sector improvements in education, health, and other quality-of-life factors can only be sustained in communities generating their own wealth, and this is only possible in communities rich in entrepreneurs.

The foundation for entrepreneurship is ownership. In *The Mystery of Capital: Why Capitalism Triumphs in the West and Fails Everywhere Else*, Hernando de Soto demonstrates the importance of legal reforms to clear ownership title to land and capital so that entrepreneurs can put these economic inputs to productive use. Muhammad Yunus won the Nobel Peace Prize for his efforts to bring microentrepreneurs into the financial mainstream through micro-credit and micro-ownership. New web tools like Prosper.com and Kiva.org are enabling almost any lender to find even the smallest and most unconventional loan opportunities. Yet thus far these innovations have facilitated a global democratic revolution not around ownership, but around debt.

Debt can be a helpful tool for entrepreneurs, but it also can be counterproductive and imprisoning. Microentrepreneurs around the world now have IOUs from unscrupulous lenders who are charging usurious interest rates. The same predicament confronts Americans who were pressured by fly-by-night financial institutions into taking on more credit card debt and larger mortgages than they really could afford. Ditto for millions of residents of Greece, Portugal, Italy, and other countries in trouble, where debtors now have little hope of paying back their debts.

What's now needed across the planet is *microequity* and other forms of local investing that shatter the monopoly of the world's financial elite. De Soto's conclusion that the historically miserable state of the law in Latin America has crippled small businesses is equally true in developed countries like ours. Indeed, the need for overhauling investment laws and practices worldwide could not be more urgent. The Earth is now beset by a growing number of crises. Reasonable people can disagree about their causes and solutions, but there's little disagreement about the mounting dangers: The climate is changing. Once plentiful supplies of cheap petroleum are running out. Species are disappearing at an accelerating pace. Fish stocks in the world's oceans are being exhausted. Farmland and prime topsoil are fast disappearing. Weapons of mass destruction are spreading into more hands. The freer global movement of goods and services means the freer global movement of germs, migrants, and terrorism. All of these dangers will intensify as the number of people placing demands on the world's resources grows, as expected, to eight billion people by 2025.

What can we do about a world that is slipping into an epoch of unprecedented instability? To a growing number of people, the answer is to *go local*: Make my community more resilient and help other communities globally do the same. William Rees, one of the architects of the concept of an ecological footprint, defines *resilience* as "the capacity of a system to withstand disturbance while still retaining its fundamental structure, function, and internal feedbacks."[3] The more communities can feed, house, educate, transport, and care for themselves, the more they can manufacture their own goods and provide their own services, and the less vulnerable they will be to the coming financial challenges. This presents new opportunities to create and expand local businesses to meet local needs. And seizing these opportunities requires new local-investment tools that rechannel our savings into priorities at home.

About a decade ago, I teamed up with a dozen other people sharing these views—entrepreneurs, investors, policy analysts, and big-picture thinkers—to form the Business Alliance for Local Living Economies (BALLE), promoting the idea that economic power should reside locally. The term *local living economy* ties together two intellectual strands. The first concerns localism, expounded in such early works as E. F. Schumacher's *Small Is Beautiful* (1973) and Jane Jacobs's *Cities and the Wealth of Nations* (1985), as well as my own books, *Going Local* (1998) and *The Small-Mart Revolution* (2006), which made the case that local ownership of business and community self-reliance are key requirements for prosperous local economies. The second is from the writings of David Korten on the importance of a "living economy" rooted in smaller, more accountable businesses. In recent years, many in the BALLE community have come to understand the critical importance of local investment, and how new practices, tools, and institutions can and should be used to achieve what we call a living rate of return—a return that's real, honest, dependable, and modest, yet big enough to enable a prudent family to secure reasonable income security before and after retirement and to bestow a decent upbringing and education for its children.

When I started working in community economics in the mid-1990s, almost no one took the field seriously. The book editor of *The Washington Post* said she would not review a book like *Going Local*, because why would a *national* audience care about *local* activities? At the first stop on that book's speaking tour, at the University of Kentucky, two people showed up—and one left early. I am now on the road almost half-time, speaking to three or four dozen communities each year, and everywhere I go, whether red states or blue states, cities or cow towns, hundreds of people show up eager to talk about their local economy. Any doubts about the penetration of the buy-local movement were put to rest when *Time* magazine put on its March 12, 2007 cover, "Forget Organic, Eat Local." The movement for local purchasing is fast evolving into a movement for local investing—which is why I recently created, with two colleagues, a new consulting company called Cutting Edge

Capital to meet the burgeoning needs of local nonprofits, businesses, and communities.

The Journey Ahead

This book shows how Americans are beginning to create their own Vall Streets to earn a living rate of return. It is about how determined, ordinary people are exploiting exceptions, loopholes, or quirks in securities law to invest locally. It also suggests ripe areas for legal reforms that could greatly speed up local investing—and stimulate a dying economy—without costing the taxpaying public a penny. While mostly from the United States, the examples here also suggest some investment tools and strategies that people living in other countries might deploy for revitalizing their own local businesses.

Chapter 1, "A Living Rate of Return," documents the financial risks of continuing to invest as we have been. It shows that the returns Wall Street has historically achieved are not the 8 to 12 percent its enthusiasts claim but rather 3 to 5 percent. Unless Americans change their investment habits—and fast—millions will be shocked to find themselves retiring in abject poverty.

Chapter 2, "Zero-Cost Stimulus," lays out the positive case for investing in local business. It reviews the evidence about what works in economic development and shows that the most prosperous communities follow three rules: They maximize the percentage of their workforce in locally owned businesses. They increase local self-reliance through the production of local goods and services, knowing that many of these businesses will grow into regional and global powerhouses. And they identify and replicate local business models with high labor and environmental standards. For this kind of economic development to succeed, the critical challenge is to channel local capital into increasingly profitable and competitive local businesses.

Chapter 3, "The Hidden Power of Cooperatives," looks at a sector of the U.S. economy that can comply with securities laws most easily. There are some thirty thousand cooperatives in the country owned by workers, producers, or consumers. They are involved in everything from housing, groceries, and credit to utilities, telecommunications, and insurance. We look at the creative ways cooperatives are borrowing from their members and reinvesting their members' capital in other local businesses.

Chapter 4, on "Institutional Lending," explores the cutting edge of business borrowing. Keenly aware that local banks and credit unions are much better at investing in local business than are global banks, millions of Americans have recently moved their money. Others have entered partnerships with their local depositories to create special certificates of deposit (CDs) to collateralize targeted small-business loans. We also see how municipal bonds ("slow munis") and state-owned banks like North Dakota's can catalyze more local business lending.

Chapter 5, on "Anti-Poverty Investing," looks at the field of community development, which has been one of the principal sources of local-investment innovation since the 1960s. Funded largely by government agencies, foundations, do-good banks, and philanthropists, the activities in this field include community-development corporations, microenterprise lending, community-development venture capital funds, and state-financed job funds. These initiatives, once dismissed as charitable aberrations, are increasingly being seen as a lucrative market niche for creative local investors.

Chapter 6 is titled "If I Were A Rich Man . . ." and looks at the remarkable options available to accredited investors. We will visit a holding company in the Pacific Northwest, Upstream 21, where investors can support an evolving network of local businesses. We'll see the work of local-investment "angels" in the small town of Fairfield, Iowa, with so many start-ups it's called *Silicorn* Valley. We'll see how a green restaurateur in Oakland raised money from local accredited investors.

Chapter 7 focuses on "Unaccredited Investing in SEC-Land." It looks at creative investment strategies local businesses have deployed to avoid or reduce the costs of securities law compliance. Some businesses like Awaken Café in Oakland are pre-selling coffee to raise money for a new store. Others are tapping into crowdfunding donations and "micropatronage" through websites like Kickstarter and IndieGoGo. A community organization, LION, in Port Townsend, Washington, builds relationships among local investors and entrepreneurs. My partners at Cutting Edge Capital are lowering the costs of direct public offerings through simple, fill-in-the-blanks forms.

Chapter 8 looks at the Holy Grail for local investing: the deployment of "Local Exchanges," Internet-based spaces where unaccredited investors in a community can trade local securities. Once operating, these exchanges will allow the creation of diversified local portfolios, local mutual funds, and local pension funds. We will learn about the history of stock exchanges from John Katovich, who until recently was a senior vice president of the NASDAQ. We will see a glimpse of the future at Mission Markets, which is prepared right now to deploy such exchanges with state and local partners. And we will look at low-budget, grassroots approaches to local stock markets in Pennsylvania and California.

Chapter 9 discusses how local investors might start pooling together to diversify their risks—hence the title "Everybody into the Pool!" We will glimpse several models of revolving loan funds that are supporting local business. We will see exciting possibilities for creating local mutual funds, local pension funds, and local business-development companies (pools of small businesses). We will learn about the No Small Potatoes Investment Club in Maine, where unaccredited investors can make loans to local food businesses.

Chapter 10, "Investing in Yourself," shows the superior returns that come from investing in one's own bank, home, energy efficiency, and a panoply of other personal needs. For many Americans, perhaps even most, these opportunities are so big and compelling that they might never need to think about their IRAs or retirement funds again. Finally, we will see how anyone, even an unaccredited investor, can take control over his or her investment life through a self-directed IRA.

The Author's Fine Print

This book is not about how to get rich quick. At best, it's about how not to get poorer by continuing to hand over hard-earned cash to the bandits of Wall Street. Readers should be mindful that the local-investment tools described in the following pages are works in progress. None is a panacea. Each needs to be tested, benchmarked, critiqued, and improved. And even the best tools are only as good as their craftsman. The success—or failure—

of the first local stock exchange, for example, may or may not say anything significant about likely performance of its successors.

This book is built upon several dozen interviews conducted between July 2010 and July 2011. My colleague Kate Poole and I transcribed the interviews, scrubbed out the "uhs" and redundancies, and asked each interviewee to make sure we captured accurately what he or she had said. Most described investment tools they were pioneering or using somewhere; in a few instances we interviewed people who had ideas for great local-investment tools in the future.

Even though you will find lots of numbers in these pages—all of them triple-checked—I encourage you to treat all of them with skepticism, especially various claimed rates of return. Mainstream investment practitioners have developed numerous tricks for exaggerating their performance, as will be seen in chapter 1, and it has taken years to put in place reliable metrics to hold them even remotely accountable. It will be many more years before we really understand how well local-investment tools work, in what circumstances, and with what risks.

What can be said with confidence is that the era of individuals, families, and communities depending *exclusively* on the Rube Goldberg machine we call Wall Street is over. We are seeing the beginnings of a fundamentally new approach to investing and managing our wealth. Because local businesses in the United States have been severely undercapitalized and many are highly profitable, some of the early pioneers could hit the jackpot. As more and more of us see backyard investment opportunities that are working and thriving, others will follow. What might first appear to be a trickle of funds going into local business could soon burst into a torrent.

What will happen when the first, say, trillion dollars of the unaccredited public's money moves from Wall Street to Vall Street? Obviously, this will benefit many local businesses. But what happens when a trillion dollars is withdrawn from the New York Stock Exchange and the NASDAQ? Fortune 500 companies, long kept superficially healthy through automatic pension fund investments, will see the prices of their shares plummet and their assets shrink. More mainstream investors will worry and look to local alternatives, which will depress prices on the stock exchanges still further. This capital flight could occur with dramatic speed and result in the largest and most monumental shift of money in human history.

As the titans of Wall Street begin to tumble, gullible government officials will be pushed to bail these companies out, as they did with big banks under TARP. I sincerely hope the temptation is resisted. Globalization, extolled over the past generation as the future of mankind, is out, and localization is in. It's time to let the financial dinosaurs go extinct and let the new era of *Local sapiens* flourish.

A Living Rate of Return

Twenty years ago, a well-manicured retirement plan representative sat down with me and a dozen of my office mates in a bare-bones conference room to teach us the financial facts of life. The rep accurately surmised that most of us were in our twenties and thirties and financially naive, and told us that we were fortunate to be able to start saving for our golden years early. If we diligently squirreled away several thousand dollars each year, if we let our cash sit quietly in one of the dozens of funds the rep's company offered, we could enjoy a beautiful and comfortable life starting at the age of sixty-five. Forgo just a little spending now, buy well-diversified portfolios of stocks and bonds, let the financial markets perform their magic, and this could lead to that fabulous place many of us learn about as kids playing the game of Life: Millionaire Estates. My colleagues asked polite, earnest questions. I suspect that most of them, like me, dutifully opted in and forked over what amounted to 5 to 10 percent of our meager income each year.

What was odd about this event, in retrospect at least, was that my workplace was the Institute for Policy Studies (IPS), a left-leaning think tank in Washington, DC. Few discussions at IPS ever escaped intense, piercing, often vitriolic dissection. Many of the people sitting in that conference room probably had multiple arrests for civil disobedience under their belts. Scarcely a remark could pass at our monthly meetings without being vetted for lurking sexism, racism, and paternalism. Some of those sitting around were leading projects on the evils of big business, CEOs' excessively high pay, and corporate profiteering. And yet in *this* discussion about our own money, where our personal stakes mattered more than our political postures, everyone nodded attentively like an innocent kindergartner.

An army of investment advisers, many with their own how-to books and syndicated radio shows, have brought the abstruse vocabulary of money-speak into the common vernacular. Ric Edelman, for example, has built a small empire around his easy-to-understand financial wisdom, starting with his 1996 best seller, *The Truth About Money*. Each of these money gurus spins a unique theory about the exact ways of maximizing wealth prior to retirement, but one message is absolutely clear: Only idiots would skip putting most of their retirement money into the stock market.

Here's a typical riff from Ric Edelman: "If you were to put your 6-year-old's education fund entirely into one investment, knowing your child will not be able to attend college if you lose the money, would you invest in the stock market?" He points to a chart of annual returns of the Standard & Poors 500 between 1926 and 1995, which shows that in 70 percent of those years, stocks made money. "In the 64 rolling five-year periods since 1926 . . . , the S&P 500 made money 90% of the time. In the 10-year interval, the S&P 500 made money 96% of the time. In fact, in every 15-year interval and beyond, the stock market made money 100% of the time. . . . Thus, the key is not *when* you invest in the stock market, nor which stocks you buy. The key is *how long* you invest."[1]

And how much money will you make if you're a dedicated, long-term investor in Wall Street? Edelman claims that an investment between 1926 and 1995 would have generated a 12.5 percent annual rate of return.[2] Like a very skilled magician, he arrives at this mesmerizing result by performing three sleights of hand. One is to count dividends. This is defensible, though dividends today constitute a much smaller part of stock returns than they have historically. Second, he uses current dollars rather than inflation-adjusted dollars, which is completely misleading, especially over a long time when periods of significant inflation are inevitable. Third, he reinvests each year's gains back into the stock, inherently making stocks look like better investments than alternatives whose gains are less easily reinvested. A fairer accounting system, which I'll use for the remainder of this chapter, should tally gains from annual returns (or monthly) and make no assumption about reinvestment; what you do with your annual gains is your own business. Undoing even two of Edelman's tricks deflates the bottom line for stocks to an astonishingly low rate of return, which I'll elaborate shortly.

For now, let's explore the less seemly side to Edelman's cheerleading for the S&P 500: The fact that your money might be sucked into McDonald's promotion of childhood diabetes or into the next BP oil rig disaster is ignored. Corporate misbehavior is someone else's problem. Your only responsibility to yourself and to your family is to maximize your dollar rate of return. As Sergeant Hans Georg Schultz used to say on the television series *Hogan's Heroes*, "I hear nothing, I see nothing, I know nothing!"

Since Edelman wrote *The Truth About Money*, tens of millions of ordinary American investors have rejected his catechism and actually begun paying attention to corporate responsibility. In response to investor demands in the 1960s and 1970s, companies like Pax World Funds and the Calvert Social Investment Fund began offering portfolios of companies screening out nasty products like tobacco, abusive practices like sweatshops or toxic dumping, or reprehensible partnerships such as those many firms once maintained with apartheid South Africa. These early pioneers have since been joined by thousands of investment practitioners. An estimated $3 trillion of people's savings now resides in such funds.[3] A lively literature—lively at least for finance geeks like me!—can be found on whether the screening of funds has a positive or negative effect on rates of return, with the preponderance of evidence suggesting very little difference between screened and unscreened portfolios.

One fine point about these socially responsible funds, however, is not widely appreciated: Like all other funds, they invest almost exclusively in Fortune 500 companies and are totally disconnected from local living economies. They might remove the worst of the worst defense contractors or child-labor purveyors, but not a few include Walmart, whose business model has transformed thousands of Main Streets across America into ghost towns. Naive investors might assume that a portfolio of "microcap" companies includes small business, but in fact the asset value of such businesses is at least $50 to $100 million. Even the occasional "nano-cap" fund involves publicly traded companies with little to no connection to any actual place and therefore disserves local living economies.

But these misperceptions about the stock market are tiny compared with the astonishing half-truths Americans have been told about how to invest for retirement. The financial industry has convinced most of us that keeping our money in the stock market will average 7 or 8 percent each year, maybe more if you were a fan of Ric Edelman. In his book *Irrational Exuberance*, Yale finance professor Robert Shiller found that by the late 1990s many Americans expected annual returns in the 10 to 20 percent range.

In fact, the market's historical performance has *never* come anywhere near these benchmarks. The rapid ascent of the tech-heavy NASDAQ market during the late 1990s convinced many Americans that double-digit rates of return were the new norm. But even during this period, expectations were wildly distorted. Human brains seem evolutionarily wired to remember those "up" years of the NASDAQ rather than the subsequent eighteen-month period when the tech bubble popped and the NASDAQ lost 75 percent of its value. Even now, ten years later, a share of the QQQ index fund, a composite of the top one hundred NASDAQ companies, trades at less than half the value it had in January 2000. Despite this, despite the housing crash, despite the financial crisis of 2008, many retain a religious conviction that if they're smart enough, they can achieve double-digit annual returns.

The Sobering Historical Record

Zvi Bodie has been studying retirement strategies since he was a graduate student at MIT's Sloan School of Management and is now a professor of management at Boston University. He warns: "Stocks are risky. To rely on them for what you really need is a bad idea."[4]

Here's why. Please sit down before you read the rest of this paragraph, because you may well lose your lunch. Between 1871 and the end of 2010, a composite of all the stocks listed by Standard & Poors generated an annual rate of return of 2.6 percent. That's not a typo: *two point six percent*. To be clear—and consistent with my earlier points about accurate accounting—I add dividends, remove inflation, and do not reinvest annual earnings. The average return on stocks is basically what you could get for many kinds of fairly safe industrial or municipal bonds.[5] Perhaps you're thinking I've picked some particularly inappropriate years—2010, after all, marked the third year of what many now call the Great Recession. Fair enough.

So before I perform the next set of calculations, let me introduce an important character for this chapter: Sam the Saver. Sam is who we all aspire to be.

He's the serious student in college who takes courses on taxes, accounting, and retirement policy, always goes to bed early, never chugs beer, and carefully plans out his marriage, his career, his 1.8 kids, and his retirement by the end of his senior year. When Sam takes his first job at the age of twenty-two, he commits to placing a portion of his income each year in a tax-deferred retirement account until the age of sixty-five. He is our textbook model of how everything should work out. Sam is "in the market" for the long term: forty-four years.

Figure 1 shows what your forty-four-year rate of return from the market would be in every month you might retire, from 1915 to 2010. If sixty-five-year-old Sam had retired in the summer of 2010, his rate of return over the previous forty-four years would have averaged about 3.8 percent. His returns improve as the years roll back, but less than you might think. His best year to retire would have been 1965, when Sam would have enjoyed an average rate of return of just over 6 percent. But in other years, including many recent ones, his performance would have been worse than 3 percent. *Put another*

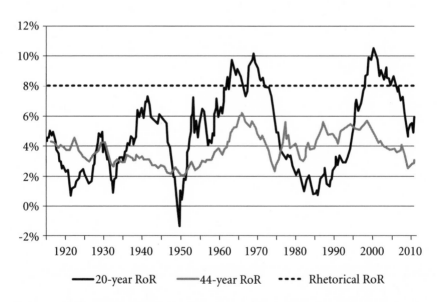

Figure 1. 20-Year, 44-Year, and Rhetorical Rates of Return from U.S. Stock Market. Note: These data represent a composite of the Standard & Poors index, as calculated by Robert Shiller of Yale University. Each point on the 44-year line represents that month's annualized real gain over the previous 44 years. Each point on the 20-year line represents that month's annualized real gain over the previous 20 years. Data available at www.irrationalexuberance.com.

way, the forty-four-year rate of return for average American retirees has never, ever
achieved anything close to the 8-plus percent the investment industry keeps telling
them to expect. In fact, the average of every month's forty-four-year rate of return
since 1915 has been 3.8 percent.

I first developed these data around Thanksgiving of 2010, when I shared
them with my family (not the smartest move to promote family cheer, in
retrospect). My sister's husband, a prominent infectious disease professor at
the University of California and a savvy investor, complained that no one
is in the market for forty-four years. He thought a more reasonable period
would be twenty years. So I added the twenty-year return line to the chart,
and, indeed, the average return of every twenty-year investment since 1891
(the first year a twenty-year assessment is possible) is just under 5 percent.
And as figure 1 shows, there are some months where you could retire with
an average twenty-year return of slightly above 10 percent per year. But there
are also many months where you would have retired with a net return in the
range of 1 to 2 percent per year.

How on Earth did we ever start thinking that a 7 or 8 percent rate of return,
let alone 12 or 20 percent, was going to be the norm? Perhaps we forgot to
consider the source. Investment companies, after all, are selling a product.
Their claims are no more credible than the late-night TV pitchmen, like the
late Billy Mays, urging us to *"order now and save!"* Professor Bodie laments,
"The investment industry persuaded ordinary people who don't know much
about market risk that all they had to do was sit back while stocks delivered
them a comfortable retirement."

Of course we all know about investors who "beat the Street" like George
Soros, Michael Steinhardt, Warren Buffett, and thousands of clever individuals you've never heard of. Even a few amateur day traders claim to achieve
rates of return of 50 percent or more, mostly by mastering the art of timing
of when to buy and when to sell. We overlook, however, that most of these
traders crave press coverage after good runs and then disappear underground
after bad ones. The real truth about money is that most of us do not have
the time, talent, or interest to become professional investors, so averages like
these over many years matter.

About twenty years ago, a number of studies revealed that the typical
returns of index funds—that is, funds indexed to proportionally mirror all

stocks on given exchanges (the New York Stock Exchange, the NASDAQ, the London Stock Exchange, and so forth) or certain broad categories of companies (like energy) or commodities (like gold)—outperformed the vast majority of funds whose well-informed managers actively played the market. In other words, human intervention was less reliable than mechanically betting on average performance. Between 1983 and 1990, in the U.S. Trading and Investing Championships, thirty-five hundred professional investors tried to outperform the S&P 500 for a period of several months, and only a handful succeeded.[6] In fact, only 22 percent made any money at all! These reports and anecdotes began to convince millions of long-term investors to stop paying high-fee brokerages for their underperformance, and to move their money into these low-fee index funds.

Today, of course, the average investor has many more options in which to invest than just the stock market. The vast majority actually carry *greater* risks than Wall Street. "One-off" investment offers—a friend asks you to become a partner in his new shopping mall—are inherently risky, which is why investment managers wisely insist that your portfolio include a variety of investments with diverse risk profiles. Many exchange-traded funds (ETFs) allow you to invest in diversified portfolios of specific commodities, specific types or sizes of companies, and specific countries; but all of these Johnny-come-lately offerings lack long-term performance data. Even alternatives with a long-term history such as silver and gold, which are assumed to be safe, are actually likely to have periods where their values inflate and deflate rapidly, like any other financial bubble.

There are certainly investment opportunities less risky than stocks, and their yields are commensurately lower. Certificates of deposit at federally insured banks, thrifts, or credit unions will earn you 1 to 2 percent per year these days, maybe as much as 3 percent if you park the money for a long period of time. Money market funds, which are slightly riskier (there was a moment during the financial crisis that this market froze up), pay about the same. U.S. government savings bonds pay 1 to 3 percent. As bond rates go higher, as you move into the world of corporate bonds, municipal bonds, and then into so-called junk bonds, expect commensurately higher risk. Professor Bodie recommends that the average investors would be smartest to avoid investment in stocks and place their money in Treasury Inflation-Protected

Securities (TIPS) and Series I Savings Bonds that currently pay 4.6 percent—just slightly less than the average stock market return.[7]

Those of us embracing the concept of a living rate of return are, among other things, striving to bring investor expectations in line with reality. So, based on historical rates of return, we could probably justify any number between 3 and 5 percent as the best return we should expect from the mainstream market. I am going to use 5 percent for the rest of this book. This is higher than the average. It sets a *ceiling* of what a reasonable investor, avoiding the usual reasonable mistakes, should expect. It also sets a benchmark that local investors should seek to match or beat. Its low magnitude also underscores why smart investors should start looking beyond Wall Street.

Deferred Dreams

We all know people who have retired early and comfortably. My dad, who worked for Western Electric (the manufacturing arm of the nation's postwar telephone monopoly AT&T), retired early when Judge Harold Greene decided in 1984 to break up Ma Bell; he lived frugally but happily off his modest pension for nearly thirty years. Other companies, particularly those with strong unions, left their employees with bigger nest eggs. A large number of military officers and federal workers could (and still can) retire after twenty to twenty-five years of service, allowing some to embark on a life of leisure in their forties. In the coming years, however, these stories will become rarer.

As U.S. corporations became more attentive to their bottom lines in the 1970s, they started jettisoning their pension programs. Global competition, corporate takeovers, weakening unions, and deregulation pushed U.S. firms to cut labor costs. Companies that once provided guaranteed pension benefits scrapped them for programs where employees voluntarily took money out of their salary for retirement. Employees instead could set up 401(k) or 403(b) plans and shelter their contributions from taxes until benefits were paid in retirement. Even self-employed people who hopped around from job to job could set up individual retirement accounts (IRAs), where their funds were similarly sheltered. All of us began to receive the kind of snow job I did at IPS. We were encouraged—implored—to take responsibility for our own retirements and start saving.

Congress didn't originally intend for the 401(k) plan to become a substitute for the traditional workplace retirement systems. The Revenue Act of 1978 created a generous perk for highly paid executives who, unlike most low-paid workers, could afford to defer part of their income. As Harvard Law professor Elizabeth Warren notes, "Much of the law governing 401(k)s was not driven by ordinary workers who were looking for a way to set a few dollars aside for their retirements. It was driven by CEOs who were looking for tax protection in order to maximize the value of their retirements."[8] When the stock market soared in the 1980s, the investment industry successfully lobbied to make the new product available for all Americans.[9] As new rules were enacted, companies were delighted to replace expensive defined-benefit programs with flexible, voluntary options that cost them almost nothing. Generous employers matched employee contributions, but most were content to arrange seminars where investment industry reps cheerfully explained that saving a little each year would be more than enough to leave you comfortable in retirement.

Tax deferral genuinely saves money. But how much? To answer this question, let's return to Sam the Saver. Living up to his name, Sam diligently puts $5,000 into his retirement account each year—a princely contribution for most of us—and invests his dollars in index funds with no fees. He patiently allows his assets to grow at 5 percent per year for over four decades. When he retires at the end of his sixty-fifth year, he has accumulated the sensational sum of $755,000.[10] Since he has put exactly $220,000 into the system, Sam's steady saving has more than tripled his assets, thanks to the miracle of compound growth rates.

Sam then decides to follow the conventional wisdom that he not withdraw more than 4 percent per year, so that he does not risk outliving his account. So, in his sixty-sixth year, Sam withdraws about $28,600. But now he has to pay taxes on his annual retirement payout. He actually gets an income of about $20,000 per year, which turns out, if Sam is living alone, to be not that far above the poverty line of $13,000 per year. If Sam has a wife or other family members living with and depending on him, the household will be struggling to avoid poverty. Sam, of course, also gets an income from Social

Security, and assuming that system is neither dismantled nor bankrupt by the time Sam retires—a bit of a heroic assumption given the "reforms" many penny-pinching politicians are proposing these days—he might do okay in retirement. Just.

Let's pause for a moment. *The average rate of return from the stock market barely gets a fabulous, way-better-than-average saver like Sam a monthly, after-tax income of $1,666.* Is this the way the system was really supposed to work?

Now suppose that, instead of contributing $5,000 a year to an IRA, Sam invested that $5,000 each year on his own in exactly the same way—only this time he decided not to place his money in a tax-deferred retirement system. So instead of placing $5,000 into his IRA, he places $3,500 ($5,000 minus $1,500 in federal and state taxes he must pay each year on $5,000 income) into the exact same index fund he would have put his IRA into.[11] At the end of age sixty-five, he will have accumulated just over $529,000 and see each year only about $14,000 net after taxes.[12] In other words, the decision not to enter the tax-deferral system made him about a third poorer in retirement. So, yes, tax deferral through an IRA or 401(k) pays. But it also turns out that if, in this tax-deferred scenario, Sam could increase his annual rate of return by just 1.5 percent, he would lose no money at all. The impact of tax deferral is therefore to increase one's rate of return by less than 2 percent. That's the best case. If you invest for fewer than forty-four years, the value of the tax deferral decreases.

The Retirement Scam

The real problem facing the U.S. retirement system, of course, is that you are not Sam the Saver. Almost no one is. Recall that Sam reached his sixty-fifth birthday, after saving $5,000 per year, with $755,000 in his retirement account. In 2007 the typical sixty-five-year-old had about $78,000, barely a tenth what Sam had saved (and no doubt, when data are available after the current financial crisis, that number will be lower). The *average* American with a tax-deferred account had $45,519 put away.[13] Almost half of all 401(k) accounts have less than $10,000. More than a third of Americans have nothing saved whatsoever. Taking the *largest* of these numbers, $78,000, and applying the recommended 4 percent annual withdrawal rate translates into about $260 per month—enough to cover two weeks' groceries.

Defenders of the 401(k) system counter that it really kicked in for most workers in the 1990s, and the real Sams saving for forty-plus years have not yet reached retirement. Because of the way that compounding works, in the early years your retirement account is mostly made up of your contributions. As the years toll—twenty, twenty-five, thirty, thirty-five—more and more of your account represents compounding returns on your investment. The difference between Sam, who saved for forty-four years, and me, who could have saved for only thirty years (I was introduced to the retirement system at IPS at the age of thirty-five), means that I will have less than half what Sam will have. Hmmm. Thinking back on my first pension-saving pep talk, I don't believe I was told that the system would fall short that way for me.

All of us have difficulty saving at Sam's rate. For the average American family barely making ends meet, $5,000 is an inconceivably high level of income to defer. This explains why there is so much resistance to privatizing Social Security. Sing all the praises you want about personal responsibility, but at the end of the day, unless the federal government or some other authority withholds that $5,000, few of us will really have the discipline to do so.

A whole generation of late Baby Boomers reaching retirement neither is covered by a defined workplace pension plan (as my dad was) nor has been in the world of IRAs/401(k)s for more than a couple of decades. (These products became available in the late 1970s, and only commonplace in the late 1980s.) Even though more Americans are saving for their retirement now than ever before, most of us will never achieve Sam's forty-four years of savings. Welcome to the other destination on the Life game board: the poor farm.

Yet another problem with the retirement system is that all our scenarios with Sam carry a bunch of assumptions that are wildly optimistic. Consider what else could go wrong:

- If taxes go up by the time you retire, the advantage of your tax deferral could be worthless (or worse). The country's long-term fiscal mess actually makes this awful scenario likely.

- If the United States enters another period of high inflation, which many believe is likely as our national and global debts mount, the purchasing power of our retirement savings will be greatly diminished. Generational theft is currently the effective policy of both mainstream political parties.
- We, like most Americans, are unaware of various hidden fees in our mutual fund accounts that could eat away more than half of our gains.
- Social Security could go bust or shrink, which would definitely leave Sam retiring in poverty.
- A belief in equities is a belief in corporate management, which, thanks to enabling politicians, has become increasingly short-term and self-serving.
- The stock market therefore could actually underperform its historic lows. If, as this book anticipates, there's a massive shift of capital from global to local business, stock prices on the mainstream markets could well plummet.
- Even if the market doesn't tank generally but only in the year before you retire, your retirement is toast. In four of the last ten years, the stock market has fallen like this.

We have set up an entire generation of Americans for a post-retirement shock. The U.S. General Accounting Office, in 2009, concluded, "If no action is taken, a considerable number of Americans face the prospect of a reduced standard of living in retirement."[14] To Stephen Gandel, in a brilliant critique in *Time*, the GAO's pronouncement is a grotesque understatement: "The ugly truth . . . is that the 401(k) is a lousy idea, a financial flop, a rotten repository for our retirement reserves."[15]

Street Repairs

Even if Wall Street matches its historical performance, millions of Americans depending on it are destined to long retirements in agonizing poverty. And that's one of the better-case scenarios. A growing number of Americans fear not just a repeat of the bursting of the tech bubble (1998 to 2001) and the recent market downturn during the financial crisis (2008 to the present), but also a sudden, cataclysmic, game-changing slide of the kind we saw on May 6, 2010. Who knows what the real odds of this happening are? Wall Street has increasingly become such a speculation-driven casino that it's impossible to evaluate the probability of this kind of implosion.

Given that level of uncertainty, smart money is beginning to look to the back roads for a living rate of return—and increasingly to local businesses. In a number of ways, Main Street investing is the opposite of Wall Street investing. While few of us ever get a glimpse of a Fortune 500 boardroom, local businesses are run by people we know and trust. Investments on Wall Street are short-term, increasingly held for mere seconds, while investments on Main Street are often held for many years. Unlike the markets on which Wall Street securities trade, which are abstract, distant, and mysterious, the markets in which Main Street investors meet are typically concrete, personal, and transparent. The lure of a living rate of return through local investing is increasingly powerful, not just because of the "push" from Wall Street's risks, but also because of the "pull" from myriad local investments that could simultaneously do better than 5 percent per year and revitalize our communities.

Zero-Cost Stimulus

Today, as I write, the American economy is in its worst doldrums since the Great Depression. The nation's unemployment rate is stubbornly stuck above 9 percent. After bailing out the big banks and the auto industry, after pushing for nearly three-quarters of a trillion dollars of new government spending to stimulate consumer demand, after encouraging the Federal Reserve to make cheaper money available, President Barack Obama has all but run out of stimulus tricks. Collectively, these measures have created stunningly few new jobs, souring much of the American public on John Maynard Keynes's theories of government-led stimulus. Instead, voters flocked to the polls in November 2010 convinced that the central problem afflicting the U.S. economy was the enormous deficit spending incurred to underwrite the stimulus. They elected eighty-seven "Tea Party" congressional representatives who, along with a Republican majority in the House of Representatives, now refuse to spend a dime on additional stimulus. The only politically feasible way forward is to find a way to stimulate the economy without spending more money.

There is, in fact, an easy way to accomplish this: Tear down the archaic regulations that stand in the way of ordinary people investing in ordinary business. A growing body of evidence suggests that local businesses are the key to economic prosperity, especially job creation. And when economic development focuses on these businesses, whether through public or private investment, the economy can begin growing again. By understanding the powerful, undervalued capacity of local business to contribute to national and local economic development, we can begin to appreciate why local investing deserves special attention from American investors today.

The Rules

Clues about how smart economic development can reduce unemployment can be found in those few places in the United States where the recession has just been a mild dip. Take the region surrounding Burlington, Vermont. In September 2010 the unemployment rate there was below 5 percent, almost half the national average, giving it the seventh lowest rate of 372 regions in the country and the lowest unemployment rate east of the Mississippi River. Most places with low unemployment, like Wyoming and North Dakota, have been the beneficiaries of rising global prices of natural resources like oil, gas, and coal. But that doesn't explain Vermont, which doesn't export any raw energy commodities.

You can certainly point to some exceptional features of metropolitan Burlington. It enjoys an outstanding public education system and has attracted more than its fair share of PhDs from Greater Boston. Its verdant geography provides rich soil for farmers, breathtaking mountains for skiers during the winter, and scenic vistas for tourists during the summer. Yet one can turn each of these arguments on its head. For example, Vermont has a shorter growing season than most states. Depending on tourism and other seasonal industries often leads to economic weakness during the off seasons. The state also enjoys a living wage law, which many mainstream economists predict should *increase* unemployment.

Bruce Seifer, who for twenty-eight years has helped lead the Community and Economic Development Office of Burlington, thinks one explanation for his region's success is simple. Instead of chasing smokestacks or bribing companies to stay in Burlington, he and his colleagues have spent decades nurturing the best small businesses with high labor and environmental standards consistent with the state's quality of life. They created revolving loan funds for affordable housing and venture funds for high-growth small businesses and helped foster the growth of the Opportunities Credit Union and the Vermont Community Loan Fund, which provide private capital to local businesses. They developed targeted technical assistance programs for women entrepreneurs, refugees, and young people. They helped put together business networks, like the Vermont Software Developers' Alliance, the Vermont BioSciences Alliance, The South End Arts and

Business Association, and Vermont Businesses for Social Responsibility. They improved Burlington's livability by putting in sidewalks and park benches, by building boathouses and fishing facilities along Lake Champlain, by rehabilitating dilapidated districts like the Old North End, and by retaining neighborhood public schools. They worked shoulder-to-shoulder with some of the best socially responsible entrepreneurs in the country, the founders of Ben & Jerry's Ice Cream, Seventh Generation, Lake Champlain Chocolates, and the Gardener's Supply Company, as each company grew from zero to several hundred employees.

Seifer understood that Vermont needed to focus its modest public efforts on local businesses. "Local businesses reinvest their money locally," he says. "They hire local people. They work with the schools, they mentor and train, they volunteer. They donate their charity locally. They serve on boards. When times get tough, they're more likely to stay and not leave town."

Seifer's argument now has strong empirical support nationally. A year ago, in the *Harvard Business Review*, a graph appeared with the headline "More Small Firms Means More Jobs."[1] The authors wrote, "Our research shows that regional economic growth is highly correlated with the presence of many small, entrepreneurial employers—not a few big ones." They further argued that the major preoccupation of economic developers—how to attract global companies—is fundamentally wrongheaded. "Politicians enjoy announcing a big company's arrival because people tend to think that will mean lots of job openings. But in a rapidly evolving economy, politicians are all too likely to guess wrong about which industries are worth attracting. What's more, large corporations often generate little employment growth even if they are doing well."

A more recent study just published in the *Economic Development Quarterly*, a journal long smitten with business-attraction practices, similarly finds: "Economic growth models that control for other relevant factors reveal a positive relationship between density of locally owned firms and per capita income growth, but only for small (10–99 employees) firms, whereas the density of large (more than 500 workers) firms not owned locally has a negative effect."[2] These results begin to explain how the Obama administration in the United States could spend three-quarters of a trillion dollars on "economic stimulus" and barely make a dent in the nation's huge unemployment rate. Like state and local economic-development programs, Obama's stimulus program focused almost entirely on big banks, big infrastructure programs, big taxpayer cuts, and big nonlocal companies. When we use a wrench to hammer a nail, we shouldn't be surprised when our efforts fail.

Economics baffles most people, and economists themselves don't make public understanding any easier by using terms like *marginal propensity to consume* or by doing most of their theorizing in inscrutable mathematical equations. And to be fair, many corners of economic prediction, theory, and practice are complicated and controversial. But on one critically important issue in economics—what works in economic development—the evidence is fast becoming clear. We now know three simple rules about local economies that, if followed assiduously, will allow a community to prosper.

> **Rule 1.** Maximize the percentage of jobs in your local economy that exist in businesses that are locally owned.
> **Rule 2.** Maximize the diversity of your businesses in your community, so that your economy is as self-reliant and resilient as possible.
> **Rule 3.** Prioritize spreading and replicating local business models with outstanding labor and environmental practices.

Stating these rules, of course, is easier than implementing them. This book addresses only one of the tools for helping communities to follow these rules: mobilizing capital. Other tools include economic planning, policy, and partnerships, especially in the fields of local food and energy (covered in the other two books in this Post Carbon Institute series). Understanding the three rules above lays a solid foundation for understanding why investors, whether billionaires like Warren Buffett or "thousandaires" like most of us, should begin to shift their hard-earned savings into local business.

Rule 1: Maximize Local Ownership

The first rule for a community seeking real prosperity is to maximize local ownership of business. While there is no universally objective definition of local ownership, a simple one might be this: The majority of owners of a company live in the community in which the business operates. Quibblers can decide for themselves whether a "community" is a neighborhood, town, city, county, or a regional cluster of counties. About 99.9 percent of all small businesses, which the U.S. Small Business Association defines as having fewer than five hundred employees, fall into this category. So do many larger businesses. Throughout rural America, for example, are regional hospitals and medical centers, run as locally rooted nonprofits, each employing thousands. There are some categories—regional chains and franchises, for example—for which it is tougher to decide whether enterprises count as "locally owned," but it's worth noting that one database that tracks ownership of these companies suggests that the vast majority of chains and franchises are affiliated with a parent company headquartered in the state.[3]

There are many reasons that maximizing jobs in locally owned businesses matters—maintaining control over the community's future being one of them. But the overarching *economic* reason is this: Every job in a locally owned business generates two to four times as much economic-development benefit as a job in an equivalent nonlocal business. Local businesses spend more money locally, which helps to pump up what is known as the local economic multiplier. The more times a given dollar circulates in a community and the faster it circulates without leaking out, the more income, wealth, and jobs are created in that community. That's the cornerstone of all economic development. What we now know, beyond any doubt, is that local businesses do this better than nonlocals.

A now classic study, performed in 2002 by a small consulting firm called Civic Economics, analyzed the impact of a proposed nonlocal Borders bookstore compared with two local bookstores in Austin, Texas. Researchers found that $100 spent at Borders would circulate $13 in the Austin economy, while the same $100 spent at the local bookstores would circulate $45.[4] Why the difference? Unlike Borders, the local bookstores had a high-level management team, used local business services, advertised locally, and enjoyed local profits. The study found that every dollar spent at the local store contributed three times the jobs, income effects, and tax benefits to the local economy as every dollar spent at the national chain store. Nearly a dozen other studies in the United States—and many others internationally—have confirmed the "local jobs advantage," as summarized in table 1.

Just as significant is the fact that *not a single study* has shown the opposite. Indeed, it defies logic that Company A owned a thousand miles away would

Table 1. Jobs from Local vs. Nonlocal Business[5]	
Study	**Local Jobs Advantage**
Austin (2002)	3.5
Maine (2003)	5
Chicago (2004)	1.6
Toledo (2004)	4
Iowa (2006)	1.6
San Francisco (2007)	1.4–1.7
Phoenix (2007)	2.9
Grand Rapids (2008)	1.6
New Orleans (2009)	2
Average	**2.6**

Note: The local jobs advantage represents the relative number of jobs (direct and indirect) produced by a given purchase (say $100) from a local business versus the same purchase from a similar nonlocal business. The local businesses consistently spend more money locally and thereby generate more jobs.

spend its money locally while locally owned Company B would spend its money out of town. In fact, the input–output model most widely used by economic developers, IMPLAN, is built on the assumption that getting businesses to spend more of their money locally improves consequent jobs, earnings, and output.

This doesn't mean that Rule 1 is uncontroversial. Many economic developers offer two counterarguments. One is that goods or services from nonlocal firms are cheaper than local alternatives. Walmart loves to cite what it calls "independent" studies (many of which it has funded) that show that the savings local consumers enjoy from shopping at "cheaper" nonlocally owned stores are then spent locally and create more local jobs.[6] The other counterargument is that local businesses pay less in salaries and benefits.

A threshold observation about both counterarguments is that they don't contradict Rule 1—they add nuance. For example, even if all local goods and services were more expensive than their counterparts at a nearby Walmart, a community would experience two different effects: the loss of local business spending (which reduces jobs), and more consumer saving (which increases jobs). Almost all the pro-Walmart studies look only at the second impact and not the first. The smart approach would be to prioritize supporting local firms that provide competitive prices, so you get the maximize impact from both effects.

But the argument that local goods and services are *always* more expensive is ludicrous, one that says more about the bigger-is-better biases of economists and economic developers than it does about reality. The U.S. economy is made up of literally hundreds of millions of products and services, and assertions about any broad class beating another are usually based on a tiny, statistically insignificant sampling. That's why we must look at broader trends, and these show, as we will see shortly, that local goods and services actually are quite competitive and becoming increasingly so.

One reason economists misunderstand the competitiveness of local business is that they confuse the concepts of *price* and *value*. The most basic models economists teach and use in microeconomics focus on the relationship of a widget's price to its given quantity. But consumers only focus exclusively on prices of goods that are "perfect substitutes," like gasoline. Few goods are like this, and almost no services are. If you believe that price is the primary driver of consumer demand, then you've never been to a Starbucks. There may be many reasons to buy your mocha latte with a shot of vanilla, but price is not one of them. What really matters is *value*. Consumers consider price alongside many other factors: What's the quality of the product? How trustworthy is the producer? What does the after-purchase service package look like? How rewarding is the shopping experience? What's the chance that I'm going to be overcharged or ripped off? How well does the company treat its workers and the environment? Does it contribute to local charities and sponsor the local Little League? The answers to these questions reveal the qualities in which local businesses often excel.

If local businesses really provided goods and services with low value, then consumers—given the real facts about more expensive and shoddy local alternatives—would flock to the chain stores. In fact, buy-local campaigns always move consumers in the opposite direction. For example, a recent survey of independent businesses found that their sales growth in 2010 more than doubled if they were in a city with a "Buy Local First" initiative.[7] The more information consumers have about local alternatives, the more they buy local. One reason is that most of us know relatively little about great deals locally, because local businesses cannot match the multibillion-dollar advertising prowess of global corporations.

The second red herring economists use to disparage Rule 1 focuses on the wages paid by small businesses. Economic developers often justify spending millions to lure an automobile manufacturer, because these jobs, unlike local business jobs, generally pay more. A variety of studies are then trotted out— all true, by the way—to show that large-scale manufacturers pay better than small-scale retailers. The problem is that these studies almost never compare two firms, one local and one nonlocal, that *produce the same good or service.* The correct comparison is not a local hardware store versus a nonlocal auto plant, but rather a local versus a nonlocal hardware store or a local versus a nonlocal auto plant. For a given industry, there is no compelling evidence that local businesses pay less than nonlocal businesses. If a community wanted to focus on, say, manufacturing, because manufacturing jobs pay relatively well, it could nurture locally owned manufacturers, thereby enjoying the benefits of higher pay *and* a stronger multiplier.[8]

Another important fact here is that the wage advantage for larger businesses is actually shrinking. One recent statistical analysis of the relevant academic literature found that between 1988 and 2003 these differences, in both wages and benefits, shrank by about a third.[9] If this trend continues, especially as many of the once high-paying larger firms continue to move factories overseas and as low-wage retailers like Walmart continue to displace existing small business, these differences could disappear altogether. But again, the smart thing for communities to do with this information is to help small businesses with the best wages and benefits expand. Hence Rule 3.

The case for favoring locally owned business actually goes well beyond the multiplier argument. Consider eight other advantages local businesses offer over the nonlocal competition:

1. **Higher Standards.** Generally, it's the nonlocal businesses that are leading fights against tougher environmental standards.[10] A good example of this is in my backyard, Maryland. Regulation of the chicken industry has been virtually impossible because the gigantic producers, Tyson and Perdue, are continually threatening to move to "business-friendly" jurisdictions like Arkansas and Mississippi.

This same problem also afflicts economic-development initiatives that seek higher wages through nonlocal industry. Yes, they may pay better, but they often fight higher labor standards for all business. Ditto for ecological protection. An Environmental Protection Agency (EPA) study found that the average amount of toxins released by absentee-owned facilities or those with out-of-state headquarters is nearly three times more than plants with in-state headquarters, and fifteen times more than single location enterprises.[11]

2. **Greater Wealth.** Because nonlocal businesses come and go while local businesses stick around for years, even generations, the latter are much more reliable generators of wealth, income, and jobs. Around the country, economic-development agencies have collectively offered an estimated $50 billion of incentives each year to attract or retain nonlocal business, and by and large these deals have been huge losers.[12] Many of these arrangements looked great on paper and promised to deliver hundreds or thousands of high-wage new jobs. But all too often, subsidy recipients stayed for a couple of years, took the incentives, and then vanished. The comings and goings of supposedly high-quality jobs turn out to be a very poor bargain for public expenditures on economic development. According to an investigative report about the cost effectiveness of tax abatements in Lane County, Oregon, the cost to the community in lost taxes was about $23,800 per job for nonlocal firms and $2,100 per job for the local firms.[13] The nonlocal jobs were *more than ten times* more expensive, because the absentee-owned firms were so unreliable.[14]

3. **Greater Stability.** The comings and goings of large, nonlocal businesses also create enormous stresses on a small community's economy. In the Katahdin region of Maine, the shutdown of a paper mill (the parent company sought to move operations to a lower-wage area) created a regional unemployment rate of 40 percent over the following year.[15] That kind of catastrophe is far less likely in a community economy built primarily around local businesses with no plans for moving to China.

4. **Better Community Planning.** Locally owned businesses are natural promoters of "smart growth" or anti-sprawl policies. Smart growth

means redesigning a community so that residents can walk or ride bikes from home to school, from work to the grocery store. It means scrapping old zoning laws and promoting multiple uses—residential, commercial, clean industrial, educational, civic—in existing spaces, because it's more sensible to fully use the town center and existing infrastructure than to build subdivisions on green spaces on the periphery. Because local businesses tend to be small, they can fit more easily inside homes or on the ground floor of apartment buildings. Also, because they focus primarily on local markets, local businesses place a high premium on being easily accessible by local residents.

5. **Stronger Identity.** Part of what makes any community great is how well it preserves its unique culture, foods, ecology, architecture, history, music, and art. Local businesses celebrate these features, while nonlocals steamroll them with retail monocultures. Outsider-owned firms take what they can from local assets and move on. It's the homegrown entrepreneurs whose time horizon extends even beyond their grandchildren and who have a vested interest in growing local wealth. And it's the local firms that are most inclined to serve local tastes with specific microbrews and clothing lines. Austin's small-business network employs the slogan "Keep Austin Weird," because it's "weirdness" that attracts tourists, engages locals in their culture, draws talented newcomers, and keeps young people hanging around.

6. **Greater Creativity.** Urban theorist Richard Florida's arguments about the importance of a "creative class" for economic success also tend to support locally owned businesses.[16] Florida argues that among the key inducements for a creative class to move to and stay in a community are its civic culture, its intellectual bent, its diversity, and its sense of self—all attributes that are clearly enhanced in an economy dominated by locally owned businesses. A local business economy seeks to celebrate its own culture, not to import mass culture through boring chain restaurants and cineplexes. It seeks to have more residents engaged as entrepreneurs, many emerging through home-based businesses.

7. **Greater Social Well-Being.** In 1946 two noted social scientists, C. Wright Mills and Melville Ulmer, compared communities dominated by at least one large manufacturer versus those with many small businesses.[17] They found that the small-business communities "provided for their residents a considerably more balanced economic life than did big business cities" and that "the general level of civic welfare was appreciably higher." The late Thomas Lyson, a professor of rural sociology at Cornell University, updated this study by looking at 226 manufacturing-dependent counties in the United States.[18] He concluded that these communities are "vulnerable to greater inequality, lower levels of welfare, and increased rates of social disruption than localities where the economy is more diversified."[19]

8. **Greater Political Participation.** Studies of voting behavior suggest that the longer residents live in a community, the more likely they are to vote, and that economically diverse communities have higher participation rates in local politics. The long-term relationships fostered by local business tend to enhance personal commitment to civic institutions like schools, churches, charities, fraternal leagues, and business clubs that are essential for local economic success.[20] As one group of scholars recently concluded after reviewing the social science literature: "The degree to which the economic underpinnings of local communities can be stabilized—or not—will be inextricably linked with the quality of American democracy in the coming century."[21] An economy with many long-term homegrown businesses is more likely to contribute to such stability than the boom-and-bust economy created by site-hopping corporations.

These eight arguments, taken together with the economic-multiplier studies, underscore why any initiative undertaken in the name of economic development, whether public or private, should focus methodically on locally owned businesses. It's not that nonlocal businesses are bad for the economy. To the contrary, most nonlocal businesses generate some income, wealth, and jobs for their home community, and they contribute some economic-multiplier effects. But we now know—with absolute certainty—that, dollar for dollar of business activity, local businesses contribute more to economic development than do nonlocal businesses. And every minute a community spends on attracting or retaining a nonlocal business is a minute unavailable for nurturing a local one, and therefore winds up generating relatively less economic development.

Rule 2: Maximize Cost-Effective Resilience

A second rule for community prosperity is to diversify your economic base and become as self-reliant as possible. This increases the resilience of your community in handling sudden global challenges—market collapses, capital flights, pandemics, terrorism, wars—over which you have no control. A diversity of local businesses boosts your skill base and maximizes the ability of your community to take advantage of future, unforeseeable opportunities for new products, new technologies, and new business designs.

Every unnecessary import opens your country, region, and community to nasty surprises that lie ahead. America's dependence on oil imports has made it vitally important to spend hundreds of billions of dollars on "regime change" in Iraq and Libya, to prop up dozens of potentates ruling oil-rich countries like Saudi Arabia and Kuwait with dismal human-rights records, and to protect ourselves from terrorist organizations hostile to these foreign policies. As oil prices have risen over the last decade, U.S. consumers have paid out literally trillions of dollars to untrustworthy outsiders. Reducing oil imports by developing local renewable resources and local conservation and efficiency solutions will naturally strengthen national resilience. Imported food is another example, in that it leaves a community vulnerable to imported pollution, microorganisms, and pests from less responsible farmers elsewhere in the world.

Despite the obvious advantages of greater self-reliance, economists wince at the term because it is seen to imply a Robinson Crusoe economy sealed off from the rest of the world. Of course, no modern community has the ability to provide efficiently for all its needs and wants. And the only way a community can access products and services unavailable locally is through trade. By selling items to outsiders (that is, through *exports*), you earn money that can then buy these unavailable goods and services (that is, through *imports*).

Early economists, most prominently David Ricardo, made a further observation that remains a cornerstone of modern economics. In his 1817 classic,

On the Principles of Political Economy and Taxation, he argued that if a community specializes in producing and exporting a small number of items, it can then use its earnings to import the goods and services that other communities can produce better. "Better" usually means providing higher-quality goods or services at lower prices. And even if you're not the one absolutely best producer in the world, specialization might still make sense because by striving to be even the one hundredth best producer on the planet, you can produce larger numbers of a given product, achieve economies of scale, and export *something*. This is, in essence, the theory of trade or comparative advantage.

There are many problems with the theory, both practical and theoretical. For example, the theory assumes that businesses don't move from one place to another. It further assumes that everyone has perfect information and every community plays fairly. But the one problem we'll focus on here concerns scale.

In the real world, no one wants to specialize too much. Suppose a family has world-class musical talent. Does it really make sense to outsource everything so that Mom and Dad can focus on their piano lessons and singing practice? Should the parents really pay other people to take care of their kids around the clock, so they can work 24/7? Do they really want servants who do all the cooking and cleaning? Many of us actually enjoy these activities and seek to develop our skills as parents and homemakers. Moreover, practically speaking, the time and expense it would take to teach a battalion of servants to do all these things just the way we want is rarely worth it.

Now let's move from a family to a small-town economy. Your son is sick, running a 103-degree fever: Sure, there may be a cheaper doctor a hundred miles down the road, but you need one right now, so you pay a little more. Your daughter needs tennis lessons, and she won't tolerate more than half an hour's trip to get there, so you go local. What's true for services is equally true for many goods. Your local bookstore probably has the book you're looking for, and if it's only a dollar more expensive than the same book at the nearest Barnes & Noble two towns over, it's hard to justify a two-hour round trip. The local credit union delivers the same basic banking services—checking, savings, borrowing—as does the Bank of America, and as best you can tell, the prices for the services are pretty much identical.

Let's generalize: The mandate to specialize dictated by Ricardo's theory of trade should be set aside whenever the value of a local good or service is equal to or better than that of a nonlocal good or service. To put this in terms that economists would recognize: If a local business provides goods or services that beat the global competition, then by definition buying local is rational behavior. Indeed, *not* buying local will leave a community poorer.

A *Time* magazine article from June 2009 reported, "Buying close to home may be more than a feel-good, it's-worth-paying-more-for-local matter. A number of researchers and organizations are taking a closer look at how money flows, and what they're finding shows the profound economic impact of keeping money in town—and how the fate of many communities around the nation and the world increasingly depend on it."[22]

Not surprisingly, economists are striking back. Take, for example, "The Locavore's Dilemma: Why Pineapples Shouldn't Be Grown in North Dakota," written by Jayson L. Lusk and F. Bailey Norwood, agricultural economists with the University of Oklahoma.[23] "A major flaw in the case for buying local," they write, "is that it is at odds with the principle of comparative advantage." They go on to claim, without a shred of evidence, that buying local is more expensive than buying global. "If local and non-local foods are of the same quality, but local goods are more expensive, then buying local food is like burning dollar bills—dollar bills that could have been put to more productive use." Duh, of course. But what if local food is higher quality and more expensive? Or—heaven forbid—local food is higher quality and cheaper? *Most economists don't even consider this possibility!*

In fact, over a growing range of goods and services, local is becoming smarter and cheaper. Consider some of the many "comparative advantages" local businesses have:

- All things being equal, a local foodstuff actually tends to be higher quality than its nonlocal alternative, because it's fresher, requires less handling, processing, or packaging, and has higher nutrition (nutrients decay over time).
- Local proprietors tend to be the true experts on local markets. Local pizza makers know just how thick the locals like the crust and what toppings to put on. Local lawyers have expertise on

local statutes, regulations, cases, and judicial traditions that their Bangalore wannabes will never have.

• Local manufacturers can make and deliver items just in time to nearby buyers, with minimal shipping or delay, and without expensive storage or inventories. Aware that "local" character *adds* value, SFMade brands goods manufactured in San Francisco—like Anchor Steam beer—that uniquely represent the region's history, culture, and aesthetics.[24]

If you think I'm cherry-picking unusual examples of local success, consider that small businesses, including home-based business, have been competitive enough to maintain their share of jobs in the overall economy since 1990.[25] *Please reread the previous sentence.* Despite dozens of sexy tomes about globalization, endless hype about the wonders of the global economy, speeches from every political quarter about the importance of attracting or retaining multinational business, nonlocal businesses in the United States have not increased their presence, profit, or power in the national economy for two decades!

Local small businesses have basically fought global corporations to a draw. And most remarkably, they did this in an environment where public officials and economic developers essentially tried to strangle them with unfairly subsidized competition. A survey I recently completed of the three largest economic-development programs in fifteen states found that 80 percent were giving most of their money to attract and retain global business—about a third gave well over 90 percent of their funds. Even a libertarian-minded state like South Carolina consistently violated its first principles to bribe companies like BMW and Boeing with tens of millions of public dollars.[26] The impact of these subsidies, if not the intent, was to make small business less competitive. And yet homegrown businesses held their own.

The tilt of public policies against local businesses goes well beyond economic-development subsidies. Generations of federal corporate welfare policies, ranging from tax breaks to outright gifts, and including trillion-dollar military deployments in the Mideast, have made fossil fuels unnaturally cheap. Public infrastructure favoring global trade like highways, airports, and ports has been generously underwritten by public dollars, while infrastructure supporting local businesses like community parking lots, intracity transit, and bicycle and pedestrian facilities has been starved. State sales taxes are largely unenforced against Internet giants like Amazon (though some states, like California, are finally trying to end this giveaway). Trade rules have discouraged communities from placing labels on products letting consumers know whether they were made locally. Antitrust laws that once would have forbidden the way that Walmart whipsaws its suppliers have been largely unenforced. Had public policy been less biased against small businesses, had our governments sought to create an even playing field for local and nonlocal businesses, globalization surely would have lost ground.

Even if foolish public policies remain in place, there are deeper trends in the global economy that actually are increasing the competitiveness of small, local business. In 1970, services made up 45 percent of consumer spending. By 2008, they grew to 60 percent. This trend is mirrored in other industrialized countries. As people make more money, they get saturated with "stuff." Once you have your third car, your fourth computer, your fifth television set, you begin to see the virtue in spending your next available dollar on more education or health care. This trend is great news for localization, because most services are inherently local and depend on face-to-face relationships with people we know and trust.

But what about outsourcing to global service providers? Thomas Friedman's bestseller *The World Is Flat* is filled with anecdotes about American firms turning to low-wage Indians and Chinese to do taxes or patent filings. But all his colorful stories turn out to be statistically irrelevant. The U.S. trade balance in services has been in surplus and steadily growing over the past decade to $146 billion in 2010.[27] In the big picture, imports of outside services have had little effect on our economy.

Meanwhile, local businesses in all industrial sectors are methodically learning how to compete more effectively. Through community-based networks, local businesses are spreading best practices—in service, in technology, in business design, in marketing, in finance—all of which are improving their competitiveness. Local businesses are learning how working together can strengthen their hand against the globals. For years, True Value Hardware stores, all locally owned, have successfully competed against Home Depots through a producer cooperative. Tucson Originals is a group of local food businesses in Arizona that collectively buy foodstuffs, kitchen equipment, and dishes to bring down their costs. There appears to be no economy of scale that local businesses cannot realize through collaboration.

Thanks to the work of hundreds of grassroots groups—U.S. examples include the Business Alliance for Local Living Economies, the Post Carbon Institute, Transition Towns, and the New Economics Institute—local business innovations are now spreading globally. Community food enterprises are increasingly collaborating through sister restaurants and technical exchanges. Global conferences are passing along innovations on small-scale energy systems, credit unions, and local currencies.

Even from the standpoint of investors looking for profit, big business has become less attractive. Sole proprietorships, the category inhabited largely by small businesses, are now three times more profitable than C-corporations, the category where large businesses are largely found.[28] Partnerships fall in between. Moreover, in all but seven of the eleven hundred categories of the North American Industry Classification System (NAICS), there are more examples of competitive small business than large business.[29]

The continued competitiveness of local business has occurred in a world where the principal fuel for the global economy has been affordable oil. Cheap, plentiful, concentrated, and portable oil has heated our homes and offices, propelled our cars and jetliners, powered our machinery, and brought the entire world into an industrial age. Periodic shortages, such as during the OPEC embargoes of the 1970s, and periodic price spikes, such as during the summer of 2008 when gasoline topped $5 per gallon, have reminded us of our dependence on crude. These events, however, were just small coming attractions of an era we can barely imagine.

Over the next few decades, and possibly sooner, oil supplies will dwindle dramatically. Many experts contend that world oil supplies have already "peaked" and that we're about to experience sharp rises in oil prices.[30] Even the critics of the peak oil concept—those who wax bullish about new reserves of oil under the ocean floor or in the remote reaches of Canada—concede that exploration of these places is extremely expensive and that prices are heading upward. The only real debate is over how quickly energy costs will rise and whether energy alternatives can ramp up fast enough to prevent critical energy shortages, economic depressions, and political upheavals.[31]

The features of the post-petroleum era will almost certainly increase the competitiveness of local business. Rising oil prices will encourage the spread of community-based energy service companies, solar equipment installers, and household geothermal services. As more people balk at skyrocketing costs of commuting to work, they will increasingly turn to home-based businesses. Our earlier family looking for a tennis instructor will have even less reason to drag their daughter long distances for her lessons. And common practices in today's economy, such as Walmart contracting with manufacturers to produce cheap consumer goods in low-wage places like China and shipping them five thousand miles to stores in North America, will no longer be tenable.

To understand the long-term impacts of rising oil prices, we need only look at the U.S. trade deficit, which has ballooned in recent years. This has occurred not because of rising imports in general—remember, we're running a trade surplus in services—but because of rising imports specifically of foreign *goods*. Of this, only about a quarter of the goods are "durable"—that is, things that last for a few years or (if we're lucky) decades. These cars, appliances, gadgets, DVDs, computers, toys, housewares—all the stuff that is increasingly manufactured abroad—only constitute about a tenth of our total consumer spending. Most of our expenditures on goods are for "nondurables" (goods that tend to be used or consumed quickly) like food, building materials, wood, textiles, clothing, office supplies, and paper products.

The distinction on durability is critical, because imports of nondurable goods are particularly vulnerable to rising oil prices. Compared with, say, durables like microchips, the nondurable goods tend to weigh more and contain less value per pound. As energy prices and shipping costs rise, nondurable imports will be the first casualties. This means that local production of food and clothing, coupled with local distribution, will once again be competitive against Walmart's cheap imported goods as rising transportation costs swamp long-shrinking labor costs. We could see a renaissance of local manufacturing of nondurable goods worldwide. The emergence of the "local food" phenomenon not only in the United States but in places like Paraguay, Zambia, Sri Lanka, and Nepal suggests that in some sectors local businesses are already becoming more competitive.

So, to recap: Local businesses have held their own against global competitors over the past generation, despite public policies tilted against them. And a number of trends, like the shift to services and rising oil prices, will boost the competitiveness of local businesses even further. The argument that we nevertheless should stop buying competitive local goods and services to focus on the handful of global "comparative advantages" economists assign our communities is ridiculous.

But how, economists skeptical of self-reliance often ask, can a community grow wealthy from exports unless it also imports the raw ingredients for its exporting industries. "Locavores seek to export goods without importing," argue agribusiness professors Lusk and Norwood, "which can only happen if the exports are given away for free—the equivalent of foreign aid." Again, they've invented a straw man. Smart locavores are not trying to abolish trade, but just improve a community's balance of trade by adding relatively more value through local labor, technology, and inputs. As the late Jane Jacobs argued, import substitution is not just a strategy to become more self-reliant—though it accomplishes that, too—but also a way to grow the next generation of exporting businesses.[32] Successful local businesses, once they start meeting local needs, naturally look to expand into markets farther away. There is no good reason why a homegrown business "going to scale" has to sacrifice local ownership.

Growing local export industries does not contradict the virtues of self-reliance. In a world of more self-reliant communities, where every community produces more of its own cost-effective goods and services, trade does not disappear. To the contrary, every act of cost-effective localization, by leaving the home community just a little wealthier, enables that community to import more things that it truly couldn't otherwise produce for itself. In a world of localization, ironically, the value of global trade could well *increase*—only, the trade would be in highly specialized goods and services. There's the additional likelihood that traded goods, due to increasing energy prices, would be much lighter and carry a much smaller carbon footprint.

Three examples demonstrate how a community can grow wealthier through locally owned businesses that meet local demand first and then gradually sell to outside markets. Fifteen years ago, Güssing was a dying rural community of four thousand in Austria.[33] Its old industries of logging and farming had been ruined by global competition. Today's economic developers would have encouraged the residents to move elsewhere. But the mayor of Güssing decided that the key to prosperity was to plug energy "leaks." He built a small district heating system, fueled with local wood. The local money saved by importing less energy was then reinvested in the district heating system and in new energy businesses. Since then, fifty new firms have opened, creating a thousand new jobs. And most remarkably, the town estimates that this economic expansion, by replacing fossil-fuel burning with clean energy, actually will *reduce* its carbon footprint by 90 percent.

"Facing a Main Street dotted with vacant stores," wrote Marian Burros in *The New York Times* about Hardwick, Vermont, "residents of this hardscrabble community of 3,000 are reaching into its past to secure its future, betting on farming to make Hardwick the town that was saved by food."[34] Farmers, businesspeople, and the town's political leaders teamed up to develop a dizzying array new food businesses. Vermont Soy sells tofu made from local beans to 350 customers. Jasper Hill Farm built a state-of-the-art aging cave for its own cheeses and for other cheese makers in the area. Pete's Greens organized thirty local farmers into a large, community-supported agriculture program, where local subscribers get regular boxes of fresh produce. Claire's Restaurant is a "community-supported restaurant," financed by fifty frequent eaters who each bought $1,000 worth of discount meals in advance. New food businesses are being developed through an "industrial park" run by the Center for an Agricultural Economy and through an incubator managed by the Vermont Food Venture Center. All these local enterprises are buying from one another, and some are investing in one another through loans. Altogether, according to Rob Lewis, the town manager, these efforts to create a local food "cluster" that meets local needs and exports world-class products have resulted in seventy-five to one hundred new jobs, at a time when similar towns across America have been falling apart.

Even a single, visionary business can lead a communitywide effort at import substitution. Take Zingerman's Deli in Ann Arbor, Michigan. On its first day of business in 1982, in a college town known more for its radicalism than for its food, Zingerman's sold about $100 worth of sandwiches. It has since grown into a community of nine businesses, each independent but linked through overlapping partnerships that collectively employ 518 people and achieve annual sales of over $41 million. Over that period the proprietors conscientiously built a local-food cluster from scratch. They carefully assessed the items going into the deli—bread, coffee, cheeses—and saw profitable opportunities for creating a bakery, a coffee roaster, and a creamery. They looked at the products being sold at the deli—fabulous coffee cakes and high-quality meats—and built new, value-adding businesses with these products, including a mail-order company and a restaurant called the Roadhouse.

These examples underscore that local businesses need not be small or unprofitable. Nor do import substitution and relocalization have to mean—as Lusk and Norwood suggest—defecting from trade, ignoring exports, and losing the benefits from comparative advantage. Just the opposite is true. Import substitution is the most powerful way to expand the value of trade while also wisely maximizing your local economic multiplier.

Rule 3: Spread High Standards

The final rule for community prosperity is to embrace businesses that operate in ways consistent with community standards. If you don't want poverty in your community, your businesses must pay living wages with decent benefits. And if you don't want polluted air, water, and land, your businesses must behave in environmentally sustainable ways. Even though there is some evidence that local businesses behave more responsibly and that greater community self-reliance reduces environmental impacts, this linkage is not automatic.[35] That's why it's worth articulating a separate rule underscoring that a high quality of community life requires high standards of business performance.

In a new era of globalization, the maquiladora approach to prosperity has become a tempting option to struggling communities. The term *maquiladora* refers to some three thousand factories on the Mexican side of the U.S.-Mexican border that U.S. businesses and multinationals use in special tariff arrangements to take advantage of cheap labor costs. These factories generally pay no better than $1 to $2 per hour (and often much less), and their output is exported primarily to the United States. While U.S. laws prohibit the kind of abysmal labor and environmental conditions allowed in northern Mexico, many U.S. communities offer business conditions that are merely a little less extreme than the maquiladora package: no unions, wages barely above minimum, looser pollution controls. Unquestionably, this is a way to get jobs, and if you have no jobs and a broken local economy, this option will seem at least temporarily attractive.

But communities opting for what some have called the low road to economic development should beware the long-term impacts. Nearly twenty years after NAFTA passed and enshrined maquiladoras in trade law, the communities in Mexico providing homes for these sweathouse factories have little to show for their sacrifices: The Mexican middle class has shrunk while poverty has spread. A 2003 article in *The American Prospect* explains that "between 1994 and 2000, maquiladora employment doubled while employment in the rest of the country stagnated," but "booming investment in exporting sweatshops of the north has created a social and ecological nightmare. Rural migrants have overwhelmed the already inadequate housing, inadequate health and public-safety infrastructure, spreading shantytowns, pollution and crime."[36] And the very modest wage rises that have been achieved through worker struggles, typically about $55 a week for forty-five hours, have simply hastened the departure of global firms to places with even more wretched conditions in poorer countries like Thailand or authoritarian states that suppress labor rights like China. In fact, in between 2001 and 2003 "an estimated 200,000 maquiladora jobs . . . left Mexico for China, where workers can be had for one-eighth the Mexican wage."[37] The maquiladora strategy is inherently short-lived, because a smart global company can always find another gullible jurisdiction that's willing to ratchet its standards downward just a little farther.[38] This pattern results in a global race to the bottom in which everyone—except the multinationals—is a loser.

Ultimately, of course, different communities will balance social and environmental considerations differently: Some, like Santa Fe, New Mexico, will pass living wage ordinances, while others, like Skull Valley, Utah, will lobby for the privilege of burying casks of nuclear waste. But it's fair to say that even those communities that choose the low road to prosperity would prefer the high road *were it available*. The only reason communities pursue the low road is that they believe it is their only option for economic development. So Rule 3 really just restates the obvious: All things being equal, the best companies for a community are those that pay good wages, treat workers with dignity, and respect the local environment. The only way a community can possibly travel the high road is if it looks for it.

There are powerful arguments for raising business performance through community regulation and *requiring* high-road behavior. Setting straightforward rules prevents the worst corporate abuses, limits the ability of bad businesses to undercut good ones, and "internalizes" some of the external costs of bad behavior. For example, one good argument for a community to pass a living wage ordinance (which raises the minimum wage so that a full-time breadwinner can earn enough for his or her family to afford the basic necessities for living) is that without it, low-wage producers simply dump the external costs of poverty onto society at large. The existence of low minimum wages encourages a multinational firm like Walmart to teach its employees how to apply for government assistance like food stamps and the earned income tax credit.[39] A living wage eliminates this effective subsidy of bad business behavior.

But I also must admit that I'm increasingly persuaded that many regulations carry unintended consequences. Regulations that are especially stringent, such as logging restrictions in the Pacific Northwest and New England, can shut down entire industries, and may even push firms with strong ties to the community to move elsewhere. Regulators with too much discretion often start to favor the most powerful companies in an industry, creating competitive disadvantages for smaller companies—which, frankly, is the way securities laws have historically mutated. And even unambiguous regulations that prevent powerful corporations from discretionary exceptions might be vulnerable to lawsuits led by the same companies, while small businesses have no alternative but to obey.

Two other approaches to improving corporate behavior are innovation and information sharing, both of which are voluntary and market-based, and both of which carry none of the unintended consequences of regulation. Technological innovation can increase the productivity of workers and allow higher pay without lowering profits, and a better-compensated workforce can lead to higher retention rates, higher productivity, and lower training costs. Other examples of innovations that improve corporate behavior are energy and water efficiency measures that lower the costs of inputs, and clean-production methods that lower costs of toxic waste management.

Information sharing also can generate competitive advantages. Contrary to economists' assumptions, consumers are not moral idiots. During the several months in 2010 when a disabled BP well in the Gulf of Mexico was spewing an estimated fifty thousand barrels of oil a day, many motorists stopped filling up at the local BP station.[40] Smart companies are conscientiously teaching consumers what matters and how their products comport with these standards. Honest Tea has taught consumers that there is too much sugar in iced tea drinks and built a minor empire around low-sugar drinks. The Body Shop has raised public awareness of animal abuses in cosmetics testing and cruelty-free alternatives. Equal Exchange has educated consumers about fair-trade issues in coffee production through its work with faith organizations across the country. Toyota has raised consumers' awareness of car fuel efficiency through advertising of its Prius Hybrid. Seventh Generation has weaned millions of consumers off of toxic cleaning chemicals.

An example of a company that has used both innovation and information wisely to improve its competitiveness is Swanton Berry Farms in Central California. Two decades ago, when Jim Cochran set out to grow strawberries organically without the pesticide methyl bromide, many of his colleagues at the University of California at Santa Cruz (UCSC) thought he was nuts. He persisted and wound up developing one of the first organic chemical-free approaches to growing strawberries on a commercial scale. When he decided to invite the United Farm Workers to represent his workers, other strawberry farmers warned him it would kill his business. And yet, today, after becoming the first organic farm in the country to become 100 percent unionized and to offer family leave, medical coverage, retirement plans, and vacation and holiday pay, Swanton Berry Farms is thriving. Cochran's two-hundred-acre operation spans five farms, four of them leased. His strawberries and vegetables are sold directly through his own farm stand, two "U-pick" locations, and fourteen farmers' markets. He also sells to six grocery chains in California and New York, including Whole Foods in the Bay Area. His annual sales are almost $2 million, and profits have been positive for years.

From Cochran's standpoint, better working conditions constitute smart business behavior. He is one of the very few farm employers to pay based on hours worked rather than weight picked. He offers low-cost housing to his workers that three out of four take advantage of. Cochran says his model "is profitable, but just not very profitable." While Swanton's profits are below the industry's average, they have consistently been in the black.

Unionizing, says Cochran, came with "a whole set of guidelines, like a contract, and includes things you wouldn't have thought of, like a grievance procedure, which turn out to be very helpful. With ten employees, you don't have much written out." Having a formalized structure for labor was like having one for organics—it holds you to a higher standard and gives you the credibility to talk about your standards in your marketing.

Swanton Berry Farm models the logic of *quality*. And with high-quality organic growing methods and a labor force highly motivated by fair compensation, its products can command higher prices. Moreover, quality and social responsibility solidify brand loyalty, which makes possible direct sales to consumers with a higher profit margin.[41]

For generations, larger businesses have been able to spread innovations like these through trade associations, partnerships, flexible manufacturing networks, and licensing agreements. Business schools played an important role in transmitting information as well, incorporating lessons from larger, socially responsible businesses into textbooks and case studies. But for smaller business proprietors, who cannot afford B-school courses or Hawaiian conventions, learning has been slower. Into the breach have stepped new business organizations. BALLE, for example, is facilitating peer learning for local businesses in "building blocks" of community economies like local food, renewable energy, green building, and local finance.

An emerging tool that rewards innovation and spreads information is a corporate rating system. For years, the Good Housekeeping Seal let consumers flooded with self-promotional information know which products could really be trusted. Then came *Consumer Reports* magazine and monthly lists of best products. Then Energy Star. Then Green Seal. Then WiserEarth. Now there's Trucost, GoodGuide, the Fair Trade Federation, the list goes on and on. By one count, there are more than four hundred rating systems for products and companies in the United States.

Will this Tower of Babel lead to a comprehensive rating system that might actually set broad market standards? One initiative that just might do this is the B Corporation label, started by three successful young businessmen. The *B* in *B Corp* stands for "beneficial," and the mission of B Lab (the label's nonprofit architect) is to help businesses benchmark their "socially responsible" performance and steadily improve it. A B Corp must complete a survey on its products and practices, and how well they serve employees, consumers, and community and environmental practices. There are two hundred points available in the Ratings System, and a company must achieve a score of at least eighty to be eligible for certification.

The B Impact Rating System is web-based and designed to be comprehensive yet user-friendly enough for most businesses to complete within sixty to ninety minutes. It's also free and open to the public. With these features, many companies, large and small, can participate. In its first year, more than thirty-five hundred businesses and consumers registered to use the B Impact Rating System. Many companies use it to benchmark their performance and set internal goals, while other organizations are repurposing it to screen investments, customers, and suppliers. Several sustainable business networks also make the assessment a requirement for membership in order to measure a group's performance and improvement. Participation in the B Corp survey process makes it possible to measure performance year after year and see progress relative to your own company and relative to other companies generally, in your community, and in your market niche.

The B Corp survey depends on self-reporting, but the survey works on an honor system, and companies found in breach will get enough bad publicity to discourage willful misrepresentation. To earn the certification, B Corporations have to not only meet the eighty-point bar on the B Impact Rating System, but also undergo a variety of credibility and assurance tests. Each company must go through the survey review process with a B Lab staff member to make sure that all answers accurately reflect the intention of the question. It must submit documentation for approximately 20 percent of its survey answers. And one out of five companies must submit to auditing during a two-year period. Performers that achieve certification are able to use this in their advertising. Already there are more than 150 certified B Corporations from over thirty industries, representing $1 billion in collective revenues and $6 billion in capital under management.

A few state and local governments have begun to work with B Lab to create policy incentives—again, not regulatory requirements—for companies to achieve good social performance. In Philadelphia, where B Lab's home office is, the city now awards tax breaks to local companies that submit to the ratings and achieve good scores. Maryland recently passed a Benefit Corporation statute that awards an official state seal of approval to any company prepared to amend its corporate charter to put social performance on a par with private profit. Other states, such as Vermont, have followed.

Our economic system historically rewarded companies on the basis of one performance criterion—profit. As conservative economist Milton Friedman once argued, "There is one and only one social responsibility of business—to use its resources and engage in activities designed to increase its profits."[42] Millions of Americans now reject this view, and the B Corp label is enabling these consumers and investors to find businesses that share their values. Effectively, the B Corp laws are creating and strengthening a brand for good corporate behavior.

This is good not only for community prosperity, but also for efficiency. Some argue that whenever companies sacrifice profits for other goals like high labor or environmental standards, efficiency is lost. Yet this conclusion depends, again, on the assumption that price is all that consumers care about. A better definition of efficiency focuses on whether consumers are getting the *best value* for goods and services. *Value* includes both the quality of the product and the quality of the company, and decisions about value depend entirely on consumer choice. An axiom of a market economy is that it functions more efficiently when consumers have the best information possible to make their market choices. That's exactly what the B Corporation label does, effectively matching consumers and investors committed to benefiting the public interest with companies that share these values.

Give P's a Chance[43]

The three rules for community prosperity challenge today's economic-development orthodoxy. The two most common words in the vernacular of economic developers are *attract* and *retain*. It's almost impossible to find a report, a plan, a document linked to economic development without these words, and even a casual conversation with your local economic-development chief will witness these magic words popping up once or twice per minute. What's telling about *attract* and *retain* is that they have nothing to do with locally owned businesses. It's an oxymoron to attract a local business. And it's usually a business with shallow roots that will stay only if the community pays it a bribe.

Despite rhetorical enthusiasm for small business, economic development is largely about the attraction and retention of big, nonlocal companies whose goods and services are totally disconnected from local markets. The lobbying work of economic development, found in organizations like the U.S. Chamber of Commerce and even the National Federation of Independent Business, seeks to improve the local "business climate" by keeping labor and environmental standards low enough to attract globe-trotting companies. In short, conventional economic development is practicing exactly the opposite of what we know creates real prosperity. The cynic might even argue that the best thing communities can do to promote economic development is to abolish economic-development departments.

It is possible, however, to imagine a new kind of economic development, faithful to the three rules of local living economies. It would focus instead on answering six types of questions:

1. **Planning.** What are the most plausible opportunities for new or expanded local businesses to meet local needs?
2. **People.** How can a new generation of entrepreneurs and employees be organized and trained for new local-business opportunities?
3. **Purse.** How can local capital be mobilized to finance these new or expanding local businesses?
4. **Purchasing.** How can the community help these businesses, once established, flourish with concerted buy-local efforts by consumers, businesses, and government agencies?
5. **Partners.** How can local businesses improve their competitiveness by working together as partners?
6. **Public Policy.** How can laws, regulations, and rules at all levels of government—local, state, national, and global—be recalibrated to eliminate the current artificial advantages nonlocal businesses enjoy?

There's a long list of creative initiatives that spring from this list, many of which are being prototyped by pioneers around the country, like Bruce Seifer, the economic-development leader in Burlington.[44] But if you had to prioritize this list, you would probably put "Purse" at or near the top. The consistent message I hear from the eighty-plus local business networks in

BALLE and from the twenty-two thousand businesses they represent is "We need more capital." More loans, with better terms. And more equity investment from customers and neighbors.

If local businesses consistently generated smaller profits than Fortune 500 companies, then those seeking a living rate of return would face some agonizing choices. But as we've seen, over the last few decades local businesses have been remarkably competitive and profitable. And given the foreseeable trends ahead—like rising energy prices and mounting global instability—their attractiveness to local investors will only grow.

But what about the *riskiness* of local investment? Every smart investor understands that a good portfolio of investments should mix different risk characteristics, so if a wheat blight adversely affects your investment in a flour company, your investment in a computer-chip company will be safe. Because investing in community capital means putting all of one's investment eggs in a single geographic basket, skeptics argue that a community-capital portfolio is vulnerable to the inevitable ups and downs of the local business cycle. Of course, given the hyper-interdependent nature of today's economy, local recessions usually are related to national recessions. And to the extent an investor is still worried about geographic risks, she ultimately could divide her portfolio among many local business funds in multiple cities around the country. Our three rules for community prosperity suggest, however, that there's another side to the risk question. Consider the many ways that investing locally can bring *down* risk and improve returns:

- Because local investors can visit the companies in which they are investing, test out the products and services, and meet the CEO and the staff, they are less likely to be swindled in an Enron-like fraud.
- Local investors appreciate that the returns from their investment are not just to their own bottom line but also to their community's, with more employment and wealth, a stronger tax base, better schools, less crime, and so forth. The social benefits, in other words, *also* wind up enriching private investors.
- Local investors tend to be less passive than other investors. Owners of a co-op grocery store, for example, are among its best marketers

and volunteers, all of which increases the probability of the business succeeding and paying a good rate of return.

- Because local businesses spend more money locally, their multipliers boost the prospects of neighboring businesses. So an investment portfolio of local businesses enjoys the benefits of a positive feedback loop, with all the businesses in the portfolio reducing the risk of any one business failing.

- A smart local investor, finally, could structure her portfolio in ways that naturally tap and enhance the benefits of investing locally. For example, she might carefully choose to invest in three local businesses that were in an industrial-ecology arrangement where the "waste" of one business became the "food" for another. A fish cannery might produce waste heat for an adjacent greenhouse, and the weeds and clippings from the greenhouse might go to an aquaculture business raising fish for the cannery. Investing in all three businesses—cannery, greenhouse, and fish growing—improves the chances that each will succeed.

The science of local investing is really in its infancy. As we develop the kinds of tools we now rely on for large-scale investments—for creating affordable investment vehicles, for evaluating businesses objectively, for making local securities tradable, for assembling diversified local portfolios—local investors will more easily be able to identify the opportunities with the greatest return and the lowest risk. How exactly they can do so is the story of the rest of this book.

The Hidden Power of Cooperatives

Who are America's investors? While we tend to think of the "investor class" as the Bill Gateses and the General Electrics of America, the truth is that almost all of us are investors. Most of us invest passively, giving our money to private companies through stocks and bonds. Even those of us who only keep our money in savings or checking accounts in a bank are investors, since we're really equipping the bank to lend to these businesses.

For most of us, however, passively investing in *local* business right now is exceedingly difficult. There's a cute little organic grocery store down the street that just opened up, and you think it's about to take off. Could you knock on the owner's door and invest, say, $100? Probably not.

If you met the standards for being an accredited investor—you earned $200,000 per year (or $300,000 with your spouse) or you had $1 million in wealth (excluding your house)—the owner might be able to accept your money. Accommodating your investment offer probably would require costly legal and accounting fees to comply with securities laws. If the grocer thought the investment was large enough to justify hiring a pricey business lawyer, you might be able to buy in. Not complying with securities laws would create a risk of fines and even jail.

If you did not meet the exacting income requirements above, you would be considered an "unaccredited" investor, and the grocer would almost certainly have to shoo you away. U.S. securities law, along with state "blue sky" laws, would force the grocer to hire an attorney to write a bunch of documents, which might cost him tens of thousands of dollars. Would it really make sense for him to do this for a $100 investment?

The difficulties here underscore why so few Americans invest in the local half of the economy, and why that local half of the economy struggles to get the financing it needs. But despite these and myriad other ways the deck is stacked against local investment, a community has one ace up its collective sleeve that easily and legally opens possibilities in most states. It can create cooperatives.

For many people, the word *co-op* evokes decades-old images of a disorganized, hippie-run grocery store, with bins of whole grains and racks of unpleasantly bruised fruit. For me, the word brings back jaded memories of several of the residential houses I lived in at Stanford University as an undergraduate. With wild names like Synergy and Columbae, we co-op'ers bought and cooked our own food and made all our decisions on the basis of consensus. After my housemates at the Androgyny co-op rebelled against the house name and spent more than two months of weekly meetings doing nothing more than debating alternative monikers (ultimately settling on the obscure Simone de Beauvoir House), I reluctantly concluded that cooperatives were for people who didn't value their time. I was wrong. And I've now come to appreciate that cooperatives are the simplest way most Americans can tiptoe around securities laws and make small investments in neighborhood businesses.

A $3 Trillion Gold Mine

A group of scholars at the University of Wisconsin recently counted nearly thirty thousand cooperatives in the United States operating at seventy-three thousand locations.[1] The vast majority are consumer cooperatives, with 343 million memberships (many people belong to multiple co-ops, hence the number of memberships exceeds the U.S. population). Another seven million memberships can be found in producer and purchasing cooperatives. Credit unions, which are essentially banking cooperatives, have ninety-two million members. Electrical utility co-ops reach forty-two million Americans. Agricultural cooperatives have three million members.

The cooperative sector owns $3 trillion in assets, generates half a trillion dollars a year in revenue, and pays 856,000 people $25 billion in annual wages. Their multiplier impact on the economy supports more than two million jobs nationally. In Minnesota, which is not only the Land of 10,000 Lakes but also the state with a thousand co-ops, another survey of just a third of them found they were contributing seventy-nine thousand jobs in the state and more than $600 million in state and local tax revenues.[2]

Cooperatives can now be found in business services, child care, hardware, telecommunications, and insurance. In 2009, as Congress was debating whether to include a "public option" in health-care reform legislation, a compromise was seriously considered that would have prioritized the creation of state-based health-care cooperatives[3]—underscoring the increasing importance and bipartisan appeal of these models. More recently Congress has been considering transforming the two home-mortgage giants, Fannie Mae and Freddie Mac, into a nationwide securitization cooperative owned by member banks and credit unions.[4]

An underappreciated characteristic of co-ops is that nearly all of them fit our definition of *locally owned*—that is, probably 99.9 percent are connected to a particular place and owned by geographically proximate members. Even large co-ops that sprawl across the country have many of the characteristics of local businesses. National producers co-ops, like Land O'Lakes and Organic Valley, represent small farmers around the country who are eager to sell, process, and distribute their products regionally. Adam Schwartz, vice president for public affairs and member services for the National Cooperative Business Association (NCBA), says, "No matter how large a cooperative is, because it is owned by the individual farmers or individual consumers or small businesses, I feel very comfortable making a case that co-ops in any form support local business."

David Thompson, a cooperative innovator based in Northern California, contends that cooperatives are critically important builders of community economies. "I've often thought about how my local Davis Food Co-op employs about 160 people. At the co-op they have their own accounting, marketing, membership, and personnel department, all of the management is local, buyers are local, the monthly newsletter is printed locally, we advertise in the local paper (Trader Joe's doesn't), the books are done by a regional accounting firm, the lawyers are a regional firm. The two Safeways in town each employ about fifty workers, have no buyers on the spot, the administration, advertising and accounting are all done from Oakland, and all of its money at the end of the day is funneled off to Oakland, where the administrative expenses occur.[5] There's another side of it, too, which is that cooperatives will never move to another town, state, or country because it's cheaper. Their owners wouldn't allow it."

The structure of co-ops can vary widely. Most are built around consumers. But some are structured around purchasing and producer members (themselves typically local businesses), some around workers, and some around combinations of all these categories. What they have in common is adherence to principles enunciated in England in 1844 by the Rochdale Equitable Pioneers Society, which was put together by a group of unemployed weavers who had lost their jobs because of the industrialization of the textile industry.[6] Among the key tenets: Anyone who wishes to join a consumer cooperative can. Profits must be split among members according to their "patronage," which refers to their use of the cooperative, not the amount of their investment in it.[7] Members elect a board that oversees the management. Unlike most U.S. companies, where voting power is based on the principle of "one dollar, one vote," cooperatives are based on the principle of "one person, one vote."

Co-ops are deeply democratic. And while many are committed to pleasing as many members as possible, few rigidly adhere to the consensus practices that made my experience in Stanford's co-ops so exasperating. If anything, co-ops transcend political ideology. As Schwartz observes, "For conservatives, cooperatives mean self-help, people doing for themselves what needs to be done. For liberals and progressives, it's social progress, people doing what the community needs."

Even though most cooperatives start very modestly, some have grown spectacularly. Familiar co-op brands include Nationwide (a mutual insurance cooperative), AgriBank (a Minnesota-based farm-credit cooperative with $36.6 billion in assets), Recreational Equipment Inc. (better known as REI, the Seattle-based sporting goods company), and the Associated Press (a newspaper cooperative). Some cooperatives have scaled up to become significant engines of economic development within their communities. The Hanover Consumer Cooperative Society, based in New Hampshire and Vermont, has twenty-eight thousand members. According to its treasurer, Donald Kreis: "We have a vibrant local ag sector, and one of the reasons is that it's anchored by our big co-op. Our co-op is a $70-million-a-year business, and it buys a ton of locally produced products. Our co-op offers these vendors favorable payment terms. In doing that, the co-op makes sacrifices, which make it less profitable. The theory is that we can go to the twenty-eight thousand households that own the business and say, you know what, we are going to return a little less to you, because we know we all want to have a vibrant local ag sector."

Another Rochdale principle is to assist other co-ops or groups who wish to start their own co-ops. Kreis tells the story of a small town north of Hanover called Littleton, an hour-plus drive away: "They came to us at one point and said, 'We love your co-op, we're members of it, and we'd like you to open a branch store in Littleton.' Well, Littleton is really a little too far away for our co-op, but we said to them that we'll help you start your own co-op. You guys can raise money in your community, and we'll assist you. The people in Littleton didn't get it at first that we were serious about totally cooperating with them and not treating them as a rival or competitor in any way. Every shred of expertise we had we were willing to share with them: Our merchandising people went up there and helped them start the store; we gave them one of our store managers who was retiring and he became their founding manager; we even subsidized his salary for a while. What was really cool was that we didn't just help this community start a co-op, we helped educate and raise the consciousness of people in the community about what cooperation really means."

The Littleton story illustrates that the capital that members put into a co-op not only supports that co-op itself but also the proliferation of other cooperatives and other local businesses. The National Cooperative Business Association is also facilitating the creation of a patient capital fund. (The term *patient capital* generally means that investors are expected to keep their money in the fund for a long time.) Co-ops like Kreis's lend their surplus capital to NCBA, and NCBA in turn lends it out to new or expanding co-ops. The Cooperative Fund of New England, another lender to start-up co-ops, gets its capital from socially responsible institutions like the Episcopal Diocese of Hartford, Connecticut.

There's a tendency for those unfamiliar with cooperatives to look down on them as the leftovers of the mainstream economy, implying that if these ideologically driven people simply reorganized themselves into "normal" private companies, they would be more efficient and productive. In fact, just the opposite is true: Cooperatives often enter into economic activities that private businesses will not take on. The most fertile period of cooperative growth was during the Great Depression. Rural electric cooperatives spread across the American plains when it became clear that other investor-owned and municipally owned utilities were uninterested in wiring up sparsely populated regions. Credit unions, as we'll soon explore, have seen an upsurge during the recent financial crisis.

One economic argument, for consumer cooperatives especially, is that putting consumers in the driver's seat helps to keep prices low.[8] The information flow from consumers to producers is direct and immediate. Outrageous executive compensation, debt-inducing acquisitions, unjustifiable dividends to lure weary shareholders, irrational price inflation and discrimination—all the crazy behavior of conventional corporations—can effectively be banned by mindful consumers in co-ops. "Members naturally have trust and confidence in a co-op," argues Kreis, "because they own it. And that has both social capital and real capital bound up in it. There's real business value in being able to look your customers in the eye and say, You can trust us, because you own us, and we're in business to do nothing other than act in your best interest."

Funerals may seem like an odd place to see the competitive advantage of co-ops, but wherever there are stratospheric profits and monopolistic practices, consumer cooperatives can bring prices back to Earth. "Pomp and circumstance are for royalty," jokes John Eric Rolfstad, executive director of the People's Memorial funeral cooperative in Seattle, "[whereas] Baby Boomers want good value, simplicity, and convenience."[9] His cooperative has eighty thousand members and performs more than a thousand funerals per year. The cost of an open-casket burial is $3,299—less than half of what the average American pays. Mindful of the huge environmental footprint of cemeteries, People's Memorial encourages members to choose cremation for $649. "Simple final arrangements focus more on the spiritual and existential aspects of life and death, rather than on ostentatious materialism," says the co-op's website. In 2009 it issued $164,000 in dividends to its members, partially through patronage payments and partially through price cuts.

A second economic argument for cooperatives is that worker participation in running the business (which is certainly the case for worker cooperatives but also is a common feature of consumer cooperatives) increases labor productivity. One study comparing plywood companies in the Pacific Northwest found that cooperatives were 13.5 percent more productive than equivalent unionized plants, noting that cooperative workers could have gone on vacation an extra seven weeks and produced as much as their private-sector counterparts.[10] The efficiencies occurred because management, by involving workers, made smarter decisions about raw materials, machinery, and production methods. Another study of the Mondragon Cooperatives in Spain (elaborated below), by Henry Levin of Columbia University, showed that with only 25 percent of the capital per worker as the nation's largest five hundred private firms, they were able to add 88 percent to the value of products per worker.[11] That's triple the productivity!

A third economic argument is especially important for local living economies: Cooperatives can help local businesses compete more effectively. An inefficient small business can team up with others through a purchasing or producer cooperative to achieve economies of scale. To put it another way, there is no economy of scale local businesses cannot achieve as long as they are willing to work together through a cooperative. Sunkist, a co-op of citrus growers, enables member growers to deploy a common brand and undertake first-class, well-financed marketing campaigns. Furniture First, headquartered in Harrisburg, Pennsylvania, undertakes collective purchasing on behalf of the small furniture dealers it represents around the country, delivering bulk discounts and volume savings that would not be possible without the collaborative platform. In rural Wisconsin, a purchasing cooperative has boosted the local food movement.

"Local food is good medicine for everyone," says Stephen Ronstrom, CEO of Sacred Heart Hospital in Eau Claire, Wisconsin.[12] "It preserves and expands family farms, provides jobs in production and processing, and keeps money in our community." To bring local food cost-effectively into the nonprofit hospital, Ronstrom's staff teamed up with local farmers to create the Producers and Buyers Cooperative. No one farmer can provide the volume needed for the twenty-six hundred meals a day the hospital must serve. But by putting together dozens of farmers, processors, distributors, and institutional purchasers into a single cooperative, the entire system performs like an exquisite ballet. Other hospitals have since joined, and the cooperative anticipates attracting more institutions in the region like public schools, universities, nursing homes, and business commissaries.

The savings from collaboration are apparent in the bulk purchasing done by the Lakes Country Service Cooperative (LCSC) in Minnesota.[13] In 1976, the state created eight regional purchasing cooperatives to provide affordable health insurance to its school districts. These have since expanded their memberships to include local governments and nonprofits and are now bulk-purchasing everything from paper to cars. Mark Sievert, city administrator for Fergus Falls, a fourteen-thousand-person town that belongs to the co-op, says the city's $250 annual membership has led to hundreds of thousands of dollars of savings. In 2009 the co-op purchased $25 million of goods and services for its members, saving them $3.5 million.

For communities struggling to create jobs, cooperatives offer an affordable way to pool capital and to start up new businesses. In most states, co-op memberships are exempt from securities registration requirements. And under federal law, cooperative memberships generally are not considered securities. Therefore, all the expensive federal and state registration requirements necessary for unaccredited investors to launch, say, a private grocery store can often be dispensed with if the store is a consumer cooperative soliciting members.

But how exactly can a cooperative become an *investment* vehicle? In a typical consumer cooperative, a new member invests in, say, a $100 share, and then gets discounts on goods and services, and perhaps a patronage refund at the end of the year. If you become a member of dozens of co-ops, covering each of your basic needs like banking, insurance, energy, food, and health care, your capital investment may add up to several thousand dollars. Usually when members leave a cooperative, they can get back their member capital. If that $100 invested in the co-op allows a member to enjoy $10 of discounts or patronage benefits each year, the rate of return is 10 percent—more than double what a typical stock fund will deliver.

In the 1975 case of *United Housing Foundation v. Forman*, the U.S. Supreme Court established that memberships in a co-op, when purchased primarily for the benefits of membership and not primarily for a financial return, are not securities under federal law.[14] Moreover, patronage distributions from co-ops that provide personal, living, or family items are exempt from federal

taxation. But state law is more complicated. Whether your specific cooperative membership is or isn't a security, whether it's exempt from state blue-sky
filings, how it is taxed, how much of a financial return members can realize—everything turns on your state's exact co-op statutes and tax and other
securities laws. And the rules are inconsistent across the country. Every state
has at least one co-op statute, and many states have different statutes governing different types of co-ops. Minnesota has seven!

But if a cooperative keeps its members and business within a state, then
at least all it needs to worry about is state law. Jenny Kassan, my colleague
in Cutting Edge Capital, explains: "The minute you cross state lines, if you
solicit investors in more than one state, federal law comes into play . . . In
Colorado, Washington, Massachusetts, and several other states, cooperative
memberships are exempt from the state securities law registration requirements. They can go out, solicit the public to buy memberships in their co-op,
and not have to worry about the usual requirement to file a registration with
the state regulators." Cooperative memberships then can open a spigot to
other local-investment opportunities.

Leveraging Member Capital

Many cooperatives solicit loans from their members (though in most states
these loans are subject to securities registration requirements). If your cooperative pays you 5 percent or more on your loan, you're doing as well as
you would on Wall Street. Adam Schwartz of the NCBA is the one analyst
in the United States who most closely tracks co-op borrowing, and he says
it's more common than we think. Co-ops need more capital than members
initially provide. "With member equity," he says, "you pay anywhere from $5
to several hundred dollars, whatever the equity fee is. That's nice and good,
but it's not enough capital to get the business launched generally. There's
a couple of national lenders, but the amount available for co-ops is very
limited."

A brief aside about those national co-op lenders: The National Cooperative
Bank, with $1.6 billion in assets, is an important place where early-stage
co-ops can turn for assistance. If you were interested in starting a food coop-

erative, for example, you could tap into two funds that the bank developed in partnership with National Cooperative Grocers Association. The Seed Fund helps start-ups by matching up to $10,000 of preliminary member capital. The Sprout Fund matches $25,000 of member capital with $25,000 of additional loans. Both funds are anchor institutions for the NCGA's Food Co-op Initiative, which aims to more than double the number of food cooperatives, from two hundred to five hundred, by 2015.[77] Other regional funds include the Cooperative Fund of New England and the Northcountry Cooperative Development Fund.

The limited size of these national loan funds is the essential reason, Schwartz argues, many co-ops must borrow funds from their members. "There's a grocery co-op in Madison, Wisconsin, called the Willy Street Co-op. They've been around since the 1970s and started out as a small organic natural foods store. There was a big push for them to open a second store. They secured a loan with Summit Credit Union, but they needed an additional $600,000 to fund the expansion project. So they went to their owners—they had about twenty thousand at the time—and they raised $600,000 in twenty-one days. They were so successful that they reached their maximum limit of a million dollars in thirty-four days. They are paying a blended interest rate of 4.0 percent over seven years. They opened the second store in Middleton, Wisconsin, which is just outside of Madison on the west part of town, and the store is doing great. Everybody is happy."

Willy Street allowed members prepared to make loans to choose the rate of interest they wanted to receive: 4, 4.6, or 5.2 percent. A fifth of the lending members chose 4 percent. "It shows you the hunger that people have for wanting to create locally owned businesses," says Schwartz.

There are many other examples of consumer food co-ops that have borrowed successfully from their members.[16] The Wheatsfield food co-op in Ames, Iowa, raised $700,000 from twelve hundred members to finance moving the co-op to a new location. North Coast Cooperatives, with two stores in California, issued a class of stock to its members that earns 3.5 percent annual dividends and can be withdrawn with a month's notice, and more than $1.7 million worth has been purchased; it also has borrowed funds from its members, totaling $555,500, on which it pays 6 to 7 percent annual interest. Weaver Street Market, in Carrboro, North Carolina, borrowed $2.8

million from its members to finance a third store in Hillsborough. The Seward Co-op in Minneapolis, Minnesota, agreed to pay its members between 5 and 8 percent annually for $1.2 million needed to relocate its store.

Schwartz would like to help co-ops go back to their members, again and again, with new ideas for further investment: "I'd like to be able to go back to those thousands of investors in Willy Street and other co-ops and say, 'Hey, we appreciate your investment in us. Would you also be interested in investing in a fund that will create a co-op like Willy Street in some towns and cities that don't have one?' I think there would be a fairly receptive audience."

Historically, the universes of cooperative investment and private investments have remained separate, but now they are colliding. An example is the Coulee Region Organic Produce Pool (CROPP), better known as Organic Valley, which is a producer cooperative owned by organic farmers across the country. With more than $333 million in revenue, twelve hundred member-owner farmers, and five hundred staff, CROPP is arguably one of the biggest and most successful producer cooperatives in the country. It specializes in organic products, including eggs, dairy, produce, meat, and orange juice. It represents over 10 percent of the organic producers in the United States. It owns and operates its own shipping company (Organic Logistics), as well as regional processing facilities. It has developed the Organic Valley brand for dairy products and the Organic Prairie line for meat products. As a farmer cooperative that follows strict IRS rules (Section 521), CROPP is eligible for special tax benefits and state and federal securities law exemptions.

Between 1999 and 2003, CROPP offered equity investment opportunities to nonfarmers. This stock was initially available only to family and friends to finance the "Freedom Fund," a credit program for the farmer-members. In 2004, CROPP began offering a wider round of nonvoting, preferred shares to underwrite general expansion. These $50 shares were designed to raise general operating revenue for the company. Because the federal tax code specifically exempts agricultural co-ops from securities filings, the legal work was manageable.[17] How did the public respond? "We originally authorized $25 million worth of preferred, Class E shares in 2003," notes Mike Bedessem, CFO. "We thought we would sell a total of $6 to $10 million worth." But by the end of 2009, they had all $25 million sold and the board has since voted to extend another $40 million of these shares.

Some 93 percent of the investors in Class E shares have been individuals—with an average investment of $15,800.[18] A third of the investors have been food co-ops or their consumer members. The Twin Pines Cooperative Foundation (described below) invested a total of $300,000, and Organic Valley returned the favor, donating $40,000 to the foundation's Cooperative Community Fund.

"Cooperatives traditionally lack access to capital," says Jerry McGeorge, CROPP's director of cooperative affairs. "We've had to be very creative."

One reason CROPP's Class E shares were so popular was that the cooperative promised to pay a dividend of 5 to 6 percent per year. "Frankly," observes Schwartz, "you don't need to pay a 6 percent rate in this environment."

Another example that impresses Schwartz comes from the National Rural Utilities Cooperative Finance Corporation. "They're a lender to electric and telephone cooperatives across the country. They were founded forty-two years ago for the sole purpose of providing equity and loans to electricity and telephone cooperatives. They raise equity on Wall Street through the issuance of bonds, and then they take that money and lend it to their members. A couple of years ago they did an equity drive among their members, roughly a thousand utilities across the country, because they wanted to improve their balance sheet and get a lower rate on the bonds they offered. They raised $400 million from their members over the course of the year."

Half a dozen states have adopted Limited Cooperative Association statutes, which allow co-ops to create a class of preferred private investors *with limited voting rights* over cooperative decision making. This is in contrast with traditional cooperatives like Organic Valley, which offered preferred shares to outside investors but denied them any voting rights. Purists in the cooperative movement are not thrilled with these developments. "I have personally voiced concerns about LCAs," says Schwartz, "because unlike preferred stock, depending on how they are organized, they could give outside investors significant control of the co-op. And you run the risk, by doing that, of negating some of the benefits of being a cooperative." That said, however, Schwartz generally favors bringing private capital into co-ops. "We need investors who have the foresight to see that the benefit of the model is that it is owned by the consumers, producers, or workers . . . and they need to let them do their job and serve their members, and by doing so it will be a good investment."

Schwartz argues that such innovations are the key to expanding the role and influence of co-ops in the U.S. economy. Critical to this objective is more capital. And Schwartz has seen too many heartbreaking instances when co-ops needing capital to survive wind up selling out to investor-owned companies. That's why he welcomes the new generation of co-ops.

Schwartz would like to go further. In 2006, NCBA organized a task force of some of the best investment thinkers in the cooperative movement to design a National Cooperative Equity Fund. The idea is that the fund would accept capital from other large cooperatives, nonprofits, foundations, and financial institutions—all accredited investors—and then provide patient capital for promising cooperative projects. A preliminary concept paper Schwartz co-authored with Mary Griffin, NCBA's director of public policy at the time, argues, "As people's anxiety and disenchantment with Wall Street grows, so does their hunger to invest in and create businesses that respond to both the economic and social needs of communities."

Co-op Power

A consumer cooperative cannot easily become a community investment fund per se. It cannot take member capital, invest in *outside* businesses, and then deliver shared returns to members. Allowing more than a hundred investors to pool their money and invest in risky enterprises without complying with the same exhaustive regulatory requirements that mutual funds and other investment companies are subject to would violate the Investment Company Act of 1940. (This is an area of securities law we return to in chapter 9.) However, the act allows states to create and regulate some investment funds dealing exclusively with in-state companies (California has taken advantage of this by creating what it calls a Capital Access Company). The SEC also allows states broad latitude on how they regulate securities issued exclusively in-state. Why not extend this waiver to cooperative investment funds?

In the meantime, a few cooperatives have noticed a loophole in the Investment Company Act. Any business, whether or not it's a cooperative, can take as much as 40 percent of its capital and invest it in other businesses without becoming subject to the onerous requirements of the act.

One cooperative that is testing that 40 percent rule, as well as taking advantage of a liberal securities statute in Massachusetts that exempts cooperatives from registration requirements, is Co-op Power, with 390 members and 7,000 other "supporters" in New England and New York. Its mission is to develop community-scale sustainable energy projects for the benefit of its members. It is organized as a decentralized network of Local Organizing Councils, each representing communities across the region. In its short five-year lifetime, the cooperative has installed eighty solar hot-water heating systems and thirty-five renewable electricity systems. It provides its members with low-cost energy audits and energy-efficiency retrofits, and with net-metered electricity from renewable sources like solar electric arrays and methane gas digesters. Members organize buying groups to secure discounts on home heating oil, propane, and wood pellets. They also can purchase, at deep discounts, energy-efficiency products like compact-fluorescent lighting, insulation, solar ovens, insulated window inserts, and window shades.

But Co-op Power has a much bigger vision. President and CEO Lynn Benander says, "It's not just a consumer-owned co-op. It's a tool for building green economies in a very game-changing way."

Benander was managing a cooperative development center when the business plan for Co-op Power came across her desk. She got so excited about it that she decided to leave her job to help start it.

One of the unique features of Co-op Power is that it asks members, not for a $25 or $100 equity contribution at the outset, but for $1,000. The fee is reduced to $750 for farmers (paid over two years), and to $500 for low-income folks (paid over five years). "The members wanted to put in $500 to $1,000," Benander explains, "in order to gather together enough equity to build the community assets they believed they needed to transition off of fossil fuels and into a more just and sustainable future. They were forward thinking enough to understand how collecting capital and investing it together could help them build valuable community energy resources. Most co-ops I know wouldn't consider investing in outside business, but this group of leaders insisted on it. Ownership matters to them. They wanted to have their own energy-efficiency businesses, biofuel plants, and renewable energy resources that they could depend on for generations to come.

"Altogether," Benander continues, "we've raised more than $300,000 in member equity. And that money comes with a tremendous amount of expertise, buying power, and volunteer labor. The people who joined Co-op Power were the thought leaders and sustainable-energy experts in the region. Whenever I need a business plan written or a solar hot-water system design problem solved, I just send out an email—does anybody feel like working on this?—and I get three or four perfect people for the job. Anytime I need a vehicle donated or a place for a new staff person to live for six months, I get several offers."

With that initial $300,000, plus another $200,000 in member loans, Co-op Power has put three energy-efficiency crews on the road, launched its own solar hot-water system installation program, and supported the development of other energy businesses collectively employing more than a hundred people.

For example, local investors partnered with Co-op Power through an innovative investment offering to build Northeast Biodiesel, a recycled vegetable oil biodiesel plant. Co-op Power invested $125,000 of its member equity. Outside investors put $830,000 in (or 87 percent of the equity) in exchange for a 25 percent ownership share. They gave Co-op Power majority ownership in order to preserve long-term community ownership of the plant. The thirteen plant workers will own 24 percent after ten years.

Co-op Power has provided the customers, training, and business-development support for five different solar installation companies. It has seeded a thermal-window installation business with its purchasing power and business development resources. It has assisted two electrical contractors to add staff and expand into energy-efficiency-related lines of business.

"We also worked with two community-based nonprofits in a limited resource community to start Energía, a multifamily and commercial building energy-efficiency company. We wrote their business plan and helped them raise $540,000 to launch the business. We have a 15 percent ownership share, Nueva Esperanza has a 10 percent ownership share, the workers own 24 percent, and Nuestras Raíces owns 51 percent of the business. Our goal was to provide quality jobs in a limited-resource community, secure multifamily and commercial energy-efficiency services for our members, and generate core operating funds for a community-based nonprofit serving the community. Energía has been in business since November of 2009 and employs fifteen people."

None of these ancillary businesses is actually a consumer cooperative. Some are LLCs, some are nonprofits, and one is a worker-owned cooperative. "We decided to help any business start that would bring quality green energy products and services to our members," says Benander. "We still partner with all types of businesses, but now we only start what we call 'community-owned businesses' that are majority-owned by a cooperative, a municipality, a local nonprofit that's member-based, or some other form that ensures accountability to the community.

"Even though we're actually helping them make some good money," insists Benander, "we don't lead with that. We're not really interested in finding people for whom that's the primary motivation, because they'll put pressure on the businesses to do things that won't be mission-aligned."

Has it been difficult for Co-op Power to find investors in its growing portfolio of businesses? Well, yes and no. Co-op Power's seven thousand supporters respond quickly to requests sent out on the mailing list. Sometimes they will recruit their friends and neighbors. But not every pitch succeeds.

"We had a very challenging time raising the money we needed for Northeast Biodiesel," Benander reports. "At first we assumed that investors and banks would provide 40 to 50 percent of the capital required to build our $2.5 million biodiesel plant. We invested all our time and money in raising capital through these traditional means. We were set to launch, but then the recession hit, and then the banking crisis, and we were unable to raise the money we needed. It wasn't until we started focusing on raising member equity and member loans that the money started coming in again. It was an uphill battle until we went back to our members."

Co-op Power's members want local green energy products and services that are not yet available in the marketplace. That means, Benander explains, that very few members actually purchase the co-op's products and services, and those who do only do so occasionally. "Energy-efficiency services and renewable energy system installations are mostly onetime purchases. Once we're selling biodiesel and electricity in addition to home heating oil and other fuels, we'll play a more meaningful role in meeting our members' energy needs."

Benander and the co-op's active board of directors have engaged members, or would-be members, in an ongoing discussion on how their business should evolve. "At the beginning there were 250 people who came together to create a sense of consensus around a vision about the way energy is bought and sold, and about how to relocalize it, make it more fair, and create jobs for the people who have been left out of the system. We've continued those conversations in our Local Organizing Councils."

The co-op has invited speakers to come and add their ideas to the mix. For example, Benander invited Richard Heinberg to keynote her Sustainable Energy Summit in 2007. Heinberg, a senior fellow-in-residence at the Post Carbon Institute, is a prolific author and speaker on the realities and consequences of the world's running out of cheap fossil fuels. He warned the Co-op Power audience that limited-resource communities will face greater challenges regarding climate change and peak oil than will wealthier communities. Because it takes ten years for a community to transition off fossil fuels even with concerted planning, he argued that poor localities will likely not have the capital or time needed to support essential transition activities. He urged Co-op Power to prioritize renewable energy, green jobs, and local business development in these communities.

Co-op Power listened. Benander ticks off some of the responses to Heinberg's challenge: "We're building more benefits for renters. We have placed dozens of people in good green jobs through our job-training and job-development programs. And now we've created a new Green Job Membership that allows people who work for Co-op Power or for one of our related business to join for $50."

Benander concedes that adding more low-income members has also meant lower sales and dividends. "We really took our time to figure out what products and services worked in a limited-resource community, what green jobs and green businesses would be a good match for a given community, and how to talk with people about energy efficiency in homes they are renting. It added two to three years to our development time line. But no one regrets this."

Another new focus is on the energy purchases of not just individual residences or businesses but of entire neighborhoods. "Some of our Local Organizing Councils are now going beyond residential projects. We've developed a power purchase agreement model, where we can own solar installations on our members' roofs, whether that's thirty- to fifty-kilowatt installations at schools and businesses or a big project for community net metering. It costs a lot less to put up one large system than to put a small system on everyone's roof. Not every roof has good solar access, and not everyone has the money to install their own system. Community-scale systems are a better use of our community capital."

Benander freely shares her investment opportunities outside her network. "It's all very open," she says, "and I think people participate in the culture with a lot of generosity and openness. That's the essence of cooperation."

A Cooperative's Loan Fund

Another way a co-op can use its members' capital to support local businesses is to set up a revolving loan fund. That's what the La Montanita Food Co-op, based in New Mexico, did in 2010. "La Montanita," says Robin Seydel, membership director, "is all about meeting the needs of the communities we serve. What we're looking for is a sustainable business model that gives people a vehicle to invest in the local system, and get some return on their money."

La Montanita is one of the local food world's great success stories. Started in 1976, the co-op has expanded to five stores: three in Albuquerque, one in Santa Fe, and one in Gallup. "We believe," says the co-op's home page, "fresh locally grown, unprocessed food provides the greatest nutritional value for your food dollar. Building relationships with small and mid-sized family farmers committed to sustainable stewardship practices helps us provide the freshest high-quality food available while strengthening the local economy." This is a vision now shared by seventeen thousand members, who support not only a regional network of stores with nearly $30 million in annual sales but also a concerted effort to build a resilient food system in the state. Its Co-op Trade food-shed project is developing purchasing relationships with seven hundred local producers (a fifth of all sales in the store are local products); providing product pickup, storage, and distribution; and creating wholesale markets. It was only natural that the co-op would move into financing this infrastructure work through a La Montanita Fund.

Two events in 2009 spurred creation of the fund. The co-op co-sponsored a Slow Money Conference in Santa Fe in September. The next month, Susan Witt of the E. F. Schumacher Society came to talk about her work creating a small loan fund for local business. (We'll learn more about Slow Money and the E. F. Schumacher Society in chapter 4.) "We thought," recalls Seydel, "that if they can do it, we can do it, too." She and her colleagues started to meet and prepare a business plan for a local loan fund.

The idea of lending to partner businesses was not unprecedented in La Montanita's history. When the co-op began in 1976, it actually had two charters—one for a store and the other for a credit union. It decided it could only do one business well, and the credit union was sold to the New Mexico Educators Federal Credit Union, which is still widely used by La Montanita members. The co-op also had a small program to prepay farmers or food processors. The loans were paid back as reductions on invoices for products purchased by the co-op in the following months. Over three years, about $40,000 was lent out this way.

But co-op members wanted to do more. "They wanted a vehicle to invest in our producers," recalls Seydel. "And so, what could we create to allow that to happen? We wanted our investors to know where they're invested, who the loans went to. And wanted them to see those products on co-op shelves, and on shelves throughout their communities, and then to be able to buy those products."

The loan fund was founded with two kinds of capital. The co-op itself bought $25,000 of A shares, which is the first tranche at risk. This, then, gave some measure of protection to the community investors—any co-op member who is also a New Mexico resident—who could buy B shares for a minimum of $250 each (the maximum is $10,000). "We just thought it was the right thing to do," says Seydel, "and we wanted to lessen the risk, because we want people to feel a sense of security. And since our decisions are being made by our loan committee, which includes some members of the co-op itself and some members of the co-op senior leadership team, we felt that to have true transparency and to let people know that we're really serious about this, we would have to take some of the risk."

Once Seydel and her colleagues nailed down the details of the fund, they needed to get it approved by the New Mexico state securities regulators.

With the help of an attorney, a back-and-forth process ensued for several months. The first offering was finalized on October 6, 2010. By the end of the year, $97,000 had been raised—only $3,000 short of the initial $100,000 goal. "That was enough for us," says Seydel. "Small is better so that we can really learn how to do this in an organic way."

By December 31, the fund had forty-two investors. The marching orders from the state were that recruitment efforts could not be done publicly, only through direct communications with co-op members. "We had a couple stories in our newsletter," recalls Seydel, "and we had our annual membership meeting party, where we rolled out the program and told people about it. We had a delicious dinner and a great band! After the offering was closed on December 31, we had a whole bunch of new people come who wanted to invest. But we couldn't accept them. Next year, we'll maybe ask to try and raise another $100,000 or $150,000."

The purpose of the fund is for grassroots investors to support grassroots businesses. "All of us want to invest in the local food system, but there's no way most of us would ever be accredited investors. We do have, I think, one accredited investor who is investing in the La Montanita Fund, but everybody else is just a teacher, a co-op worker, a gardener, an irrigation specialist."

La Montanita is prototyping loans that will diversify the local food system so that it's possible to increase the level of local goods sold in the co-op from 20 percent to perhaps 35 or 50 percent. "If we got more local growers, if we had more products, if we could make the nutritional palate more complete for people . . . Our commitment is to local, organic, sustainable foods, and the local economy. That's who we are as an organization."

Interest payments to the Class B shareholders in 2011 will be small. "This first year, everybody is very clear that they're not going to get anything but a money market rate—but at least we're getting a better rate than if we hadn't pooled our resources. So that's where we're starting." Ultimately, the goal is to give at least 5 percent per year back to investors.

Seydel's long-term vision? "We're thinking that if an underserved community in rural New Mexico needs a co-op location, sometime in the future, we might respond with an offering of half a million or a million dollars, get all that through local money, and then pay the interest back to the investors.

It just really maintains the circle of investing and reinvesting, keeping the money in the community in a deeper and broader way."

Workers' Capital

Despite their successful strategies connecting with local investors, consumer co-ops suffer from one of the same capital gaps that afflict every business in the economy: Their workers are putting their retirement money in mutual funds made up almost entirely of Fortune 500 companies. "I'll put this in a very personal way," says Adam Schwartz of the NCBA. "I'm just sick and tired of my hard-earned dollars going to buy the equities of companies that I do not know, do not agree with, and whose fund managers are making tremendous amounts of money but not adding anything to our economy. I was once giving a speech to a group of credit union executives and I asked how many of you have 401(k) programs at your credit union, every hand went up. I then asked if they knew how the money was being invested? Most hands went up—these are financial people, after all. I then asked if any of the money was going to buy the stocks of large national banks. Again most hands went up. Finally I asked if any of them would open up a savings or checking account at one of those banks. No hands go up. I concluded by saying: So let me get this straight. You would never do direct business with competitors who are trying to put you out of business, but every day we and our employees pour hard-earned retirement savings into funds that buy their stocks. Psychiatrists have a word for that: insanity!"

Schwartz has consequently made it a priority to create a co-op capital fund that could qualify for 401(k) investments from the million or so people working for cooperatives. "I often tell the story of how I am an avid recycler of trash but I only became one when they brought the service to my curb, because it became easy to do the right thing. We need to do the same thing with our financial investments."

One kind of co-op that does reinvest employees' savings within the cooperative universe is the worker cooperative, which is relatively uncommon in the United States. The worker cooperative that most inspires awe worldwide and suggests new directions for the evolution of co-ops here is Mondragon in Spain. The Mondragon Cooperative Corporation (MCC) was started in 1956 by a priest who wished to put the legions of unemployed in the Basque region back to work. One of its earliest businesses was a bank, into which many Basque residents, with prodding from the local Catholic Church, moved their savings. This capital enabled workers in Mondragon to start other businesses within the cooperative. Mondragon has long maintained a full-employment policy: If a business is losing ground or fails, workers are reabsorbed into new or expanding businesses. In 2009, according to its website, Mondragon had 256 companies—half of which were *not* cooperatives—employing eighty-five thousand workers. These businesses spanned the entire economy and included finance, manufacturing, retail, consumer services, software, and construction. Global sales were 14.8 billion euros ($20 billion), and its assets were over 33 billion euros ($45 billion). The co-op offers its workers a safety net with health-care clinics and social security. Part of workers' pay goes into a MCC retirement fund, which underwrites the growth of the company.

A close student of Mondragon has been Ted Howard, executive director of The Democracy Collaborative, a research and policy center based at the University of Maryland. Since 2007, he has been working to replicate some of Mondragon's features in a cluster of pioneering worker cooperatives in Cleveland, all linked to a laundry.

The Evergreen Cooperative Laundry bills itself as a worker-owned, industrial-scale, "green" operation and targets the laundry needs of major health-care-related institutions in Cleveland like nursing homes and hospitals.[19] Six months after joining the co-op as a worker-owner, an employee receives a raise of $2 an hour, from which 50 cents per hour is withheld to purchase over time a $3,000 ownership stake in the company. A typical worker-owner can expect to build up a $65,000 equity stake from profit distributions in eight or nine years. Like Mondragon, Evergreen also has its own financial institution: The Evergreen Cooperative Development Fund, capitalized with more than $5 million from foundation grants, provides capital for each worker co-op in the cluster. The laundry itself received $750,000 from the fund and was able to use it to leverage seven times more capital from a variety of sources. Other cooperatives seeded by the fund include: Ohio Cooperative Solar, a large-scale installer of solar panels; Green City Growers, which is building a

230,000-square foot hydroponic greenhouse to grow food year-round; various recycling businesses targeting the medical waste stream of local hospitals; and a document scanning and data storage company. Each affiliated co-op agrees to pay 10 percent of its pretax profits back into the fund.

"The cooperative businesses we're building," says Howard, "have a very clear social mission, which is to stabilize and revitalize low-income neighborhoods that have experienced radical disinvestment over the past few decades. There's very little business activity, very few jobs in these neighborhoods, the poverty rate is off the charts. In the neighborhoods we're targeting, there are approximately forty-three thousand residents with a median household income below $18,500. Because of where we are siting our cooperatives physically, and because of the income levels of the people we are hiring, we have access to low-cost capital, particularly federal funds and New Markets Tax Credits, to build these businesses."

New Markets Tax Credits were initiated by President Bill Clinton as a way to provide equity investments, loans, and technical assistance for businesses in impoverished areas. Taxpayers are invited to patiently put money into these funds for seven years, and over that time they receive an astonishing 39 percent credit against federal taxes. (That's better than the stock market, even if the investment itself generates zero return!) The U.S. Treasury Department, which oversees the program, has authorized nearly $30 billion of tax credits since the program began. Among the key investors in Evergreen tax credits have been commercial banks, which otherwise would be reluctant to make loans. Key Bank, for example, is underwriting major parts of Ohio Cooperative Solar.

The Evergreen Cooperative Development Fund has attracted capital from a number of wealthy institutions and individuals committed to the future of Cleveland. The Cleveland Foundation, one of the largest community foundations in the United States, has played a catalytic role. Its board of directors and senior management have committed significant grant funding, assigned key program staff to assist the project, and funded experienced national consultants to help build the cooperative network. And since community foundations manage multiple funds of wealthy individuals who either live in the community or are connected to it, the Cleveland Foundation has been able to encourage many of its donors to add their own funding.

Howard hopes that the Evergreen Fund will attract investment from foundations and individuals all over Ohio and even beyond. "Around the country, wherever I go, I meet people who were born in Ohio but who left to look for work and opportunities in other cities. These last few decades have seen a kind of Ohio diaspora. But they still have a fond feeling and connection to Ohio. Many have families remaining in the area."

The Cleveland Clinic, the University Hospital, and Case Western University have each contributed $250,000 to the Evergreen Fund. "The CEO of the Cleveland Clinic," explains Howard, "has often said, 'You know, the word *Cleveland* is in our name. We have a vested interest in helping our community to be safe, healthy, and prosperous.' People aren't going to want to come to Cleveland for their health care if they think the city's hospitals are in the midst of this vast sea of poverty and disinvestment and it's unsafe in the community. Through our Evergreen strategy and partnership, we work very closely linking our cooperatives to the supply chain and procurement side of these large, place-based anchor institutions. That's good for the community and it's good for the business model of the anchors, a real win–win."

To coordinate the multiple co-ops in the Evergreen system, Howard and his colleagues are putting in place a holding company that will own minority positions in each company and maintain certain rights, including the right of veto if any co-op tries to exit the Evergreen system or wants to "demutualize" (convert to a noncooperative entity). The holding company board will be made up of representatives of the member co-ops, the donors, anchor institution partners, and other representatives of the community.

Incentivizing the cooperatives and their workers to remain in their community is very important to the Evergreen organizers. "How do you keep people in place," asks Howard, "so that they can really help fight for and build and organize their community to stabilize it and revitalize it? We don't think you should penalize or fire people because they move, but we want to provide incentives for them to stay. We're looking, for instance, at an Evergreen employer-assisted housing program, whereby a company might extend a $5,000 to $10,000 loan to a worker who wants to trade up into a better house or a safer part of the neighborhood, and if they stay in that house for five years the loan will be forgiven. In Cleveland $5,000 to $10,000 is enough for a down payment on a really nice house."

Howard is already introducing this model elsewhere. He has been meeting and consulting with organizers in Atlanta; Springfield, Massachusetts; Pittsburgh; Detroit; Richmond, California; and Washington, DC. "You know, there's no cookie-cutter approach. We've always been committed to making a difference here in Cleveland, but secondarily, we think we have a responsibility to share the lessons we're learning and to provide assistance where we can to help others in developing their own wealth-building and ownership strategies."

Mondragon itself, it's worth adding, also sees the potential for replicating its practices in the United States. It has reached out to the United Steelworkers Union, in the words of Josu Ugarte, president of Mondragon Internacional, "to combine the world's largest industrial worker cooperative with one of the world's most progressive and forward-thinking unions to work together, so that our combined know-how and complementary visions can transform manufacturing practices in America."[20] The Steelworkers have been one of the most creative unions when it comes to reinvesting worker pensions—though not yet in local business—so this collaboration could generate many new kinds of local-investment experiments.

The Present Future

"I grew up in Blackpool, England (fifty miles from Rochdale, the birthplace of the cooperative movement)," says David Thompson, "where both my parents worked for the local co-op. Our local co-op, the local Blackpool Industrial Cooperative Society, had about forty stores; it had its own farm, dairy, and bakery where my dad worked. It had its own department store where my mom worked, it had a social club, soccer fields, and its own housing estate. It was an amazing organization. I grew up knowing that as Christmas got nearer, the most important thing was going to the co-op store, standing in line with my mother, and getting our annual dividends, which the co-op paid out just before Christmas. We would get back $200 or so, which was a huge amount of money in the 1950s. One of the options the co-op had was, if you spent the dividends in the store, you got an extra discount. So my mom and I would go around the store, and we might buy clothes or a gramophone player or we might buy a new piece of furniture or something for the kitchen . . . She would use that money paid out at Christmas time to create a better life and a better home for her family."

Thompson now fancies himself Santa Claus delivering the goodies of co-ops to every community in America through his national advocacy. But he knows that will be impossible without more equity or patient capital. "That has been a problem almost since 1844 when the first cooperative started, because cooperatives are composed of people who don't have much money."

Thompson points out that some state laws place strict limits on how much a consumer can invest in a given cooperative. In California, for example, it's $300 per person—hardly enough to start a new grocery cooperative. The solution, as Thompson sees it, is a co-op IRA "for people to put money aside in an IRA that then gets directed toward the development of cooperatives across the country." Two years ago, he served on a task force of the NCBA to consider ways of achieving this goal.

In the meantime, Thompson has been pioneering a philanthropic solution through the Twin Pines Cooperative Foundation. Under his leadership, Twin Pines has helped twenty-seven food cooperatives across the country set up Cooperative Community Funds (CCFs), which in turn work alongside the national and regional cooperative banks to launch new projects.

"Our Community Cooperative Funds program operates as a family of endowments. When someone wants to start a CCF, we offer a $5,000 match, and that match comes from, for example, Equal Exchange, Organic Valley, Blooming Prairie Foundation, or from other cooperative organizations. The new cooperative comes into the program, they put up their own $5,000, and we give them that grant of $5,000 to kick-start their fund. And from that $10,000 they then have the task of growing that fund. The largest fund we have at this point is the Hanover CCF, which has now grown to $300,000. The twenty-seven funds we now have under management are now approaching $1.1 million in total size. Add in Twin Pines' own assets, and we have just over $2 million in assets."

Unlike most foundations, which invest 95 percent of their endowments conventionally to give 5 percent away each year innovatively, Twin Pines and the CCFs target all of their resources toward the development of other cooperatives. "We're the only charitable organization in the nation that has 100 percent of its assets reinvested back into cooperative development," explains Thompson. "That entire $2 million creates a leverage ratio of 10 to 1, so our funds have created $20 million of capital access for cooperatives."

Thompson believes that charitable giving is a huge, overlooked potential source of community capital. "Every co-op could use this, but I will use as an example the Sacramento Natural Foods Co-op (SNFC). We have approximately twelve thousand members, and the median income for a family of four in Sacramento County is $52,000. That means that SNFC members earn $624 million per year, over half a billion dollars. We know that people at that income level give 3 percent of their gross income to charity, which means they give away $18.7 million. Who do they give it to? They give it to people that ask them for money. Do co-ops ask them for money? Not really, we're uncomfortable and shy about doing that. But what if we did? Let us say, we only got 1 percent of that. It would be $187,000. So $187,000 a year, coming from fifty storefront cooperatives in metropolitan areas the size of Sacramento, and you'll have $9.3 million in new investment capital for cooperative development. You could then leverage $93 million."

Cooperative innovators like David Thompson believe that their sector can gradually attract more consumers, workers, and small businesses who have given up on the mainstream economy. Whether they are looking for better prices, more efficient platforms for business collaboration, or just more social solidarity, cooperatives are providing practical solutions to Americans' economic problems. But to grow from a percentage point or two of the economy, cooperatives need more capital. A lot more.

The investment tools outlined here—memberships, member loans, and private equity investment—allow Americans in almost every community to participate in this growing universe of local-investment possibilities offered by co-ops, and more tools may well be available in the near future. "My feeling," concludes Thompson, "is that we don't have to change much of the world to be able to change the world."

Institutional Lending

What's the first institution that comes to mind when you hear the word *money*? The answer is probably "bank." Why? Because, most of us believe, banks are where most of our money resides; they are the neighborhood financial storefronts open to everyone, rich and poor; they are the principal places into which we can walk, deposit our savings, and borrow whenever we need to. In fact, none of these beliefs is true today.

Banks, whether local or not, are no longer the most important financial institutions in our lives. Recall from the introduction that the long-term savings of households and nonprofits—stocks, bonds, mutual funds, pension funds, and insurance funds—totaled slightly more than $30 trillion at the end of 2010. By comparison, all assets in banks, credit unions, and thrifts were about a quarter as large: $6.4 trillion in savings, $1.1 trillion in money market funds, and a mere $326 billion in checking accounts and cash. So our traditional (and often local) financial institutions have become overshadowed by the titans of Wall Street.

In theory banks are open to everyone, but thanks to massive consolidation the local part of banking is fast becoming as rare as an Indian-head nickel. According to the Federal Deposit Insurance Corporation (FDIC), at the end of 1992 there were 11,463 commercial banks that held $3.5 trillion. Banks with assets under $1 billion accounted for a third of all assets. At the end of 2010 the nation had 6,259 commercial banks with $12 trillion in assets, meaning that nearly half of its banks disappeared in two decades. Banks with assets under $1 billion now account for less than a tenth of all assets, while the top ten bank holding companies account for more than a quarter. The leader of the pack, Bank of America, has nearly a trillion dollars in assets—*as much as all small and medium banks in the country put together*. The near quintupling of bank assets after 1992 went almost entirely to a shrinking number of nonlocal banking behemoths.

The story of savings and loan institutions, so-called thrifts that are also insured by the FDIC, is similar. In 1992, 2,390 thrifts held $1 trillion, with 64 percent held by institutions with assets over $1 billion. At the end of 2010 about half as many thrifts, 1,128, held $1.3 trillion, with 80 percent held by institutions with assets over $1 billion.

Even credit unions have seen a dramatic thinning of the herd. In the 1960s there were more than ten thousand federally insured credit unions. Today there are fewer than eight thousand. As noted in the previous chapter, nearly ninety million Americans are members of credit unions, but their assets at the end of 2010 totaled $679 billion—less than 6 percent of the total assets of commercial banks.

These trends have been accelerating for more than a generation. Banking of all types increasingly has moved beyond single brick-and-mortar outlets into multistate operations. The inescapable problem with large banking chains is that deposits drift from one bank to another, leaving some branches winners and others losers. Banks naturally want to dispatch their money to serve their best customers.

By the late 1970s Congress had become alarmed that banks were moving money from poor neighborhoods to rich ones, and more disturbingly from African American and Latino neighborhoods to white ones. It sought to end these "redlining" practices with the Community Reinvestment Act (CRA), which gathered records of banks' loan patterns and conditioned government approvals of bank plans to expand across state lines or to merge on good local reinvestment performance. Most observers regard the law as a mixed success. Banks have moved trillions of dollars into community investments that they otherwise wouldn't have. But if the CRA had really been effective, place-based banks would have stabilized and community investment could have expanded by an order of magnitude more. Instead, thanks to consolidation, thousands of communities have lost their local banks altogether.

Conservative critics also blame the CRA for the recent financial crisis by forcing banks to invest in less creditworthy customers. But it's a stretch to hold the CRA responsible for predatory private lending by firms like Countrywide Mortgage, for the collusive behavior of the management of

Fannie Mae (lowering lending standards for federally insured loans), and for the derivatives, swaps, and other exotic financial instruments that Wall Street concocted to hide bad credit risks. The CRA, moreover, only requires a bank to reinvest in its neighborhood, not in bad credit risks. Most neighborhoods, even poor ones, have *some* good borrowers. And nothing in the CRA requires lending at all. If banks saw only bad risks, they could have sat on their money and collected interest in overnight accounts (which is essentially what most banks are doing now to ride out the recession).

A third misunderstanding about banking today is that any credit-worthy individual can get a loan. In fact, as banks have consolidated, they have decided to put less of their money into their customers and more into higher-risk investments that promise higher rewards. In other words, we've allowed our Main Street institutions that once were the key supporters of local business to be hijacked by global gamblers. One catalyst was the dismantling in 1999 of the Glass-Steagall Act, which for decades had placed an impermeable wall between depository banks (which were prohibited from making risky investments) and investment banks (which weren't). When this wall came tumbling down, many banks happily invested federally insured depositor money in all kinds of high-risk activities.

Why Community Banking Matters

Even before the recent financial meltdown, small businesspeople have come to expect less from their banks. Banks naturally prefer loans with security. They'll extend a mortgage for commercial real estate because, ultimately, they own the land and the buildings. They'll extend a loan for a business to purchase machinery and furniture, because if the company goes belly-up, it can resell the tangible property. But unsecured working capital? Forget about it. Unless of course the entrepreneur puts his own house on the line, which might open the way for a guarantee from the Small Business Administration (SBA).

A recent SBA report shows that even though nine out of ten small businesses currently have loans, more than half these loans are secured by real property, vehicles, equipment, or a lease.[1] "Lines of credit" are unavailable to more than 80 percent of businesses with fewer than five employees. Given this reality, it's understandable why small businesspeople turn first and foremost to their own personal assets—their savings, their credit cards, and their houses. Then they might turn to their family—their spouse, their uncle, maybe their uncle's uncle. In close-knit ethnic communities, such as the Korean population in Los Angeles, broad networks of families also lend to one another.

Historically, the kind of financial institution most likely to extend a loan to a local business was a locally owned one. As Stacy Mitchell at the Institute for Local Self-Reliance recently observed: "Although small and midsized banks ($1 billion or less in assets) control only 22 percent of all bank assets, they account for 54 percent of small-business lending. Big banks, meanwhile, allocate relatively little of their resources to small business. The largest twenty banks, which now command 57 percent of all bank assets, devote only 18 percent of their commercial loan portfolios to small business."[2]

Mitchell is one of the best friends the local business community has. Her New Rules Project (www.newrules.org) collects cutting-edge public policies that can help local business, and her most recent book, *Big-Box Swindle*, has been a bible to local activists fighting Walmart and other chain stores. Her passion over the past two years has been the Move Your Money campaign, led by activist Arianna Huffington (who publishes online the popular *Huffington Post*) and financial televangelist Suze Orman. The campaign has encouraged Americans to take their cash out of big banks and put it into local banks in the name of community revitalization.

Mitchell argues that smaller banks and credit unions are inherently more open to extending credit to local businesses: "One reason," she writes, "is that big banks rely on computer models to determine whether to make a loan. Because the local market conditions and circumstances surrounding each borrower and his or her enterprise are so incredibly varied, this standardized approach does not work very well when it comes to understanding the nuances of risk associated with a particular small business."[3]

Smaller banks rely on a real-world understanding that comes from having relationships with borrowers, knowing their history, family, and ties with the community. This judgment, while difficult to reduce to a simple, machine-assembled score, is actually a much better predictor of the riskiness of a given loan. Consequently, smaller banks and credit unions actually have lower default rates on their small-business portfolios. In 2009, the peak year of the financial crisis, big banks had to write off 2.7 percent of the value of their loans, while small banks and credit unions only had to write off 1.2 percent.[4]

In August 2010, Thomas Hoenig, president of the Federal Reserve Bank of Kansas City, testified to Congress that "data show that community banks have done a better job serving their local loan needs over the past year. Community banks, as a whole, increased their total loans by about 2 percent, as compared to a 6 percent decline for larger banks . . . Business lending in particular stands out, with community bank loans dropping only 3 percent as compared with a 21 percent decline for larger banks."[5] Even though smaller banks and credit unions were largely uninvolved in the mortgage-backed securities that brought the system down, the crisis has exacted a particularly heavy toll on them. Like all banks, the values of their mortgages sunk. To maintain their legal loan-to-asset requirements, they had to pare down credit lines, call in loans, and hold back on making new loans. Their smaller size, however, meant they had less room to maneuver, and hundreds of small banks have failed or been shut down by federal regulators.

Despite this, the Move Your Money campaign has been a stunning success. Credit unions added 1.5 million members in 2009, a level of growth commensurate with the previous fourteen years combined![6] They expanded their business lending that year by 10 percent, while big banks were contracting business lending by 22 percent. The immediate impact of the campaign, however, has been blunted by several other nasty consequences of the financial crisis. Two of the largest (and least place-based) credit unions that performed back-office services for local credit unions were heavily invested in mortgage-backed securities, lost billions, and went into conservatorship. The National Credit Union Share Insurance Fund covered the bill, but now all credit unions must cover the loss. This has brought down their net earnings. Regulators currently consider 6 percent of the nation's credit unions "undercapitalized," which means they are close to failure, and all of them are constrained in their ability to make new loans.

Over time, as consumers understand the relative advantages of local banks and credit unions, many more Americans may Move Their Money. We know, for example, that local financial institutions generally pay more on savings accounts, charge less on checking accounts, and use more of their deposits to lend to their members. Moreover, some of the more superficial reasons consumers might have once preferred bigger banks—Internet services and free ATMs—have become almost universally available. Credit unions have developed their own sophisticated web-based banking platforms and collectively make all their ATMs, some twenty-eight thousand nationally, available to one another's members without charge.

For the relatively small number of consumers who live in those communities with no local financial institutions at all—primarily inner-city neighborhoods or sparsely populated rural regions—the fastest route to more credit may well be to open a new banking institution. Conventional wisdom suggests that a financial entrepreneur needs about $1 million to start a bank, but only $100,000 to start a credit union. (Anyone interested in doing the latter should obtain the excellent how-to manual put out by the National Federation of Community Development Credit Unions.)

But for the majority of us who already have some local banking options, the immediate challenge is different: How can we work with our local institutions to *increase* the flow of capital to local business?

Turbocharging Your Local Bank

The CEO of your local bank has many reasons to say no to more loans to local business. There's not enough capital in the bank, not enough collateral for the loans, and the businesses are seen as too risky. But suppose you were to approach your banker with the following proposition: "How about a group of us place additional money in your bank. You use that money to process and service the loans that meet our social and ecological criteria. If a loan goes south, you take our money. If the loans go well, we'll share the interest payments. Either way, you win. Deal?"

That's essentially what the New Economics Institute (formerly the E. F. Schumacher Society) did when it created the Self-Help Association for a Regional Economy (SHARE) in Great Barrington, Massachusetts. Influenced by the ideas of economist E. F. Schumacher, whose book *Small Is Beautiful* became a best seller in the 1970s, the institute has prototyped dozens of social experiments ranging from the first community-supported agriculture (CSA) farm in this country at Indian Line Farm, to one of the most ambitious local money systems in the United States, BerkShares, which has partnered with fourteen branches of six locally owned banks to put over $3 million worth of local scrip into circulation since its launch in 2006.

The institute is directed by Susan Witt, a brilliant, intense, sunny woman in her sixties. The late Robert Swann, her partner, was its founding president. In 1977, Witt began volunteering at the Institute for Community Economics in Cambridge, where Swann was pioneering the concept of community land trusts, which take land off the market and place it into regionally organized trusts, and then lease the land for housing and other productive uses. He and his colleagues were also trying to develop an investment fund to finance these land trusts, as well as alternative energy projects and worker cooperatives.

"Up until that point," Witt recalls, "there were investment funds that had social purposes, but they were stated in the negative. *No* to investment in South Africa, which at that time was infamous for its apartheid policies, *no* to investment in alcohol, *no* to investment in weapons (that was Pax World Funds). But there weren't investment funds focusing on the positive. We created three limited partnerships, in which sophisticated investors—that is, investors with substantial wealth—could put in certain levels of funding, with the institute serving as the general partner."

Witt was asked to be the staff person for these partnerships, which became known as the Community Investment Fund (CIFund). This entity had an extraordinary board of directors that included noted philanthropists like Charles Knight of the Haymarket People's Fund, respected investment advisers like Bob Zevin (then with the U.S. Trust Company), the investment genius Wayne Silby (who had recently founded the Calvert Fund), co-op experts like Ed Kirshner, activists like Terry Mollner, and lawyers like Rochelle Korman of *Ms.* magazine. The board created criteria for the fund with specific social and ecological standards that are still being used in social-investment circles today.

Board members were able to get Witt meetings with the investment liaisons at universities, foundations, and major church groups, but she consistently got the same response: "Our job is to make as much money as possible so that others can do good things with it. Don't bother us about how we are investing." After eighteen months, the CIFund had raised only $1 million—a third of its target. "We had done a lot of education, we had started a movement, but we had run out of operating funds to keep the door open."

What stayed with Witt from this experience were the questions she consistently got asked about local investment. She realized that these new, socially motivated investors wanted to see exactly what their money was doing in their own backyards. "If they knew the people involved and could watch how the business was run, then they did not experience the loans as risky. They felt close enough to influence the success of the business. What we needed was a fund that would connect local investors directly with local projects. That's why we created SHARE."

In 1980, Witt and Swann moved to Great Barrington, Massachusetts, to put their ideas about community land trusts and local financing programs into practice and to found the E. F. Schumacher Society, the precursor of the New Economics Institute. They incorporated SHARE as a nonprofit, locally based membership organization that provided residents in the Berkshires with an easy to manage way to extend needed, low-cost credit to small businesses in the region.

In her testimony before the House Select Committee on Hunger in 1988, Witt said: "We discovered that in rural areas, where many small businesses begin in the home as cottage industries, a very small amount of capital will go a long way in providing new jobs and encouraging the local production of goods formerly imported from outside the region. A knitting machine for a mother working in the home while caring for a family, a table saw for the carpenter, and a commercial-sized oven for the local baker are all low-cost technologies that are quickly repaid with the increase in productivity."[7]

Witt went on to explain to the committee the inherent barriers she saw facing small businesses seeking credit. "After all, from one point of view, it is more efficient [for a bank] to take on a $250,000 loan than it is to make one hundred $2,500 loans. The small rural borrower, often without established credit references, finds himself or herself competing with international corporations for financing. When the small loan is approved, it is at the penalty of a higher interest rate—a rate that is often so high as to make the emerging business unfeasible."

Witt and her colleagues thought about creating a credit union but worried about the expense of the overhead. She also observed that most credit unions, controlled by their consumer members, naturally prioritize personal loans for housing, cars, and college over business loans. Another mechanism was needed to bring capital to local entrepreneurs. So they decided to create a new mechanism *within* an existing bank.

They approached the bank in town with the best CRA performance record, Great Barrington Savings (now Berkshire Bank). In a first meeting with the bank's president and four vice presidents, the reaction was mixed. "'Too costly to manage,' we heard from the vice presidents. 'Small deposits and small loans. Just a lot of bookkeeping.' Our hopes faded. But then the president spoke up. He had been raised in the area, had worked his way up in the bank from a position as teller, and could remember the time when loans were made on the character of the borrower, with little paperwork. He instructed his vice presidents to 'work out all the details of the proposal with these people, so that we can have the SHARE program at this bank. They are planning to do what we should be doing and are no longer able to do.'"

The details were ironed out in a month. A Berkshire resident could open a passbook savings account at the bank as a joint account with SHARE. The account remained fully owned by the depositor, who earned 6 percent per annum, below the then-standard rate of 7 percent. Each member also entered a contract with SHARE, agreeing that the passbook could be pooled with others as collateral for loans that met SHARE's criteria. As deposits in SHARE accounts grew, the bank made more loans recommended by SHARE, charging 10 percent interest, well below the nearly 18 percent interest that was typical of small loans at the time. The 4 percent "spread," between cost of the money and income from the loan, was the bank's to keep to cover administrative costs.

By the time Witt testified to Congress, the program had seventy depositors and, through rapid turnover, had made fourteen loans of $3,000 each. The first loan helped Rawson Brook Farm, which made a soft chèvre cheese from its goat herd, bring its milking parlor and cheese room up to state standards. Another loan enabled a home knitter to purchase yarn in bulk as well as a new knitting machine. An appliance repairman got a loan to buy extra parts for washers and dryers. In all, the program created forty new jobs without any loan loss.[8]

"While in form SHARE was simply a loan collateralization program," Witt explains, "in practice it proved to be much more. Members received quarterly letters describing which businesses received collateral support. They then took a personal interest in the business. They brought their grandchildren to see the new goat kids at Rawson Brook Farm; they rooted for Spike and Rosie at the local draft horse pulling event; they recommended Marty to a friend when a washing machine was in trouble; and they boasted that Terry, whose loan went to buy a piano, was the best music teacher in the area. They chose Monterey Chèvre cheese before national brands and asked for it at shops where it was not yet available."

Witt designed the program to tap the wealth of summer dwellers in the Berkshires, but she was surprised at how many of the people opening up SHARE accounts were relatively poor: "People working for their living, not with a lot of excess cash, were just putting their whole savings into a SHARE account and that just flipped my mind. And then I realized that they perceived it as helping people like themselves. They were glad to do it. They weren't thinking in terms of risk, they were thinking in terms of particular people and particular projects that they knew. It was a different way of thinking about investment."

After a whirlwind run, Witt and her colleagues closed the program in the 1990s. New CRA regulations encouraged banks to do more neighborhood lending. Interest rates were lower. And SHARE had helped local banks become more familiar and comfortable with making small-business loans—so much so that SHARE money was just sitting in accounts unused. (Anyone interesting in trying out this program in their own community can download SHARE's legal documents at www.neweconomicsinstitute.org.)

In retrospect, Witt wishes SHARE had focused as much on nurturing entrepreneurship as it did on mobilizing capital. "It was not lack of capital, but lack of good business plans, that prevented the program from growing. Working people find it hard to take time to develop plans for a new import-replacement business. SHARE would have benefited from a team of 'social entrepreneurs,' retired businesspersons, and other concerned citizens working together to create a library of business opportunities. We wished for great business plans focusing on basic necessities of food, clothing, shelter, and energy that met a high standard of social and ecological responsibility."

SHARE laid the groundwork in the Berkshires for other local financing initiatives like the Deli Dollar and Berkshire Farm Preserve Note self-financing scrips, and later BerkShares. Meanwhile the story of SHARE circulated broadly in community banking circles, especially in a community several hours' drive to the west.

A Social Action Credit Union

Alternatives Federal Credit Union in Ithaca, New York, where Cornell University is located, opened in 1979. To become a member, all a resident had to do was set up a savings account with at least $5. By the end of 2008 assets at the credit union had grown to $55 million, and it was servicing businesses and institutions throughout eight counties surrounding Ithaca. Around 1996, the then-CEO of Alternatives, Bill Myers, was impressed not only with SHARE but also with the Self-Help Credit Union in North Carolina, which invited outside nonprofit organizations to put money on deposit and then co-managed loans those organizations made to clients they were trying to serve. He asked Mary Ziegler to study the Self-Help model and adapt it for their area. That was how the Community Partnership Lending program at Alternatives was born. Like SHARE, outside groups could place capital on deposit and determine who would receive loans, while the credit union administered the program. The new features Alternatives added were to focus on nonprofits and to match every dollar put on deposit with a credit union dollar.

Ziegler, now director of projects for Alternatives, recalls, "We developed a contract and materials that went along with it, and we sent out invitations to nonprofit organizations in the area, and had probably about half a dozen who became serious candidates." Two of the nonprofits they signed up worked with small-business owners. Another was Catholic Charities of Tompkins County, which helped people moving into an apartment come up with the first month's rent and a security deposit. Most of the loans ranged from $2,000 to $5,000.

Community Partnership Lending encourages each participating nonprofit to develop its own lending policy. "We expect the nonprofit to find the clientele," says Ziegler, "to answer a need, and to determine who of their clients will receive the loans and who will not—where their lines are drawn. A lot of organizations ask for help with this; they think they have no idea how to do something, but typically they find out they really do. Who do you want to loan to and under what circumstances? What's the maximum dollar amount, how would you like it to be repaid? That's all a loan policy really is."

As in the case of SHARE, the funds that an organization deposits at Alternatives Federal Credit Union serve as the reserves to cover any losses. They stay on deposit for the duration of a loan. Ziegler clarifies that "a lot of organizations seem to think that if they give us the money, every time we give out a loan we're taking funds from them—but that's not what happens. The funds we give out in loans are all Alternatives Federal Credit Union funds. The deposit sits there untouched unless there is a loss. The deposits can earn interest or not, depending on the organization." The organization gradually develops a revolving loan fund because, as clients repay, the funds become available as loss reserves for new loans.

Alternatives ties the interest rate it places on these loans to the interest rates demanded by its nonprofit depositors. Thus far, almost every organization, eager to maximize its lending portfolio, has chosen to receive zero return. "A lot of organizations are really focused on giving a really good interest rate to their clients, which is fine, and we're also always willing to point out that the difference in payment between a 6 percent interest loan and an 8 percent interest loan is pretty minimal. It's okay if you want to earn some interest." If a nonprofit wants to cover administrative costs, they will consider charging an application fee.

The key to successful lending, Zeigler believes, is strong relationships. "We serve a higher-risk population. So the idea of having a partner organization is that they know their clients, and they have sensible criteria that a financial institution doesn't impose. For instance, for the car loan program, a partner might require that you have a clean license, that you haven't had accidents, and that you have a mechanic inspect the car that you're buying. Knowledge of the client really helps, first when they're making the loan decision, and second, if they see that a loan is falling behind. Yes, the credit union will go after delinquent borrowers when it needs to, but first the partner will call up and talk to that person, and encourage them to speak with the credit union and make some kind of payment. That helps reduce the loss level."

Does the decision to match each lent dollar put the credit union at risk? No, says Ziegler, because the first "tranche" at risk for any failure is what the organization itself has put on deposit. "To put the credit union at risk we would have to reach an over 50 percent loss rate. Most people want to repay what they've borrowed. You can almost hand out money blind on the street and be able to collect half of it. Still, that said, we do evaluate an organization, and include provisions in our contract to suspend lending if necessary. With some of the organizations that are just getting started with a loan program, we don't match in the first year. If too many loans become delinquent, we call a halt to new loans while the loan approval guidelines are considered for revision."

Leslie Ackerman, a colleague of Ziegler's at Alternatives, would like to explore ways to apply the partnership lending model to community investment in local business. Ackerman directs Alternatives' small-business resource center, Business CENTS (Community Enterprise Networking and Training Services), and oversees its curriculum of courses and coaching services that help entrepreneurs conduct feasibility studies, prepare business plans and marketing strategies, learn finance and management skills, and network with other small-business owners. Ackerman believes that the partnership model "*could* be adapted to many small-business-lending uses—and this is what excites me!" She wants to focus on local agricultural businesses, and she points to a similar model in New England that's going gangbusters with one particular foodstuff: coffee.

Arranging Your Own Bank Loan

Daniel Fireside has spent his life working on the cutting edge of social enterprises, everything from a magazine on progressive economics (*Dollars & Sense*) to community land trusts. Today he's the capital coordinator for Equal Exchange, a worker-owned for-profit that helped introduce the United States to the concept of fair-trade coffee and is doing more than $40 million in sales per year. Educated as an urban economist, Fireside spearheads the company's program for raising money from specialized CDs at a local bank. But before elaborating this innovative investment scheme, we should take a moment to review the history of Equal Exchange.

Equal Exchange started in 1986 as a "solidarity project" with smallholding farmers in Nicaragua, at a time when the U.S. government was trying to overthrow the Sandinista government by arming the Contras. The idea was to purchase coffee directly from family-farmer cooperatives. By cutting out the middleman, fair trade puts more income into the pockets of the growers. Today the company has expanded its fair-trade operations to tea, chocolate, bananas, olive oil, and snack foods, though most of the business still centers on coffee.

Equal Exchange is based in metropolitan Boston. The founders of the company were committed to its being a financial success, so they organized it as a for-profit. The pay for workers is good, with full benefits, and the ratio between the highest- and lowest-paid staff person is only four to one. Every single worker-owner gets the exact same profit-share (or loss) at the end of the year. Another intriguing company feature is that it is virtually impossible for future owners to sell out. The bylaws state, according to Fireside, "that if Starbucks ever drops a check with too many zeros on it and says 'Hey you guys did your hard work, now go out and buy your fair-trade yacht,' we have to pay back our bank loans, pay back our investors the amount they put in, and then all of the net proceeds have to be donated to a nonprofit that works for fair trade."

The company's thinking is imbued with the vision of stakeholder ownership. The founders, according to Fireside, argued that every participant "has the right to benefit from the company: the people who work here, the farmers who sell to us, the co-ops and other partners who buy from us and sell our products, and people who invest and lend to us. The true value of the company is created by everyone, and so it's not for the people who happen to be here at any particular moment to cash out. We hold the company in trust for everyone who has created it."

The business ethos of the company is to make money, but not too much; always keep the core values first. For both worker-owners and investors, says Fireside, this understanding is "incredibly liberating." It allows the company to make choices others couldn't or wouldn't.

For example, several years back Equal Exchange entered a partnership with a European fair-trade group to start selling bananas in the United States. The company was hemorrhaging money. "We had to decide," recalls Fireside, "if we were going to pull the plug and call it a noble experiment, or invest half a million dollars, revamp the sales structure, and keep it going. This decision was brought before the entire worker-owner group, over eighty people at the time. The facts suggested that, if we lost half a million dollars of our money, it would be a big black eye of business failure. It wouldn't sink us, but it had very little upside. There wasn't an easy path to success. This venture was never going to be a huge moneymaker, because fair-trade, ethically produced, environmentally sound bananas simply cost more. It ultimately came down to people saying, You know, this is a really bad business decision but it's the right thing to do. This was the same business case that people must have faced when Equal Exchange was starting up. And so if we're not the ones who are going to try this, then who is?"

Equal Exchange voted to put half a million dollars more into the European banana company and has since become a 90 percent owner of it. It hasn't made its investment back yet, but the business is still viable. Although the margins are razor-thin, Equal Exchange now sells more pounds of bananas each year than it does coffee, all from small-farmer cooperatives in Peru and Ecuador.

Equal Exchange brought these same values to its decisions about how to secure capital. "The conventional model," says Fireside, "is to go out and raise a bunch of venture capital money. No matter how well intentioned those people might be, a lot of them want to get rich quick, want 40 percent annual returns, and want you to go public—and those are the kinds of pressures that really shape your business decisions. We didn't want that kind of funding. And even when you're successful, you get bank loans and other kinds of financing that place all sorts of conditions on your company. We have access to that kind of money, but we much prefer to get it from people who are really committed to what we're doing."

So as a worker cooperative, Equal Exchange adopted some of the techniques we saw in the previous chapter. Like Organic Valley, it created a preferred shareholder class. Fair-trade coffee actually requires a lot of up-front capital. "Because we're fair trade," explains Fireside, "we take possession of the coffee as soon as it's harvested. We also provide for pre-harvest financing. So we're paying and financing the stuff we're selling long before we can ever sell it. We believe that manufacturers and sellers of coffee products should be carrying those costs, not the farmers. But that means we have millions of dollars of our working capital tied up in inventory."

To avoid registering as a publicly traded company, Equal Exchange has had to keep the number of shareholders in its preferred class to fewer than five hundred. Some unaccredited investors are allowed, but the SEC rules require that they never number more than thirty-five per offering. These stock offerings have raised more than $10 million.[9] But over the years, as the amount of capital sought from these five hundred shareholders has risen, the company has had to redeem shares from smaller shareholders to make way for bigger ones.

The stock has been fabulously successful. There's a five-year minimum holding period, and the annual dividend is typically 5 percent. "It's not guaranteed and it's not cumulative, so we don't promise to make it up if we ever miss a dividend. But we have paid a dividend for every year in the last twenty-two years. There were two years when it was a little bit below 5 percent and four years when it's been above 5 percent. All the rest it has been exactly 5 percent, so our average annual payout has been a whisker over 5 percent."

Fireside whips out a chart that makes one of the central points of chapter 1: With a steady 5 percent return, Equal Exchange is outperforming Wall Street. Over ten years, from 1998 to 2008, a $10,000 investment in the S&P 500 yields a couple of hundred dollars' gain. A similar investment in Equal Exchange Class B stock yields a gain of $6,444! "I tell people that we're not out to make anyone rich," says Fireside, "but we want this to be a viable investment. Otherwise we're just a charity."

But the most significant entry point for unaccredited investors, especially as the minimum-investment threshold for Class B stock has risen, has been its CD program. Fireside's predecessor, Alistair Williamson, had a brainstorm to do something similar to E. F. Schumacher's SHARE program. People interested in supporting Equal Exchange could buy a CD and earn the normal rate of return on it, and the bank would use it as collateral for a low-interest loan to the company. Williamson approached Wainwright Bank (now Eastern Bank), which had a good track record for supporting socially responsible companies, and they agreed to create a special three-year CD, requiring a $500 minimum deposit, and made it open to accredited and unaccredited investors alike. The CD is FDIC-insured against bank failure, but it is at risk if Equal Exchange ever defaults on its loan.

Fireside points out that the risk to CD holders actually is quite small: "In the grand scheme of things, the greatest risk, if the company were to go out of business, is held by the worker-owners. If there weren't enough to cover all of our debts and obligations, there's a pecking order of who gets paid back. The banks are always first. Then our preferred shareholders. Last in line are the worker-owners. So we're very careful. We don't take on more credit than we feel comfortable with."

Defying the logic of neoclassical economists, the CD holders don't demand any increased reward for the extra risk. They are paid at exactly the same rate as the holders of conventional CDs. "What they're getting," says Fireside, "is a social return. They're saying, Hey, this is really the only vehicle I know of where my bank is telling me exactly what they're doing with my money, and it's a really great thing that's in line with my values, and for me that's worth the tiny extra risk." After three years, the program has attracted over $1 million from more than one hundred depositors.

Even though the bank is paying Equal Exchange CD holders the same rate as it pays on other CDs, its margin is tighter. Superficially, the spread it has—currently between 3.25 percent it takes in from the loan and 0.85 percent it pays on the CD—is the same as it enjoys on other CDs. But the bank's costs of administering the program, Fireside admits, are greater. "The bank is taking on some extra work. It's really a sign of the commitment from them and their values that they're willing to do this. I also think they see it as a real plus. They include it in some of their advertisements. People come into the bank and say 'Wow! This is cool that you're supporting fair trade!'

"But it's not charity on the bank's part," Fireside adds quickly. "It's providing a real service to depositors, who want to see their money do double duty."

Some depositors who would have difficulty making an equity investment in Equal Exchange, Fireside suspects, nevertheless are comfortable buying the CDs. The barrier to becoming an equity investor is mostly psychological. "Financial professionals have this belief that investing in a company like Equal Exchange is riskier than putting your money in Wall Street, despite the fact that we've outlasted several stock market crashes and the Great

Recession. We're working hard to change that perception, but a lot more of them seem to feel comfortable with the CDs."

The agreement between Equal Exchange and the bank stipulates that the holders of the CDs remain confidential. "It's really two separate transactions," explains Fireside. "Individuals make a deposit with the bank, and then they're agreeing to let the bank lend the money to us. It's not ideal from our point of view. We would like to have direct connections. The bank does allow us to provide them with annual reports, coupons, and a cover letter, and the bank then sends the materials out to all of the depositors. For us, it's really important to make social returns something tangible."

But many of the depositors make themselves known to Equal Exchange. The Union for Radical Political Economics (URPE), for example, is an association of left-leaning economists with a very successful journal that generates extra cash for them. For years, they invested that cash in CDs at Bank of America. "Here it was, in the midst of the bank bailouts, with all of the pulling back of the floorboards and seeing all the cockroaches of the financial system, and here they were, the most vocal academic critics of this, with all their money in the place they're most criticizing. We were a natural fit for them. They went through our materials and put $20,000 into our CDs."

Equal Exchange plans to continue growing—with more offices (they've already expanded to Portland and the Twin Cities), more cafés, and more products. And they expect to expand their capital-raising techniques as well. They're listing some of their securities on the Mission Markets trading portal (elaborated in chapter 8). They have loans from the Calvert Foundation, the Cooperative Fund of New England, several progressive religious orders, and Everence Community Investments (described in chapter 9). Fireside is also exploring ways the company can sell preferred shares to more than five hundred people and "go public" without the company veering from its mission. Perhaps the key will be to build an association of cooperatives that lend to one another.

Fireside admits he lacks the background in high finance that might be required for the work ahead. "But frankly I've found that this is helpful, since what we're trying to do here is generally not something that has been done. There really aren't models for us to follow, so I think about how things should be."

Blue Dots and Blue Sky

Another entrepreneur who dreams of tapping the power of existing banks for local investment is Gino Borland, an online marketing specialist based in the Pacific Northwest with a passion for saving the world's environment through renewable energy systems. One of Borland's biggest clients was Microsoft, where he once worked with his longtime friend Paul Garner, a group program manager. "Paul and I decided to do a new start-up together, and we said, Let's have some cake and eat it, let's make the world a better place and make money at the same time."

Borland and Garner wanted to connect investors to smaller-scale clean energy projects. Following the Microsoft playbook, they were interested in creating a model that could be easily replicated and scaled globally. "There are some solutions on a local scale, but we want to scale globally locally, the *glocal* thing."

Enter their idea for Blue Dot, inspired by their friend Aaron Fairchild: Mobilize millions of investors to put their money into bank CDs, and in exchange get the banks to agree to plow equivalent dollars into cost-effective neighborhood power generation, including small-scale solar, wind, hydro-power, and biomass. With enough volume, Borland reasoned, banks should be willing to pay Blue Dot a fee for delivering millions of new deposi-tors. Borland and Garner immediately partnered with Jae Easterbrooks of ShoreBank Pacific (now One Pacific Coast Bank) to build a prototype of the product.

Why the name *Blue Dot*? "We've got a mental map connecting money to projects. The money side ranges from low-end consumers investing only $25 to big-money investing multimillions of dollars. The project side ranges from small projects like rooftop solar to big projects undertaken by utilities. We are in the middle, putting together a marketplace to connect those dots."

Borland is convinced his scheme will be attractive to consumers: "You pick the project you want to be connected to, but the money is going still to a bank, and through the bank it's going to these projects. We show you which ones." Blue Dot depositors would get details about the projects they were indirectly financing. Borland demonstrates this on his website with a project called Farm Power: "So you get to see photos, here's the bank giving them the big check, there's the cows, they show the construction, you're feeling connected, they put out a video. So we would do this for every single project, we'd allow them to tell their story. That's where the connection comes from."

"The pitch to you, as a customer, would be this: You could put a thousand dollars into a Bank of America CD or you can put that same thousand dollars into a Blue Dot CD and feel connected to a local energy project. Same interest rate, same deal—our value proposition to you is that you feel good about your money."

The business, however, is now stalled. "Blue Dot *would* work," says Borland with exasperation, "if we weren't in such a strange interest rate situation." Today interest rates are so low that most banks are not prioritizing getting new deposits or depositors. When interest rates rise again, the model might pencil out. Until then, Borland is tinkering with another idea, Blue Dash, which would connect large institutional investors like banks, investment funds, and utilities directly with small-scale energy projects. This framework drops bank CDs.

Underlying these choices, of course, are the intricacies of securities law. Borland's dream of using banks for Blue Dot is driven by the fact that banks already have all the regulatory approvals they need to connect unaccredited investors to worthy investments. "We talked to securities lawyers. We didn't have any banking backgrounds or financial backgrounds, we're software guys. And the solution is partnering with those who can, which is the banks.

"Until interest rates change," Borland concedes, "Blue Dot remains on the shelf. In the meantime I'd be happy to license it to nonprofits, or anyone else who wants to use it in the short term. For example, it could be applicable to Slow Money, an organization promoting investment in local food businesses."

Slow Munis

Slow Money is a nonprofit exploring ideas that could expand bank and credit union lending for local food business, including the use of municipal bonds for collateral. The origin of Slow Money is Slow Food International, founded by an Italian visionary named Carlo Petrini in 1986. Its name conveys what it's against—the pernicious impacts of fast food: the creation of vast "food deserts" in inner cities and rural areas that leave nutritionally starved residents increasingly vulnerable to obesity and diabetes; the destruction of family farms and linked networks of regional and local food processors, packagers, distributors, wholesalers, and retailers; and the replacement of family-nurturing dinners where children learn the relationship-building virtues of gardening, shopping, and cooking with instant meals eaten in front of mind-numbing television sets.

"Slow Food," says its website, "stands at the crossroads of ecology and gastronomy, ethics and pleasure. It opposes the standardization of taste and culture, and the unrestrained power of the food industry multinationals and industrial agriculture. We believe that everyone has a fundamental right to the pleasure of good food and consequently the responsibility to protect the heritage of food, tradition, and culture that make this pleasure possible."

This philosophy has spread to some one hundred thousand practitioners around the world. One of its disciples has been Woody Tasch, a visionary investor who has been at the forefront of developing and spreading tools for mission-related and patient-capital investing for two decades. In 1992 Tasch decided to ply his financial acumen to Investors Circle, a learning network of angel investors, foundation members, fund managers, and other investment advisers committed to supporting socially responsible business. At its regular conferences, Investors Circle members hear pitches from cutting-edge entrepreneurs, and thus far they have channeled $150 million into 230 of these enterprises, many of them focused on organic food.

Tasch articulated his worldview about local investing—his dream that 1 percent of all investing go to reviving family farms and local food systems—in his 2010 book, *Inquiries into the Nature of Slow Money*. He then announced to friends and followers that he would start to hold gatherings to discuss the concepts in the book. He was stunned when hundreds of people showed up in person and thousands more virtually. Thus was born Slow Money, the nonprofit.

Slow Money's proposal to create municipal bonds to spur lending from local banks and credit unions—what Tasch calls "slow munis"—fit perfectly with a local food project I was working on in Cleveland. A little background about my own locavore roots: In the late 1980s, I received a three-year leadership fellowship from the Kellogg Foundation. Among the forty midcareer professionals in my class were two agriculture professors from Michigan and Nebraska, Oran Hesterman and Rick Foster, respectively, who went on to work at the Kellogg Foundation and grow the largest philanthropic programs in the country supporting local food. Both taught me about sustainable agriculture and food systems, and over the last two decades I've completed half a dozen or so studies on local food systems. One of my most recent efforts was in Cleveland, where I teamed up with two other researchers—Brad Masi, founder of the Cleveland-Cuyahoga Food Policy Coalition, and Leslie Schaller, research director for ACEnet in Athens, Ohio—to prepare a strategic plan for expanding local food in the region.

The sixteen-county North East Ohio (NEO) region already had a remarkable local food system. The environmental website SustainLane recently ranked Cleveland the second best city in the country for local food and agriculture (Minneapolis was number one), with the following explanation: "Cleveland takes second place in our bakeoff with 12 farmers' markets and 225 community gardens reported, serving truckloads of fresh food to its population of over 450,000. A nearly 600 percent increase in the total number of farmers' markets and a sizable increase in community gardens since 2006 explain Cleveland's ascent in this rankings category."[10]

We examined the impact of the region moving just a quarter of the way toward total food localization. Our research found that a 25 percent shift could create twenty-seven thousand new jobs, enough in principle to reemploy one out of every eight unemployed workers.[11] It could increase regional output each year by more than $4 billion, regional wages by $1 billion, and regional tax collections by $126 million. It could increase the food security of hundreds of thousands of people and reduce near-epidemic levels of obesity and Type II diabetes. And it could significantly improve air and water quality, lower the region's carbon footprint, attract tourists, boost local entrepreneurship, and enhance civic pride.

We also identified obstacles standing in the way of the 25 percent shift. New workforce training and entrepreneurship initiatives are needed to prepare the managers and staff of these new or expanded local food enterprises. Land must be secured for new urban and rural farms. Consumers in the region must be further educated about the benefits of local food and the opportunities for buying it.

But the biggest obstacle of all, as we saw it, was capital. More than $1 billion of new capital was essential to finance the 25 percent shift. From one perspective, this was a modest requirement. A billion dollars represents about 1 percent of the short-term savings NEO residents have in their banks and credit unions, and about a quarter of 1 percent of the long-term savings they have in their pension funds and related investments. Still, as is true across the country, the financial crisis had all but turned off the spigots of credit to local businesses, including those focused on food.

Our top recommendation was Slow Munis. Specifically, we proposed creating a NEO Food Authority (NFA), an entity that would issue Slow Muni bonds, providing loans to and mobilizing in-kind support for those local enterprises with the greatest catalytic potential to help the region realize the 25 percent shift. For example, we envisioned the NEO Food Authority prioritizing: infrastructure businesses such as incubators, food hubs, and shared-use facilities; clusters of businesses involving one or more food businesses, so that the success of one business would spur the success of many; and what we called "metabusinesses," by which we meant economic-development programs supporting a wide range of local businesses (like a local gift card) that could pay for themselves.

We used the word *authority* not to suggest heavy-handed regulatory powers, but to indicate that the proposed entity should have some kind of official support from the Cleveland City and Cuyahoga County governments. This might enable the NFA to issue municipal "food bonds" with interest payments to bondholders exempt from federal taxation. And like most such bonds, anyone, including unaccredited investors in the region, could buy them. Those funds could be used—like a SHARE or Alternatives program on steroids—to stimulate lending to food businesses throughout the region. And as the loans were repaid, the bondholders would be repaid as well.

Municipal bonds often are used to bolster the private credit market. Industrial development bonds, for example, are frequently sold to underwrite industrial parks and major corporate expansions. Why not local food businesses? In fact, why not all kinds of local businesses? The whole idea is to deploy the full faith and credit of a community to stimulate economic activities that serve the entire community.

The timing of this proposal, of course, was less than ideal. After the recent financial crisis, state and local governments across the country are practically broke. The national stimulus package pumped federal dollars into state coffers during the first two years of the financial crisis, but as the stimulus has wound down, many states now see oceans of red ink ahead. Their bond ratings have plummeted, and new bond deals are off the table. Even Slow Money has put Slow Munis on the back burner.

It's ironic, and tragic, that the foolish investment policies that state and local authorities embraced with such gusto—investing their pension funds and surplus revenues in exotic derivatives that went bust and nearly bankrupted once financially strong jurisdictions like Orange County—now prevent them from taking the simplest of steps to move in a new direction. But the current bad patch in state and local finance will sooner or later come to an end, and then Slow Munis might begin to get the kind of attention they deserve. In the meantime, there may be other, more direct ways state governments can stimulate institutional lending to local businesses.

Good Banking in the Badlands

In 2007, state and local governments in the United States spent slightly more than $3 *trillion*. About a sixth came from the federal government. The rest, because state and local government operate under strict balanced budget requirements, came from taxes, fees, royalties, and other revenue sources. Like any business, a smart government entity doesn't spend money the moment it's collected. At any given time, state and local governments have a trillion dollars or more sloshing around in reserves.[12] That money is not sitting in the governor's or mayor's safe. It's usually placed in portfolios of globally traded securities. In other words, all the potential stimulus that could come from government reserves is essentially lost to Wall Street.

But another direction is possible, as suggested in a recent article in *U.S. Banker*, a trade journal for banking professionals:

> Consider this tale of two cities: Grand Forks, North Dakota, suffered massive flooding that left it economically crippled in April 2007. So

did East Grand Forks, just across the river in Minnesota. Three years later, Grand Forks had lost 3% of its population, and East Grand Forks had lost 17%.

Those who are pushing for states like Illinois and Washington to create a publicly owned bank insist this difference in economic recovery is no coincidence. They give much of the credit for Grand Forks' resiliency—only one minute by car from its Minnesota counterpart—to the 92-year-old Bank of North Dakota, the country's only state-owned bank. Its help came in many forms, including a quickly established $25 million line of credit for the city itself.[13]

Ellen Brown, a lawyer turned writer, is president and chairman of the Public Banking Institute and a leading advocate for state-owned banks like North Dakota's. She reflects on another victim of the 2007 flood, the city of Fargo: "It was a big flood, just like the New Orleans flood on a relative scale, and the bank just stepped in and took care of it. It put a moratorium on foreclosures and acted in the public interest. It saved the city."

"It takes a crisis to change the system," she adds, referring to the recent financial crisis, "and I think we're at that point now."

The Bank of North Dakota is the only state-owned bank in the United States, but at least half a dozen states are seriously looking at the model. It's important to clarify that the most important function of a publicly owned bank is not to put privately owned banks and credit unions out of business but to provide them with capital and services that can improve their performance. It basically places state and local money on deposit at the right local banks, at the right time.

The Bank of North Dakota was founded in 1919 with $2 million in state money, after local farmers found it impossible to obtain credit from out-of-state lenders. Its mission was "to deliver quality, sound financial services that promote agriculture, commerce, and industry in North Dakota." Today its capital assets have grown to $270 million. Since 1945, it has generated $555 million in profits for the state, and it's one reason many observers think the state has had one of the nation's lowest unemployment rates and biggest budget surpluses.

Individuals and companies can set up their own savings and checking accounts at the bank, but these only account for about 1.5 percent of the bank's deposits. Most of its capital comes from public entities. State agencies are required to use the bank to hold funds, and many local governments choose to do so as well. Yet-to-be-used federal dollar transfers to North Dakota also are kept in the bank.

The vast majority of the bank's funds are currently used for federally guaranteed student loans, though this is changing because of recent congressional legislation. It also performs the exhaustive paperwork for community banks in North Dakota to handle FHA and VA residential mortgages. The bank balances its relatively safe activities with riskier loan portfolios for farms, ranches, livestock, health technology, water facilities, and various small businesses. It loans directly to priority projects and also guarantees loans originating from other banks in the state.

One of the most important functions of the bank has been to strengthen North Dakota's local banks. For example, it provides loans to residents and institutions to buy stock in local banks. It also strategically places its capital in various local banks to improve their loan-to-asset ratios, which in turn increases their willingness to engage in more lending.

The Bank of North Dakota takes money that might have been placed in a multinational bank, where it might have done economic-development work in, say, Singapore, and makes sure that the funds are doing that same work back home in North Dakota. It also allows the state to take advantage of some of the unique opportunities available to a bank. For example, while most states these days must pay 4 to 5 percent on the bond market to borrow funds for various projects, banks can borrow from one another or from the Federal Reserve at an extraordinarily low rate of 0.2 percent. Plus, banking allows a state to multiply the impact of its deposits. Every deposited dollar can cover more than $10 of loans.

Sam Munger, managing director of the Center for State Innovation at the University of Wisconsin–Madison, which has been issuing a flurry of papers analyzing what this kind of bank might look like in other states, says, "In the wake of the recession, people started talking about the public banking idea. They are able to act counter-cyclically to ramp up lending at a time when banks cannot or will not." The center's paper on a proposed state bank for Oregon found that it could create sixty-nine to eighty-eight hundred new small-business jobs, primarily by stimulating $1.3 billion of additional lending in the state.[14] It further estimates that an initial capitalization of $100 million could create a profitable institution within three years and generate more than $1 billion of revenue for state coffers within forty years.

Jared Gardner, a former mortgage banker, has partnered with the Oregon Working Family Party to lead the effort to create a state bank in Oregon. "In January of 2009," he recalls, "we hosted an economic crisis town hall, and about nine hundred people came. People were really riled up about the big banks. So we started channeling that energy into focus groups and brainstorming groups. We learned about community banks and credit unions, and we developed a Move Your Money campaign that highlighted the value and benefit of community banks.

"When we borrow from community banks," Gardner continues, "the whole back-end structure is dominated by the large institutions. That'd be everything from loan participations to correspondence services or federal funds management. Small banks are often having to borrow overnight, short-term loans from the big banks to manage their books. And we came across the Bank of North Dakota model, and started realizing that it provided community banks with a lot of the support they needed—so they didn't arbitrarily have to pull credit lines and operating lines, or not refinance viable businesses. We started exploring that model, organizing conference calls with Bank of North Dakota executives and community bankers, talking to our legislators and treasurer to see what support there was. That process has taken about two years."

Gardner is keenly aware that most job creation comes from local business. "Since community banks are the most likely to support small business, anything we can do to expand their capacity or to level the playing field will get more small businesses loans. A state bank is kind of a large Move Your Money campaign."

The jury is still out on whether Gardner and his colleagues in Oregon will succeed. Ellen Brown thinks their effort has the best odds among half a dozen campaigns under way nationally, because they have sold it carefully to banking officials throughout the state. "The first reaction of any banker, or anybody really, is that it won't work: Why do we need another bank that's going to compete with us? But Gardner and his group went around and talked to the small bankers, asked them what their problems were, and showed them how this proposal would solve their problems."

Brown is hopeful that success in one more state, like Oregon, could trigger a national movement: "If just one state did it, it would be so obvious that it was an improvement—and then everyone else would follow."

Even if these states do not embrace a full-scale public bank, the debate may well open political space for other innovations. Another model being talked about—in some ways similar to Slow Munis—is the Connecticut Development Authority, which issues industrial-development bonds and then uses the proceeds to help local banks with economic-development lending, by guaranteeing their loans, for example. The authority was initially capitalized by the state but now is self-financing.

The Future of Community Capital

For the foreseeable future, local banks and credit unions will remain among the most important places where local businesses get their capital. The innovations described in this chapter could increase the flow of capital to these critically important businesses. The expansion of local banks and credit unions, fueled by Move Your Money campaigns, can inject new capital into the very financial institutions with the best track record of assisting local business. The creation of additional lending platforms within these institutions, along the lines of the SHARE program or Alternatives Federal Credit Union programs, can accelerate this flow, especially to businesses regarded as most critical to self-reliant local economies. Even if Blue Dot never gets started, similar enterprises will undoubtedly form to link depositors to local energy or food businesses. The addition of still-larger capital vehicles to guarantee these kinds of loans, such as slow munis and state-owned banks, could dramatically spur the flow of more community capital, especially during times of disaster or recession.

For those of us who deposit our money, these options underscore that where we put all of our short-term money—our cash, our checking funds, our savings, our money market accounts, our CDs—really matters. Indeed, removing our money from the nation's diminishing number of bankosaurs, whose insatiable appetites to grow may hasten the extinction of the communities they inhabit and thus themselves, may be the single most important act of localization that any individual or family can make.

Localizing banking need not be an act of community charity. Interest rates right now are extraordinarily low, reflecting national policy makers' embrace of "loose money" to pull the nation permanently out of its financial tailspin. But they will rise in time. Moreover, as we saw with the Alternatives example, programs can be set up to ensure that depositors obtain whatever rate of return they are looking for. To be sure, their savings are at risk, but no more so than they would be on Wall Street. The spread of Slow Munis and state-owned banks may create hundreds of new entry points, with higher rates of return, for local investors. The result could be a return of banking to its once core mission of supporting the local economy.

Anti-Poverty Investing

One of the pioneering forces for local investment has been the community-development movement, spurred on largely by government and philanthropic dollars. President Lyndon Johnson's War on Poverty underwrote nonprofit community-development corporations (CDCs) across the United States, many of which supported local businesses and housing projects. Community-development credit unions became more common. Community-development banks like the South Shore Bank of Chicago were launched to provide credit to underserved populations.

These activities got a huge boost when the Clinton administration signed into law the Riegle Community Development and Regulatory Improvement Act in 1994. The bill created a process whereby various financial institutions—banks, credit unions, loan funds—could apply for a federal designation as a Community Development Financial Institution (CDFI) and qualify for infusions of federal capital. It also enacted the New Markets Tax Credits, which provided investors who put funds into federally approved Community Development Entities (CDEs) with tax credits amounting to nearly 40 percent of the investment. According to the website of the Department of the Treasury, which oversees these programs: "Since its creation, the CDFI Fund has awarded $1.4 billion to community-development organizations and financial institutions. It [also] has awarded allocations of New Markets Tax Credits which will attract private-sector investments totaling $29.5 billion."

The accomplishments of community-development initiatives since the 1960s have been impressive. More than forty-six hundred CDCs are operating nationwide, and they have created half a million jobs. Each year CDCs are developing an average of eighty-six thousand new housing units and 8.75 million square feet of commercial real estate space.[1] Community

Development Financial Institutions currently manage $25 billion in assets and in 2006 could claim to have created sixty-nine thousand housing units and thirty-five thousand jobs.[2]

Underlying the community-development movement was an assumption, which some now question, that mission-related businesses are necessarily wobbly. Poor communities were seen as not having the capital to fully finance their own community-development initiatives, credit unions, and banks. Even with outside funding, these institutions were deemed higher risk, because they catered to poor homeowners who were more likely to default and to poor businesspeople who had sketchier credit records. The belief that community-development initiatives require periodic infusions of outside capital became the justification for federal investments. But government budgets are notoriously unreliable, as administrations with different political philosophies change every four or eight years and as the nation cycles through the inevitable down troughs of the business cycle. State and local dollars, which must comport with balanced budgets even in recessions, are even less reliable.

Among the first nongovernmental investors to step forward to supplement government programs were charitable foundations. Those with community-development missions were happy to support nonprofit CDCs and CDFIs with annual grants. A few were also prepared to make program-related investments (PRIs). The Ford Foundation was one of the early practitioners, giving generous grants and PRIs to anti-poverty banks (like South Shore), credit unions (like Self-Help in North Carolina), and community-development support organizations like Local Initiatives Support Corporation (LISC).

A word about PRIs: By law, foundations must give away at least 5 percent of their assets each year in grants. The charitable giving side typically operates independently from the investment side that manages the other 95 percent (though everything is technically overseen by a common executive director and board). Some in the philanthropic world have observed that, at best, this means only one-twentieth of a foundation's resources are actually doing mission-related work.[3] Worse, the giving and investment departments may be working at odds. Of the hundreds of foundations supporting community development these days, almost none screen out from their own investment portfolios stocks of the Walmarts, Home Depots, and Costcos that have undermined thousands of downtown local businesses.[4] PRIs are a partial solution to this problem; they allow a foundation to invest in certain mission-related businesses and then, if those investments fail, count them toward the legally required 5 percent annual payout. Despite the promise of PRIs pouring billions into "social impact" for-profits, recent data suggest that only one-tenth of 1 percent of U.S. foundation assets are being invested this way.[5] That said, community developers remain hopeful that, sooner or later, foundations will find their PRI mojo.

But even if PRIs expanded spectacularly, foundation resources could only play a modest role in addressing the country's social and economic problems. The assets of all U.S. foundations put together is around half a trillion dollars, less than 1 percent of the total assets of all U.S. households and nonprofits. And foundations give only a tiny percentage of their grants to community development, with the lion's share going to vanilla-flavored cultural, civic, and educational activities. Addressing the needs of the tens of millions of Americans in poverty cannot possibly be done without a strong partnership with the private sector. Into this breach have stepped a few mission-oriented, "social impact" investors. Some have been large institutions like churches, labor unions, and fraternal organizations. Others have been well-heeled individuals. All of them have been prepared to accept lower or even negative rates of return. That was the brilliance of the New Markets Tax Credits program, which made otherwise marginal investments highly attractive to private investors.

The expansion of public, charitable, and private funds for mission investing, in turn, has nurtured a new generation of community-development entrepreneurs. One of the most successful has been Ron Phillips, whose Coastal Enterprises Inc. (CEI) in Wiscasset, Maine, now runs revolving loan funds, a venture capital fund, and technical assistance programs. Since its founding, CEI has provided 2,104 businesses with loans totaling $677 million, and it estimates that these loans leveraged another $1.7 billion in capital for the beneficiary businesses.

"When we started Coastal Enterprises in 1977," Phillips told a public television interviewer in 2000, "I would characterize the economic problems facing Maine as very much the same problems that third-world countries face: being a natural resource state, being based on more extractive industries with less value added than you'd like to see. Maine really faced the question of how it could create a vibrant local business economy to market its products at competitive prices, and with value added to those products. Back in the '70s, Maine was really at the much lower end of the spectrum in terms of per capita income . . . compared to national averages."[6]

One of the first CEI projects targeted the fishing industry. "At the time," says Phillips, "we estimated that only 15 percent of the fish landed in Maine was actually being processed in Maine. This created a framework for us to look at how we could work with that industry and grow it to a more value-added type of activity. So we got involved in a strategy to actually make investments in small-scale fish processing cooperatives or community-owned fish processing plants. The first was in Bar Harbor and then we did a second one in Vinalhaven."

An intriguing opportunity CEI offers accredited investors today is CEI Ventures, led by Nat Henshaw. Not many high school students are avid *Businessweek* readers, but that's how Henshaw first learned and got excited about venture capital. He studied economics at Duke, where he also earned an MBA, and worked for the Venture Capital Group of Chemical Bank, Intersect Partners, and Kitty Hawk Capital. He returned to Maine in 1988 and after responding to a newspaper ad was hired by CEI as a loan officer, mostly making microloans and guarantees. In 1991, he and an intern sketched out a venture fund prospectus, and three years later he created for CEI a for-profit subsidiary that became the general partner for a series of venture funds.

For readers hazy on what exactly the term *venture capital* means, recall the ideas of Blue Dot's Gino Borland in the last chapter. A Microsoft veteran, Borland was keenly aware that the key to Bill Gates becoming the richest man in America (second richest in the world) was scalability. Once Gates created the first version of Windows and got it licensed into IBM's computers, the licensing fees started to roll in by the millions and then the billions. The mantra of venture capitalists is "We're looking for the next Microsoft." They invest large chunks of money in companies that they think can grow spectacularly. They obtain working control of the company, often replace the management team, and once the beanstalk starts growing, they take the company public and exit. A typical venture fund will have ten to twenty companies and will expect only a handful to succeed. The challenge is, as the old saying goes, to know when to hold 'em, and know when to fold 'em. Investors in venture funds must be patient, because the beanstalks may talk five to ten years to sprout.

Henshaw went on to establish three venture funds for CEI. The first was capitalized in 1996 with $5.5 million and invested in twenty companies, although thus far it has lost money. The second fund closed in 2000 with $20 million invested in seventeen different companies and has done better than most venture funds started that year. Henshaw has just finished raising $10 million for a third fund, a heroic feat given the current investment climate. The principal investors in these funds have been foundations, large commercial banks, various federal CDFI funds and Maine state funds, and a handful of wealthy individuals. Over time, CEI hopes to be able to add unaccredited money into its funds through a community notes program.

The investment bias of all these funds is to stay in Maine. "We're born here and grown here," says Henshaw. "A lot of our investors are from here. So we're very interested in Maine. But we don't exclusively invest in Maine and we do have some investors from outside Maine, including regional banks. We think it's good from a diversification standpoint."

The motives of CEI's investors, Henshaw reflects, are varied. "Some of them invest for financial return. All of our investors have an interest in the socially beneficial aspect of creating jobs in their communities and seeing their local economies do better. One of our largest investors said he wanted to do something tangible for Maine. Sometimes it's for tax credits. Our bank investors are looking for CRA credit."

Asked to cite a success story, Henshaw immediately mentions Looks Gourmet Food, which makes Looks and Bar Harbor brand chowders, clam juice, and canned seafood. It was a ninety-year-old business that had almost gone bankrupt. A native Mainer, Mike Cody, bought the company after a long career at Pepperidge Farm, Odwalla, and Coke. He made its products all natural and got them placed in Whole Foods and Wild Oats, using only his own savings. Cody needed additional capital, and CEI Ventures invested.

The results? "We ultimately got the product sustainably certified," says Henshaw, "and grew sales dramatically. We sold our stake to the company's master distributor, leaving management in place, and doubled our money in a couple of years. The company grew from eight to twenty-six employees and sustainably sourced its natural harvested products, and so that's an example of the three E's of investing. There's social equity. It's economically feasible. And it's environmentally beneficial. That's what we're trying to do."

Microcapitalism

The assumption that community-development investment could not generate profitable returns was challenged in the 1990s by an enterprising Bangladeshi banker named Muhammad Yunus. His Grameen Bank provided very small loans, often under $50, to help women with tiny businesses. For example, a roadside vendor could carry more food for a longer period if she could purchase a small refrigerator. Observing that women were generally more likely to spend money they earned on family well-being than men (too many of whom were willing to squander their income on drinking or gambling), Grameen focused exclusively on entrepreneur peer groups that each involved half a dozen women who had known one another throughout their lifetimes. When the first woman in a group repaid her loan (with peer support), the second woman would receive a loan, and so forth. Grameen achieved an astonishing 97 percent repayment rate and proved that the poor were "bankable."

Community developers across the United States took notice and began to create their own Westernized versions of microlending with larger loans, higher interest rates, and more diverse borrowers. One early leader in the field was Claudia Viek, who today directs CAMEO, the California Association for Micro Enterprise Opportunity, a statewide network of microlending nonprofits and entrepreneurship centers. Viek got involved in microenterprise development in the late 1980s when she started to teach an entrepreneurship class for low- and moderate-income aspiring entrepreneurs in Los Angeles. Out of this grew the Renaissance Entrepreneurship Center, one of the first microenterprise-development programs in the country—and one of the very few to train both men and women.

Today CAMEO has eighty-five member groups spread up and down California, thirty of which focus on lending and the rest on training and business technical assistance. Collectively, they fund two thousand microloans (under $50,000) and prepare another twenty-five hundred clients for bank loans in the state. Based on surveys of her members' needs, Viek aims to triple this number and assist one hundred thousand California businesses per year. California is one of fifteen states with well-organized microenterprise networks. Oregon has a network called OMEN, for example, and Georgia has one called GMEN. They all collaborate through the DC-based Association for Enterprise Opportunity (AEO).

Despite the financial crisis, or perhaps because of it, CAMEO membership growth has remained on track. In 2010, says Viek, "we facilitated new investments of over $12 million and we raised more than $3 million in new grants for our members' services—three times as much as I thought we would. We're also exceeding our investment goals, because we're seeing more capital coming in from the CDFI fund, the SBA, and the U.S. Department of Agriculture. There's a huge need for capital among microentrepreneurs. And if we don't meet it, entrepreneurship and all of the good things that make our country great will be stifled."

Where should the capital for microentrepreneurs come from? Viek believes this is what a smart government stimulus package would focus on. "Recent research shows that almost all new jobs are created by start-up businesses. In California, we have a very high unemployment rate, 12 percent, and that's just the official rate. We believe it's closer to 25 percent for Latinos and African Americans. So job creation is really very important. What better way to create jobs than through our traditional entrepreneurial spirit? We believe that meaningful and longer-term sustainable job creation can happen when you support locally owned microbusinesses."

By *micro*, Viek means businesses with five employees or fewer. She argues that they are particularly important for expanding employment, because when microbusinesses get assistance, 80 percent will add an average of two jobs after start-up and a few will grow spectacularly. "Plus, minority-owned businesses tend to hire other minorities, and it's an important way to expand employment into communities of color. This creates more stakeholders in the community."

For many years microlending supplemented mainstream banking, but now its role is expanding. "In California we're seeing banks pretty much not lending under $100,000 to businesses anymore. We used to think of microlending as amounts around $10,000, but now the SBA has expanded its notion of microloans, so a microloan in California can be anywhere from $500 to $50,000. The big banks are just not servicing that segment at all—except, I guess, if you want to get a credit card and pay 25 percent interest rates. Microlenders are now becoming the lenders of choice. But we still operate on a very small scale."

Microloans, Viek emphasizes, are not gifts. "Our microlenders require borrowers to have some financial statements to show that they are able to repay, and also to have a fairly good credit ratings. They don't have to be as squeaky clean as banks are requiring, but banks aren't even making loans to squeaky-clean people."

Viek is skeptical whether microlending can, or should, be viewed as a profit-making business. She argues that, to succeed, the low-income recipients of microloans require a lot of front-end work to retool their business plan, to analyze their market, and to consolidate their debts. A typical applicant requires ten to twenty hours of this kind of technical assistance to get "ready" for a loan. This costs money. That's why most microlenders require grants and gifts. The only alternative is to charge borrowers very high fees and interest rates. Which is exactly what some for-profit microlenders have starting doing, drawing howls of outrage from the traditional community-development providers.

Viek admits that pricing loans fairly poses a real dilemma. "In California, we have very tight usury laws and also a strong values system that says you should not charge more than 14 percent —and even then, some of my members disagree with their peers who do that. So we rely on government grants to fund the operational overhead, whether it comes from the SBA, from the CDFI fund, from the U.S. Department of Agriculture, or HUD. Those government grants are critical to being able to operate community-based nonprofit loan funds."

Funds also come from commercial banks that seek good scores under the Community Reinvestment Act (CRA). "Wells Fargo," says Viek, "has been the gold standard, but it is gratifying to see that more banks are stepping up both investments and grants to microlenders. If your organization is a member of CAMEO and you have a seasoned loan fund operating, Wells Fargo will consider making between a $250,000 and $1 million investment in you at 2.5

percent over a seven- to ten-year period. This is a great form of patient capital. And at such low rates you can then charge 8 or 10 percent interest to the small businesses and still cover some portion of your operating costs."

Viek has been able to harness Wells Fargo's hunger for CRA credit to recruit new partners like the Fresno Regional Foundation. "The Valley Small Business Development Corporation had been lending to disadvantaged small and microbusinesses in Fresno and the Central Valley. They had never met a soul at Fresno Regional Foundation, and had never gotten a grant from the foundation. But then the foundation's board and managers started seeing storefronts shuttering, and they were really concerned that the banks weren't lending anymore. I went down to Fresno, met with the foundation a couple times, had a lot of phone calls, and brought the three parties together. Finally, their board moved to accept an investment of $1 million from Wells Fargo bank and then pass it through to Valley. I liken it to when you give your computer more RAM—that's what we did when we plugged Valley into the foundation, and injected additional assets. This is all about relationship building: The bank likes to have access to high-net-worth people in communities, and the foundation likes having access to the bank—in fact they invited their local Wells Fargo banker to join their board. Now they're all going to each other's fund-raisers, and Valley Small Business is looking for other banks to connect with the foundation as well."

Viek is untroubled by taking funds from publicly traded, nonlocal banks. Their larger scale means they have staff with expertise in community lending, and they clearly have the resources. She also is happy to press large companies to contribute to microlending, such as the California biotech giant Genentech. Her biggest complaints concern foundations: "They get a huge tax deduction, they're supposed to be investing in helping to eradicate poverty, but instead we see them putting their money in the traditional arts, the ballet, museums, and universities like Stanford. I'm not saying these institutions aren't worthy, but it's the rich who largely benefit from those institutions, not the poor. The poor can't even afford to go to museums anymore. And certainly they are not going to Stanford, which already has one of the biggest endowments in the world. I think we need to tweak the tax system so that foundations get more credit for investments in the poor."

The dominant role of banks, foundations, corporations, and federal agencies underscores that anti-poverty lending does not envision a bit part for unaccredited investors. Viek would at least like to make it easier for individuals to *donate* money to local microenterprise nonprofits. "Let's say you read an article about somebody who started their own business and got a small loan for $5,000 or $10,000—that's still the average loan size, around $10,000—and you said, 'I really want to support people just like that where I live. How can I do that?' You could go to the CAMEO website where you can access a map and see which organizations are serving that community. You could then read a profile about the group, and actually make a donation right there through CAMEO."

But what about helping unaccredited Californians invest in microenterprise businesses in the CAMEO network? "Frankly," Viek admits, "there aren't really too many avenues at this point, although Kiva is starting to work with U.S. microlenders." Viek is intrigued with using peer-to-peer (P2P) Internet lending platforms like Kiva and Prosper, which are discussed in chapter 7. Unaccredited individuals also may be able to put money on deposit in community-development banks and credit unions and, in the ways described earlier, stimulate commercial lending. The entrepreneur in Viek is struggling to find a better revenue-generating model.

The Country's Fifty Biggest Laboratories

Another source of capital in the community-development universe is state and local government. Any government agency qualifies as an accredited investor. A recent survey conducted by the Corporation for Enterprise Development found six hundred revolving loan funds sponsored by state or local governments around the country. While these entities strive to be self-financing, with the interest from early loans covering expenses of the fund, most require periodic infusions of public money from local, state, or federal agencies. Like other community-development efforts, the risks are high. These funds are usually the lenders of second resort and cater to riskier businesses. The expectation is that public funds must periodically cover losses.

A small number of these revolving loan funds also are trying to capture the upside of the risks they are taking. They might take an equity position in a company. Or they might insist on a convertible note, which gives them the option of turning debt with a successful business into equity. Or they might insist on a share of revenues, profits, or royalties.

One state that has created a community-development institution focused on helping local business has been—unsurprisingly—Vermont. In 1995, the state legislature created the Vermont Sustainable Jobs Fund (VSJF) to accelerate the development of Vermont's green economy. Originally established to show that being pro-business and pro-environment were not mutually exclusive, the VSJF was tasked with focusing on renewable energy, environmental technology, forest products, sustainable agriculture, and waste management market sectors. The VSJF currently receives between $220,000 and $250,000 per year from the state (which covers a portion of its general operating expenses), and it uses these dollars to leverage nearly $1 million of capital per year from federal agencies, foundations, and individual donors. These funds are then used to provide grants and technical assistance to Vermont small businesses and organizations in the priority sectors.

What type of business or project is of interest to the VSJF? Its most recent annual report tells the story of a grantee, Carbon Harvest Energy (CHE), which is converting methane from an old landfill in Brattleboro into electricity, food, and biofuel. CHE plans to use methane to generate electricity, which then will pump waste heat into an adjacent greenhouse and aquaculture fish farm, the latter of which will produce algae that will then be harvested for its oil to make biodiesel. The VSJF's Vermont Biofuels Initiative has provided CHE with a total of $235,000 in grants, largely from funds it received from the U.S. Department of Energy (thanks to an earmark pushed by U.S. senator Patrick Leahy). CHE is also beginning to replicate its business model in other landfill sites in New England.

The director of the VSJF is a wide-eyed, fast-talking dynamo named Ellen Kahler. Ten years ago, Kahler ran a statewide nonprofit pressing for livable wages and other economic reforms. She commissioned a paper from Doug Hoffer, an economist based in Burlington and one of the sharpest grassroots policy analysts in the country, on the most significant economic leaks from the state: namely, local dollars lost to imports of energy and food. Today she sees leak plugging as an essential part of the fund's agenda.

"One of the core things that we're trying to accomplish," says Kahler, "is a relocalization of the economy for those goods and services that we can produce ourselves. For instance, our biofuels work is premised on the idea of local production for local use. If you're a farmer and two of your largest input costs are diesel fuel for your tractor, which comes from foreign oilfields, and feed for your animals, which comes from the Midwest, could you actually produce some or all of the fuel and feed you need yourself for less money and be more self-reliant in the process? We think you can. So we're helping farmers learn how to grow oilseed crops and turn it into biodiesel for their tractors and feed for their animals. We can't replace everything imported into Vermont, but we can produce a greater percentage of our food and fuel right here. So these sustainable-market-building values are informing our biofuels-related grant making, and influencing how we plan for growing our local food system through our Farm-to-Plate Initiative."

To locavores, Vermont is a paradise. According to the U.S. Department of Agriculture, Vermont has more direct food sales to consumers per capita than any other state in the country—with the next largest state having a tenth as much local purchasing. The Vermont Economic Development Authority (VEDA), which was originally capitalized with state dollars, now goes out on the bond market to underwrite low-interest loans to family farms. Recall the story in chapter 2 about the town of Hardwick, with a population of three thousand, whose consortium of private investors and local food businesses— among them High Mowing Organic Seeds, Cellars at Jasper Hill, Vermont Soy, and Claire's Restaurant—created a hundred new jobs at a time when most of the country was losing jobs.

"There was a lot of stuff hopping here in Vermont in the local food movement for a number of years," explains Kahler. "The foundation was laid way back in the 1970s when NOFA [Northeast Organic Farmers Association] was established, and it's been building ever since. The state legislature was feeling overwhelmed by how much was happening, but we didn't have any kind of a statewide plan to evaluate what we were doing well already, what we could do better, and what opportunities we could capitalize on to strengthen our local food system and create jobs. So two years ago, they asked us to create a ten-year strategic plan for doing just that. The economic impact assessment that was completed showed that for every 5 percent increase in the consumption of locally produced food, fifteen hundred new jobs will be created, $135 million in new annual economic output ($177 million if you count the multiplier effect), and $110 million in new annual income will be generated—in a state of 620,000 people."[7]

"In the work we've done on the whole Farm-to-Plate process," adds Janice St. Onge, deputy director of the VSJF, "we've identified a lot of organizations and individuals in Vermont, along with high-net-worth individuals, who are recognizing the value of investing locally in their community and in their food system. A couple of things have come together all at once. One is the locavore movement, which is finally coming of age at a national level. Another is the notion of eating healthier. Then there's the reality that keeping your dollars locally in the economy has a multiplier effect. I think Vermonters have been seen as more progressive on these fronts—that's just the nature of who we are. But now it has escalated, and these things are converging, especially as people have seen their investment portfolios disappear."

For St. Onge, these trends help explain VSJF's newest initiative: the creation of a low-profit limited liability company called the VSJF Flexible Capital Fund (Flex Fund). This is actually the VSJF's first foray into local investing per se. The initial goal is to raise $4 million to capitalize this fund, and they are already halfway there. The mother ship put in $700,000. The rest came, according to St. Onge, from "our foundation partners, nonprofit organizations, and high-net-worth individuals who are looking to invest a small piece of their investment portfolios locally, but hadn't, to date, found a mechanism they felt comfortable with. They like the idea of putting a small amount, maybe $100,000, of their endowment into an organization that's going to do the work for them, in terms of finding the deals, conducting due diligence, underwriting, and maintaining the relationship with the local companies. Investing in an intermediary also allows them to spread the risk across a portfolio of companies. So we, as an intermediary, fill a niche for an organization like Shelburne Farms or the Vermont Land Trust that hasn't done much, if any, of this kind of local investing before."

In a way, the Flex Fund has become a catalyst for institutions and foundations in the state to begin considering investing locally. "These organizations began to explore mission-related investing some time ago," says Kahler, "but they had not yet found the right vehicle. We made the pitch as to what the value might be for them, that this is a local investment, that we're not expecting you to put all of your investment portfolio with us—but wouldn't it be a great fit with your mission if you put a small piece into something that you can see and touch and feel right in your own community."

The big investors see a good alignment between the Flex Fund's mission and their own. "A major component of the Vermont Land Trust, for example," says St. Onge, "is land conservation. So our mission of helping businesses grow to preserve the working landscape, to help build healthy food systems, fits right in their sweet spot. The same is true for Shelburne Farms."

The mission-driven nature of the Flex Fund led to the decision to structure it as a low-profit limited liability company, or L3C. Vermont became the first state in the country to create this new category of business in 2008, which legally recognizes the social mission of the company and that its objective is not to maximize profit. These features are designed to fulfill the Internal Revenue Service requirements that foundations can only make program-related investments to mission-oriented businesses with below-market rates of return. "Honestly," admits Kahler, "the jury is still out as to whether the L3C is really accomplishing what it's meant to accomplish. Had we been an LLC, the foundations that we work with locally may still have looked to invest in us, but this made it a little easier."

The investors in the Flex Fund, all accredited, are drawn not just to the Vermont businesses and community-building focus but also its anticipated profitability, and in this respect the fund may represent a new generation of community-development institutions. "Our projected return for the fund over its life," says St. Onge, "is between 4 and 6 percent. It could very well be more, depending on how well the companies we invest in perform. We're different than a traditional venture fund, in that we'll be using debt instruments, like subordinated debt and royalty financing, not equity investment. We'll offer more flexible terms than our companies could find with traditional lenders. For example, we will take a subordinate, or second, position in terms of collateral security.

"Given that we're taking on a little bit more risk, we're looking for a little bit of an upside with a royalty payment, which means we'll take a percentage of revenue over a period of time to achieve the rate of return we agree upon with the borrower. We share in the revenue of a business if they're successful—not in the ownership—and we won't force an exit strategy to pay us back. In addition, we offer CEO mentorship opportunities through the VSJF's peer-to-peer collaborative program because we know it's not just about the money. In the end, we're looking for businesses that are 'built to last' as opposed to 'built to flip.'"

Still, if these businesses were such good investments, why are existing banks and investors not supporting them? "They often can't get equity financing," answers St. Onge, "because they don't have high enough growth rates. But they're still good companies with strong management teams and a solid growth plan. And they're just getting left by the wayside because they're not sexy enough, or they don't target national markets. From our perspective it's not necessarily that there's a shortage of capital; it's that there are not enough types of capital a business can find out there that match their size, scale, and stage of growth."

The niche of the Flex Fund, like that of its parent, the Vermont Sustainable Jobs Fund, is to invest in value-added agriculture, sustainable forest products, renewable energy, green technology, and waste management. "From talking to entrepreneurs and other investors and lenders in state," says St. Onge, "we could see that a business gets to a point where it's growing rapidly and to get to the next stage they need to take on higher-risk capital that was just not available at a Vermont scale. They needed equity-like capital but in smaller amounts and at lower returns than traditional equity financing. On the other hand, these businesses couldn't take on much more debt, because it would constrain their cash flow and their ability to grow. Or lenders wouldn't talk to them because they didn't have sufficient collateral or operating history."

Leverage is very important for the Flex Fund. "Because we're a small-scale, limited-size fund," says St. Onge, "we're going to be selective in companies we invest in to ensure that they have some ability to fill a gap or meet a need in the supply chain. A company must have not only a good product or service, but also a product or a service that another local business needs."

Kahler hopes the Flex Fund offers Vermont investors a solid, locally focused intermediary. "Investment takes a lot of work. And I'm seeing this firsthand as we create an entire new company and we raise our own capital, and then we've got to go out and be responsible with other people's money. All the people and organizations who invested are accredited investors, so they are going into this with eyes wide open, and we're very clear that they may not get their money back."

As a dispenser of money, the VSJF has become a trusted steerer, convener, and advocate for the growth of sustainable businesses in the state. "We recently did an access-to-capital workshop targeted at service providers and funders interested in farm viability," says Kahler. "It was amazing. You wouldn't think to invite your local equity investor or venture capital person to a farm viability conference, but we did. And we invited the Federal Reserve funders, the state government funders, the alternative lenders, the bankers, the nonprofit grant-making entities, the tax incentive folks, and the revolving loan folks from the municipal and regional corporations. The fact that these people didn't know each other was in itself a huge statement (especially in Vermont where everyone knows everyone). If they don't know that there's a whole continuum of capital available to small businesses, then how can they know how to best match that business with the right kind of capital? This cross-pollination of information among funders is really important.

"Part of what caused the financial meltdown," reflects Kahler, "besides greed, was the fact that decisions were being made in high-up corporate offices in Manhattan, on Wall Street, with absolutely no personal connection to the people affected. Whether it's the company that is bought out through a hostile takeover, or it's all these mortgages that get flipped or packaged and bundled up and sold, they're just numbers. And if you take a look at commodity-scale agriculture and the way in which the average American buys food in the supermarket, where they have no idea where that food comes from or who grew it, there are a lot of similarities. What is so different about the local food movement and the local money movement, like Slow Money, is that it is relationship-based. You can touch it, you can feel it, you can see it working. And in the case of food, you can see where it's growing and you can get to know the farmer.

"Why," asks Kahler, "are these individuals and organizations putting $50,000 or $100,000 a pop of their precious savings or endowment funds into us, at a time when they've lost so much asset value from the global stock market collapse? It's because they trust us. It's because they trust our board, and that we've gone through a very thoughtful process about ways to mitigate their risk. That all flows from the power of relationships."

Moving from the Margins

Since its inception in the 1960s, community development has largely been about investments in marginal institutions focused on marginal people and projects with, at best, marginal financial returns. It has been a world dominated by mission-oriented players—government agencies, foundations, socially conscious banks, and philanthropists—who never expected to profit. Its practices and philosophy have shaped much of the public perception about the field of local investment.

Each of the stories here, however, shows how quickly the field is evolving. An odd consequence of the recent financial crisis is that millions of Americans, once regarded as solid members of the middle class, have fallen far enough to qualify for community-development programs. The size of the businesses considered micro is growing, as is the size of loans that qualify as micro. The financial tools being offered to these businesses are becoming more diversified. And in some cases, expectations that some of these programs could be profitable are growing as well.

If I Were a Rich Man . . .

For about one of every fifty Americans, local investment is a piece of cake. Wealthy individuals, families, and institutions are free to invest in any business they wish, global or local, with minimal legal requirements. The law trusts those with the deepest pockets. They are presumed to know what they are doing (even if they don't) and to be capable of absorbing losses from their folly (even if they can't).

But as Tevye might have sung in *Fiddler on the Roof*, if you were a rich man (or a rich woman!) . . . you could invest directly in any local business that will take you as an active partner or as a passive shareholder. You could team up with an entrepreneur, alone or with other investors, to start up new local companies or buy up existing ones. You could put your money into private investment firms that assembled portfolios of local businesses. You could create a local venture capital fund that actively incubated promising local businesses and then sold off the most successful ones.

Few wealthy investors, however, actually do any of these things. Despite their presumed wisdom, they suffer from the same illusions as the rest of us, believing that their best returns will come from globally traded stocks, bonds, funds, derivatives, options, currencies, commodities, you name it. Only a few have dabbled in local investment, embracing the *Star Trek* philosophy—"to go boldly where no one has gone before"—and their work is the focus of this chapter. Most of these local-investment pioneers believe that their investments in mainstream small businesses will, like their investments in Community Development Financial Institutions, generate submarket returns. The most astute, however, are starting to realize that maybe, just maybe, smart local investments can generate better returns than Wall Street.

The Christian Theology of Local

When I was writing my last book, *The Small-Mart Revolution*, the only invest-ment fund manager in the country I could find who was struggling to undertake local investment for her clients was Leslie Christian, who runs offices in Seattle and Portland and serves clients primarily in the Pacific Northwest. Driven by her "realization that the global economy is problem-atic with respect to sustainability and equity," Christian developed several creative funds for accredited investors who wished to invest locally. "Without strong local and regional economies," she insists, "there can't be a long-term successful global economy." But after more than a decade of experimenta-tion, she is still struggling to figure out the right approach.

Christian is one of the very few top-flight financiers who questions the traditional paradigm of infinite growth. A student of the writings of econo-mist Herman Daly, she says, "We look at the pressures on our ecosphere, ecological limits, and we see that the trajectory of the global economy is not a positive one. We cannot continue growing, physically, the way we have been, in a finite world. So that was the origin of our mutual fund, Portfolio 21. As limits are reached, as resource limitations and climate changes inten-sify, companies are going to have to really step up to increase their efficiency and decrease their through-put of energy and materials."

For Christian, this was not enough. "We went into a thought process as to what Portfolio 21 investments could do to support local economies, and to support the needs of our clients who are interested in investing in local economies. We wanted to resolve another problem we were witnessing, which was small local companies essentially being bought out and dissolved by larger companies or just going out of business, because the owners or the founders were ready to retire and there wasn't a clear exit for them. So we decided to create a regional holding company that could step in to buy companies that were ready to transition, and additionally where the employ-ees were not ready to buy the companies or take over."

That was the birth of Upstream 21. Like B Corporations, Upstream 21 has written into its articles of incorporation that the company must consider the long- and short-term interests not only of shareholders but also of the employees, customers, suppliers, community, and environment. It currently has two small, subsidiary forest-product companies: Jefferson State Forest Products and Roguewood Furniture. The intention is to add local companies from other sectors—perhaps another seven or eight. Investors in Upstream 21 must be accredited. And one of the biggest investors in Upstream 21 is actually Portfolio 21 Investments.

Christian says that the companies in Upstream 21 struggled during the recession, though they have now returned to profitability. The big challenge was to adapt to rapidly diminishing sales while maintaining progressive, innovative manufacturing operations. In the case of Jefferson State, which makes wooden displays for produce, for example, Upstream 21 decided to shut down the company's plant in Hayfork, California, and reopen it in Grants Pass, Oregon. This drew strong criticism from Hayfork residents and from the company founders who had sold the company. Christian defends this decision as a necessary one for the business to survive. "Basically, the company had been established when the economy was roaring along, and it had been built with the support of one big client. When we bought the company, we realized that we needed to diversify its client base and improve the plant's efficiency. The recession hit us hard. The large client pulled back. And Upstream 21 found itself contributing more capital for a couple of years, even though it was operating at a loss."

Another one of Upstream's companies, Roguewood, had better equipment that it was not fully using. "So," explains Christian, "it made a lot of sense to move Jefferson State to Grants Pass where they could share the facility and the equipment of Roguewood. But for the severity of the recession, Upstream 21's capital could have been used to upgrade the equipment in Hayfork, rather than keeping Jefferson State in a survival mode."

Christian concedes that the impacts on Hayfork and the workers at the plant were negative. "But," she counters, "our environmental analysis was positive. Our customer and supplier analysis was positive. And our long-term analysis for employees in general was positive because we could not continue to operate Jefferson State as it was and stay in business much longer. By relocating the company to another small community that had been hurt both by the recession and by declines in the timber industry, and that had an unemployment rate of over 16 percent, we were able to retain jobs and set a foundation for adding more."

One lesson is that supporting local business does not obviate tough business decisions. And sometimes a business that is failing in one locale will, if moved, succeed in another. Yet how one saw the decision depended a lot on the vantage point. For Christian and her investors, the locality whose interest was paramount was the region. If the residents and employees of Hayfork had bought out the company, their judgments about the business problems and solutions might well have been different. But could they have found enough capital to keep the company operating through the recession? Perhaps. The Mondragon Cooperatives have managed hundreds of subsidiary businesses over fifty years without laying off a single worker.

"There's some real differences of opinion," reflects Christian, "with respect to local ownership. What exactly does local mean? How important is it? Can you still have outside capital coming in?"

Christian cites another example where Upstream 21 could have saved jobs that were destroyed by a *more local* owner. The first company Upstream 21 considered acquiring was a manufacturer of bicycle trailers and bicycles based in Eugene, Oregon. Upstream 21 proposed expanding and improving the Eugene manufacturing operations to strengthen its competitive edge. Just prior to the deal closing, however, a local investor made the case that his money and management would be more local than Upstream 21's (in Portland, 120 miles north). He won the deal and immediately cut the workforce, laying off more than forty longtime employees and offshoring all the manufacturing. Those jobs are gone not only from Eugene, but from the region. And the local and regional suppliers to the former manufacturing operation lost a valuable customer. Ouch.

"So," argues Christian, "it raises the question of whether it is constructive to have rigid rules about ownership, or whether it's more important to have rigid rules about the best interests of all the stakeholders. It's a good example of how 'local' doesn't always mean 'aligned with values.'"

At the Roguewood factory, Christian is now putting into practice her views on localism. The plant there, which has been sourcing much of its hardwood from the East, is working to source more from the Northwest. "That's part of our whole goal: to build the local capacity and to relocalize as much as possible. We are steadfast in our commitment to purchase our goods and services locally."

Another reform at Roguewood involved its dealers. "When we acquired them they were doing most of their business with one big client. We have helped them to reestablish connections with their network of dealers with more one-on-one relationships, locally, regionally, and some nationally.

"Our general principle, in terms of our manufacturing process, is local local local. Where can we get these parts, where can we get the wood, where can we get the workers . . . we think local first."

Christian believes that demand for local-investment opportunities by the unaccredited public has grown "radically higher" but says that her decision to open Upstream 21 only to accredited investors was the only rational choice. Creating a mutual fund open to unaccredited investors faced too many regulatory barriers, and becoming a publicly traded company was much too expensive. But she is continuing to think about ways of creating new local funds for unaccredited investors. Well, she hesitates, maybe *new* is the wrong word. "I hesitate to call local investing a new idea. It's really going back to the basics."

The Angels of Iowa

The word entrepreneurs have for deep-pocket investors who will write a check for many thousands of dollars is *angels*. Like their biblical counterparts exquisitely painted on cathedral ceilings, the angels of finance swoop down with magical powers to help earthly innovators realize their commercial dreams. Many fly solo, each with a quirky personal philosophy about the right entrepreneur, the killer app, and the smartest exit strategy. Sometimes they flock together, learning that by sharing information and resources, their dollars can reach more entrepreneurs, more quickly, with less risk. They might form clubs where, as the lunch or dinner wraps up, local entrepreneurs have a fifteen-minute opportunity to pitch their business plans. For entrepreneurs, getting an invitation to one of these angel soirees is the equivalent of an actor being called to audition for a blockbuster Hollywood feature film.

One of the first and best known of these clubs is the Band of Angels in Silicon Valley. And one of the first rural entrepreneurs to score big there was Burt Chojnowski, who was launching one of the first Voice over Internet

Protocol (VOIP) companies in 1999. Unlike most of the other entrepreneurs pleading for help, Chojnowski was decidedly not a local. True, he had worked in California for nearly two decades as a successful investment banker, but now he was sold on living and building his next venture in Fairfield, Iowa.

Fairfield has a population of 9,509 and got its name by organizing and hosting the first Iowa State Fair in 1854. The city is surrounded by farms growing soybeans, corn, cattle, and hogs, but *The New York Times* has described Fairfield as a town that "thrives largely on its abundance of start-up companies." It has created thousands of new jobs in firms making tofu, designing software, brokering oil sales, providing telecommunications services—so much so that the locals call it Sili*corn* Valley. And one of the keys to this success has been Burt Chojnowski.

Chojnowski first came to Fairfield in 1974, when he was part of a team that put together Maharishi International University, an institution linked with the Transcendental Meditation movement that later became Maharishi University of Management. He was one of the school's first graduates and a poster boy for "consciousness-based education." Chojnowski recalls, "I decided to return to Iowa in 1996, in early days of the Internet, when I recognized, before the term was coined, that the world was 'flat' and you could do anything basically from anywhere if you had a decent communications infrastructure. So I moved back with my young family to Fairfield, mostly because the quality of life was good here, and there was a thriving business community doing some very innovative things in telecommunications, software, marketing, and media."

Chojnowski's pitch to the Band of Angels was simple: "Fairfield, Iowa, is a digital suburb of San Jose, California, and a dollar invested in a small company in Iowa goes about five to ten times farther than one invested in a California-based company. Our overhead is lower, and we also have access to highly skilled technology employees who won't jump ship every three months to go on to a new venture."

Once his business was up and running, Chojnowski moved on to other opportunities. He organized a boot camp for entrepreneurs in Fairfield that drew 125 people and flew in speakers and investors from all over the country (including representatives from the Band of Angels). In 2000, Ed Malloy, who had been head of the Fairfield Entrepreneurs Association, was elected mayor and asked Chojnowski to step in and take over the organization. Chojnowski was then appointed by the former governor Tom Vilsack (now the U.S. secretary of agriculture) to be on the Iowa Capital Investment Board and manage tax credits for angel and venture capital investment in the state. One milestone for the board was the creation of the Iowa Fund of Funds, which invested in venture capital firms rather than directly into individual businesses.

One might assume that accredited investors are rarer in rural Iowa than blue whales, but Chojnowski spots them everywhere. "The strength of our town is that it's social and it has a business network. We have more restaurants per capita than San Francisco. Everybody goes out for lunch, and every restaurant is a business incubator. Everybody is doing business over lunch. Our downtown area is filled with cars, people are hobnobbing and putting deals together. About a week ago, I was in a local café and bookstore, Revelations, and at the table next to me there were some young guys who were pitching a movie deal to another guy who's from Fairfield and has some notoriety because he won some big bucks on the World Series of Poker on ESPN."

Chojnowski became a founding board member of IowaMicroLoan, which provides loans of up to $35,000 to small businesses. The capital comes from Wells Fargo, the U.S. Small Business Administration, the Northwest Area Foundation, and the State of Iowa Department of Economic Development. Applicants must first be turned down by a traditional financing institution. "In Iowa, most of the banking is done through small community banks. They know how to loan with collateral, real estate, agriculture, things like that. But they have not done well, or had much experience, with start-up businesses. So we created this microenterprise loan program. It's a higher interest rate because it's a higher-risk loan, but we also build some support services. Loan recipients get a $500 stipend every year to offset some of their consulting or business coaching expenses. We're also now creating a regional microenterprise loan program that's an affiliate to the statewide program."

Even though Chojnowski sees small loans as essential for start-ups, he sees equity funding as equally critical for small businesses. "You don't want to have them encumbered by debt. And if the business doesn't succeed, you don't want to leave the entrepreneurs so burdened that they will ruin their credit rating and can't go and start a new business. It's a dead end for small businesses, especially in rural areas, if they get an SBA loan but have to put up the owner's house as collateral." Accordingly, Chojnowski helped organize Iowa Community Capital to make equity investments in food-related small businesses and co-ops in a ten-county area in southeast Iowa. It operates under the U.S. Department of Treasury as a Community Development Financial Institution, which entitles it to receive additional government grants.

Chojnowski is now creating the Silicorn Valley Investors Fund to facilitate a broader range of angel investments and other funds to join his deals. He is an active member of the Chicago-based Seyen Capital. He also helped facilitate a major commitment from the Iowa Fund of Funds, which was looking to expand its support of Fairfield-based companies. And he cemented a relationship between the Iowa Fund of Funds and Seyen Capital, "because Seyen had a successful track record in Series A [first-round] investments, and had identified Fairfield as a fertile market for new deals."

"The best way to do an angel fund," insists Chojnowski, "is to have it piggyback on the deals put together by other funds—that's what the Band of Angels does. The problem with most angel investor networks and funds, and we've seen this across the Midwest, is that they think, 'Oh we want to be the lead investor, we'll invest in a small business because it's going to create some jobs.' But it often doesn't pan out. They're not really taking a tough look at the return on investment, the scope of the business, the management team—all the critical things you need to evaluate in a professional investment decision. It's smarter just to tag along or piggyback on an investment fund that does the due diligence."

Chojnowski's and Fairfield's track records are impressive. "We've raised, at last count, a combination of local investment and out-of-town investment, upward of $300 million in about twenty-five years or so." Most of that, Chojnowski admits, has come from outside investors, but the beneficiary projects are decidedly local. "We've done a really great job of creating what I call the entrepreneurial class. Not only are they starting businesses and creating jobs, they are also social entrepreneurs and benefactors. What we need to do next is create more sophisticated literacy on what it takes to be a successful investor, and target those investments, as much as you can, to benefit the local community. And I think we're doing that with the Stage Door Cinema."

The Stage Door Cinema is one of Chojnowski's first efforts to involve unaccredited investors. Control will reside in three hundred members paying a buy-in fee of $250 each, with the rest of the capital coming from outside investors. "It's a movie theater and event venue based upon cutting-edge digital media. We'll show documentary films, local films, foreign films, independent films, but we're also going to be the home base for TED (which invites speakers to present innovative solutions to tough global problems in short, punchy speeches). We've got the license for TEDxFairfield—we're the smallest city in the world to get one. We can also receive high-quality live broadcasts from, say, the Metropolitan Opera. If you couldn't be here, we could Skype you in or do a live video chat with you, wherever you are in the world."

One can sense that this project is Chojnowski's halfway house to exploring community ownership. "Personally, the movie theater might make me a little bit of money. But I just think it's a cool idea, given what it does for our community. It sort of knits together an interesting asset of digital media and moviemaking skills and movie-going-out. It will put us not only on our local map, but certainly on the regional and national maps as well."

Another new business Chojnowski is trying to start is a food innovation center. It will convert an old grocery store into a test kitchen and an "aggregation center" for local foods. "The goal is to create a bunch of new, year-round food businesses and get back to a local supply chain with products like organic ice cream or gluten-free bread. We'll work with Iowa Community Capital, Iowa State University, IowaMicroLoan, and the USDA to foster a facility that alone could generate twenty jobs directly and a couple hundred indirectly."

Chojnowski understands the value of keeping the companies he nurtures locally owned. "Fifteen years ago, we had a local company that went public. A lot of people—they had about three or four hundred employees—had the opportunity to buy stock in the company, as did people in the town. The stock did really well in the short term. But the company wasn't managed that well. A few months later, there was a lot of pressure from the investment bankers to sell their shares. The stock was thinly traded on Wall Street, and the price dropped quickly. It didn't work out very well for our people.

"When you do an IPO or you sell the company—we had a big company that was sold to Reader's Digest, their biggest acquisition ever—you can almost turn on the timer, and it might be two or three or four years, and the company and the jobs disappear."

Chojnowski recently put together a magazine called *The Fairfield Edge*, which profiles forty locally owned companies and explains their competitive advantages. Two of the case studies are the biggest employers in Fairfield, Dexter Apache and Cambridge Investment Research.

"Dexter Apache makes commercial washers and dryers. They ran into problems in the '80s, and nobody would buy their products. They did an employee stock ownership buy-out, an ESOP, and they still give the line workers the opportunity to buy in. They really have a dynamic, creative management team, because all the team members are owners of the company. They are also one of the greenest businesses in town—leaders in producing commercial energy- and water-efficient commercial washers and dryers, partly because their customers demand it. It's another case where the stability of that company is based upon local ownership.

"Cambridge Investment Research could have sold out any number of times to bigger financial concerns, but they have maintained local ownership. They've expanded like crazy, but never really needed any venture capital; they didn't bring in outside investors. They bootstrapped everything, grew out of their own cash flow, and they're a really stable company."

While proud of Fairfield's biggest performers, Chojnowski reveres the community's smaller firms. "Most new jobs are created by companies less than four or five years old, the new emerging businesses. And the fastest-growing segment is sole proprietors and home-based businesses. These businesses do not necessarily need so much in the way of financing, but they do need know-how."

Chojnowski is trying to provide that know-how through a cooperative incubator for home-based businesses that would use a common infrastructure and operational staff. "These businesses might each have a share in a co-op. As the co-op thrives, they will thrive. This was how it worked out for farmers here who started some of the early ethanol plants. They sold their corn to the ethanol plant, and the ethanol plant made its own income and spun it back. In fact, the difference between those farmers that got into an ethanol co-op and those that didn't has in some instances meant the difference of $500,000 per year in income."

Imagine every town in the United States with at least five or ten thousand people nurturing its entrepreneurial class the way Fairfield does. Imagine a hundred Burt Chojnowskis in every state, mobilizing local investment from the angels lurking in the shadows. Local entrepreneurship is a powerful force that feeds on itself. "We're ranked the number one community in Iowa in per capita giving," notes Chojnowski, "because the most successful entrepreneurs have really given back to the community, not only money, but time, effort, and ideas."

Chojnowski's kind of leadership is rare. More typically, the movers and shakers for local investment are entrepreneurs who are trolling for cash.

Locavores Gone Wild

When Ari Derfel was told by his lawyer that he could only ask for money from accredited investors, his immediate reaction was: "That's bullshit! That means only the people with means can invest in new business. That's just wrong. How can that be true?"

Derfel was a successful caterer specializing in delicious, healthy, organic food from local sources; he had just won a highly competitive bid to build a restaurant on the ground floor of the new David Brower Center, right in the heart of downtown Berkeley, California. Between December 2007 and April 2008, Derfel raised $1 million in large chunks from accredited investors—but he needed $2.5 million.

"All of a sudden the economy tanks. The million dollars we had shrank when several investors pulled out or significantly reduced the amount that they were investing. We were under quite a bit of duress, because we had a signed lease, we had an expected opening date, and we needed the money. So one day my business partner and I were sitting down and we said: Why are we doing it this way? Why don't we go more Obama-style, grassroots, democratic? Why don't we go to a hundred people or two hundred people in our community, and get them each to put in $5,000? Let's invite the whole community to own this institution.

"But," Derfel adds with frustration, "our attorney said you can't do that. He said the maximum number of investors you can have is thirty-five, and those people need to be accredited. No one is allowed to participate in a private equity deal unless they're accredited." That's when Derfel got creative.

This is the point where we must pause, go to the blackboard, and sketch the basics of securities law. Get a strong cup of coffee before reading the next page or so. The most basic federal rule for an entrepreneur seeking investment, according to the Securities Act of 1933, is that you can only avoid most of the legal paperwork if you privately, without public advertising, solicit funds from accredited investors. The moment you solicit money from even one unaccredited investor, you must prepare a detailed private placement memorandum (PPM), which summarizes your business plan and contains an encyclopedia of legal language that says, in a thousand different ways, *you may lose everything.* (You actually have to prepare a PPM for accredited investors as well, but there are no requirements about what it must contain.) Because a PPM for unaccredited investors could cost at least $10,000 for a lawyer to prepare—many will charge $25,000, $50,000, or higher—the penny-wise entrepreneur will usually say, Fine, let's stick to accredited investors.

Federal law defines a *security* in sweepingly broad terms. It includes any financial instrument—debt, equity, royalty—sold with the possibility that the holder will realize financial gain. The law presumes that any security must be registered with the Securities and Exchange Commission, unless it falls into an exception. And the most commonly used exception is a private placement where 100 percent of the purchasers are accredited. Under this exemption, the securities are "restricted," which means they cannot be freely resold.

There are actually four exemptions especially relevant to small business.[1] The layperson might assume that *exemption* means that the law does not apply, that you're home free. In fact, it only means that there are different, lighter, and less expensive legal burdens with which you must comply:

1. **The intrastate offering exemption** applies if you limit offers and sales of shares to people just living in your state, and if your business mostly takes place within that state. However, if you offer a share to even one person residing out of state, the exemption is lost. Ditto if one of your shareholders does this without your permission. Plus, you still must comply with state securities laws, many of which are at least as onerous as the SEC's.

2. **Rule 504 under Regulation D** establishes a very light filing process, if you wish to raise under $1 million in a twelve-month period. You must comply, however, with the securities laws in every state in which you make an offer, many of which, again, are quite demanding. This process has been simplified somewhat by the Small Company Offering Registration (SCOR) Form U-7, which a number of states accept as part of their registration requirements.

3. **Rules 505 and 506, also under Regulation D,** ramp up the filing requirements if you wish to raise under $5 million (Rule 505) or over $5 million (Rule 506), and both allow you to have up to thirty-five unaccredited investors. The SEC concedes on its website, however, that the disclosure documents required under these rules are, if you make an offer to an unaccredited investor, "generally the same as those used in registered offerings," so it's not even clear why these rules are called exemptions.

4. **Regulation A** allows a company to raise up to $5 million in a twelve-month period from an unlimited number of accredited and unaccredited investors. The filing requirements are demanding but less so than a full-blown SEC registration. In concrete terms, lawyers will extract $25,000 to $50,000 for this assignment. Most states also require an audit of the company's finances, which can add another $10,000-plus to the bill.

Is your head ready to explode? Okay, let's return to Ari Derfel's story. In case you didn't notice, his attorney gave incorrect advice. He said that Ari could only have thirty-five accredited investors. In fact he could have as many as five hundred. (Under securities law, if you have more than five hundred investors in a single class of securities and at least $10 million in assets, the company automatically becomes subject to federal reporting requirements for public companies, which are too costly for most small businesses to comply with.) And he said that Ari could not have any unaccredited investors, when in fact, relying on Rule 505, he could have had at least thirty-five. Did Ari's attorney mix up that the number thirty-five applied to unaccredited investors, not accredited ones? Who knows? The lesson is that most attorneys have a poor understanding of securities law, which underscores why it imposes such a huge burden on small businesses, which cannot afford the pricey attorneys who are experts in the field.

Being an entrepreneur, Ari kept exploring. "Around the same time I had gone to the first Slow Money event in Northern California. I brought up my situation at the event and someone walked up to me and said, Hey, there's this thing called Regulation A. Then I called my accountant and asked, What's Regulation A and what else is out there? My accountant, a friend, was just getting started in his father's firm, so he was a bit hungry and curious about the way the world works. Lo and behold he called me back and said, Hey, your attorney's wrong. Long story short, there's this thing called Regulation D. It requires more reporting, but you can have an unlimited number of accredited investors and up to thirty-five unaccredited. Well, gosh, that will do it! A lot of people around here are accredited but they just won't give us more than $5,000."

Back to the board. Note that under existing securities laws, even Ari Derfel—the one-in-a-thousand entrepreneur who really, really wanted to sell most of his shares primarily to unaccredited locavores—decided it was not worth the hassle. Instead, he would stick to the under-thirty-five limit. Small-business people understandably have a million things to worry about, and the less time wasted on gathering the start-up funds, the better. Ultimately, Derfel was lucky. He secured the money he needed to start his restaurant from sixty-five people—twenty-six of them unaccredited. Nearly all the unaccredited investors were friends.

Okay, it wasn't luck. It required a Herculean marketing campaign, as Derfel retells it: "The Bay Area community, especially those involved in progressive social, environmental, and financial work, is relatively incestuous. Because we had been the caterer for many progressive organizations over the last seven years, there were a lot of folks that we knew either directly or indirectly through one degree of separation. So it was basically a tireless effort of talking to friends, finding out who knew who, trying to unearth more people, going to events, hobnobbing, socializing, finding out who the movers and shakers were in the room. I just did that over and over again until I was able to find enough people. There were probably three or four hundred people who made it onto a list at some point, and we ended up with sixty-five."

This laborious process of recruiting investors radicalized Derfel. "The discovery that only a certain class of people are allowed to invest—wow, that's profoundly undemocratic. Sure, I can understand how the rules keep a real loser from putting together a phony investment opportunity and then robbing a thousand grandmas of their last thousand dollars. But our laws and guidelines ignore the situations where it would be very appropriate to invite unaccredited investors to participate."

Today Derfel's restaurant, called Gather, is a smash success. A readers' poll in a popular weekly, the *East Bay Express*, called it the best new restaurant in 2010, and national magazines like *Esquire* and *Food and Wine* have praised it. But Derfel's painful experience with securities law persuaded him to take a less glitzy day job, during much of 2011, as the acting executive director for the nonprofit Slow Money to crack the code of securities law for other local businesses and open up the universe of accredited investors to them.

Under the leadership of Derfel (who recently stepped down as executive director to tend to an ailing parent) and founder Woody Tasch, Slow Money has now begun advocating that all kinds of investors, even unaccredited ones, put more of their money into local businesses. The Slow Money Principles, which envision, among many things, investing 1% in local food systems right now and ultimately "50% of our assets within 50 miles of where we live," have attracted 22,000 signatures. The goal is have a million people take the pledge. In the meantime, Slow Money conferences have spawned dozens of chapters around the country, each pioneering new ways mindful investors, irrespective of their wealth, can support local businesses and collectively mobilizing $11 million in local investing in just eighteen months. An affiliate in Boulder, Colorado, for example, has raised $1.5 million for an investment fund to support food businesses. A Slow Money chapter in North Carolina helped mobilize $465,000 in loans for various local food enterprises in the state. These kinds of cutting-edge tools—and the revolution they are beginning for unaccredited investing—are the focus of the next chapters.

Unaccredited Investing in SEC-Land

It's hard to believe that Lewis Carroll never worked for the Securities and Exchange Commission. Down the rabbit hole of securities law is a jabberwocky of regulations that allow the rich to get richer, while the Red Queen screams "off with their heads" to any unaccredited investors who dare to have tea with small businesses. Only a Mad Hatter could insist that the least powerful businesses in society dole out a small fortune to attorneys before they even can knock at the doors of potential investors, including *accredited* investors.

Defenders of the twisted logic of SEC-land say these rules are needed to protect innocent Americans from getting taken in by the shysters selling shares of Florida swampland. We have to be sure, absolutely sure, that securities are the real deal before they go to market. On the surface this is a reasonable justification. But try applying this hypercautious thinking to potential consumers of new products. Why should we care more about protecting an investor from losing $100 on a badly run business than a shopper from losing $100 on a badly designed product? Shouldn't we forbid all advertising until the said business registers with a variety of federal and state agencies? And why stop there? Shouldn't we insist that, say, a home-based tree-ornament maker get each and every plastic reindeer, snowman, and bobble she makes tested for toxins, strength, endurance, and so forth at a government-certified laboratory before they go to market? And why not insist that the company have a full audit before it does business?

If we applied the logic of securities law to consumer goods, commerce as we know it would come grinding to a halt. Small companies would never get started. Advertising would largely disappear. (Okay, part of me thinks *that* wouldn't be such a bad thing.) Our marketplace would be limited to a small number of lumbering, government-approved behemoths, letting consumers know about their wares through carefully vetted, grim, black-and-white listings in the back pages of newspapers.

The truth is that federal and state laws do impose lots of requirements on the producers, distributors, and sellers of goods in the United States, and much of our political wrangling is over what's a sensible level of regulation. Our tree-ornament maker does have to comply with laws prohibiting certain toxic materials, her sales must follow the guidelines of the Uniform Commercial Code, and fraudulent advertising on the Internet (assertions that the ornaments could cure cancer, for example) might be punished by fines or jail time. But notice the main difference from securities law. In the consumer context, *freedom to engage in commerce is presumed.* Small companies have permission to get started, to sell products and services to anyone, and to advertise anywhere. In securities law, *the presumption is against selling shares to investors until permission is granted.*

Securities regulators like to suggest that the alternative to these totalitarian rules would be anarchy. The consumer analogy demonstrates, however, that's nonsense. Freedom to create, market, and sell securities could be presumed, and simple anti-fraud statutes could be strengthened to punish abuses. Individuals and companies could be rated and held accountable for the quality of their securities, just as they are for the quality of their products on eBay. Those who flout the law could then be banned from selling securities ever again. There are a million ways to approach this problem short of forbidding unaccredited investors from participating in small-business finance.

The current logic of SEC-land envisions business proceeding at a slow, methodical, snail-like pace more suited to the early nineteenth century. You create your securities. Then you create an offering statement. Then you receive approval from federal and state regulators. Then, and only then, are you allowed to sell your securities to potential investors. Today's rules weigh down against action, against entrepreneurship, against the modern speed of commerce. They were written in an era when there was no Internet, no computers, no televisions, and no fax machines. Most people in the 1930s got their information through static-filled radios, text-heavy newspapers, and word of mouth. The architects of securities laws can be forgiven for viewing business communications as a rather static domain that the government could and should control. But how can this be defended today, in the twenty-first century?

Nevertheless, within this legal landscape, there many ways entrepreneurs can dance around—or with—these outdated securities laws to involve unaccredited investors:

- **Pre-Sales.** Not every instrument that puts money into a business is a security. Advance sales of a product at a discount, for example, might not be securities. A café in Oakland has relied on this exception to generate much of its start-up financing.
- **Profit-Free Transactions.** Funds given with no expectation of a return are also not likely to be considered securities. This opens up several kinds of "crowdsourcing" approaches, which have been runaway successes on such websites as Kickstarter and IndieGoGo.
- **Local Networking.** A community group can become quite deliberate about building relationships to facilitate one-on-one investment ties, which is what an innovative group called Local Investment Opportunities Network (LION) does in Port Townsend, Washington.
- **Peer-to-Peer (P2P).** Using a growing number of peer-to-peer websites, which have themselves made extensive securities filings, community-minded investors can begin to set up LION-like circles throughout the country.
- **Low-Cost Public Offerings.** Through direct public offerings, a local business can go to large numbers of unaccredited investors. Several new companies are bringing the once stratospheric legal costs of issuing these securities back down to Earth.

We'll explore these options in this chapter, and then conclude with some thoughts about the most promising way to get around the SEC rules— namely, to overhaul or repeal them.

Not Quite Securities

Awaken Café in Oakland was born from an epiphany of its founder Cortt Dunlap after President George W. Bush narrowly won reelection in November 2004. He had invested a lot in that election and was heartbroken with the results. He started thinking: "As a nation, we put so much energy into this national election every four years. What if we were putting that same energy, right here, into Oakland?"

That was Dunlap's awakening. He decided to throw himself into creating a community space, a hub, where locals could dream up the next great businesses in Oakland, the next great nonprofits, and the next great projects: "What is it that people commune over? The arts came up. And we started thinking about beer and wine, about coffee and tea, and about the other kinds of things that inspire people to sit down and hash out a plan on a napkin."

At about the same time, he met a couple who had just moved from Seattle and had been a part of that city's now world-famous gourmet coffee culture. They had this idea of treating coffee like a wine, where you source the best-quality beans from sustainable farms, roast them carefully to bring out the subtle flavors of each region, and serve each cup in a way that enhances the customer's taste experience. The idea of Awaken Café was to use gourmet coffee as the financial engine for the community hub. The café opened as an eight-hundred-square-foot espresso kiosk in downtown Oakland. Dunlap planned to expand in the building, but that did not work out. After three years he decided to move the café into a new, larger space.

The last thing Dunlap wanted his new Awaken Café to be was just another East Bay coffee shop. "They tend to get kind of library-esque, people are in there with their laptops, quiet, you feel almost uncomfortable having a conversation with a person sitting across from you. People aren't interacting. We have to counter what one of my partners calls *Laptopistan*. That's why we must train our staff to learn who people are—not just their names but what they're up to—and to introduce them to other people in the community."

Dunlap wants his new café to have speakers on local investment. It should attract artists working on group projects. It should hold local TED conferences parading great ideas through short talks. Between serious presentations the stage might have dance performances, movies, jazz groups, and stand-up comedians. "The tagline of Awaken Café is to launch movements," Dunlap says. "We're literally on the footsteps of city hall in downtown Oakland. We want the café to become a place where thinkers and artists go and meet and really give birth to a local independent living economy in downtown Oakland."

Why downtown Oakland? "This was once a very grand downtown area," explains Dunlap. "When we opened the first café three years ago, it was filled with empty storefronts, run-down and forgotten. We were on the very front line. Jerry Brown, who's now the governor of California again, had been our mayor for eight years and started to bring more residents here. Now there's all this residential growth, but still a lot of empty storefronts. We're a part of this growing movement of people opening new businesses, and by and large they're not big-box multinational corporations. They are little, local retailers, restaurateurs, and club owners. And they give the community, I think, real flavor and a soul."

To raise the $100,000 of capital required for the new café, Dunlap began educating himself about securities laws and saw an intriguing opportunity. "I had been a customer at a local restaurant called Café Gratitude. I noticed, at the original San Francisco location, a note on the table that said: 'We're looking to open in the East Bay. If you'd like to help us out, you can buy a thousand-dollar gift card and we'll give you twelve hundred dollars to spend at either of our restaurants.'"

Dunlap discovered that these prepaid discount cards did not trigger any of the nasty limitations of the SEC.[1] "What a great idea, I thought! So your customers say, 'Hey, I want your restaurant in my neighborhood, and I'm willing to bet I'll spend a thousand dollars there when you open. I'll give you that money in advance, and you'll give me a discount.' You can vote with your dollars in advance. It's nice, because it allows someone to buy in for a small amount of money. They don't have to have $5,000 or $100,000. Before we opened, we had sold about $20,000 worth of prepaid purchases. Since then, we have continued to sell them. I think to date we've sold something like $35,000."

Dunlap set the discount level so that, even if customers fully used the coupons, he would be making money. He also built higher discounts for larger advance purchases. A $100 advance purchase got a 10 percent discount. A $1,000 advance purchase got a 25 percent discount. Unlike Café Gratitude, where you could use the discounts at the existing café, Dunlap's customers had to wait patiently for the new Awaken to open.

All kinds of people bought the cards. "You know," says Dunlap, "friends and family, of me and my partner. People who lived downtown and wanted more businesses to be there. I would say 90 percent [were] people we knew already. Maybe 10 percent had read about us in the paper or walked by the café and hooked into it. Once we opened, the people who were buying were our regulars."

The other benefit of the prepaid accounts, totally unanticipated, was that it introduced Dunlap to the people who would become his most serious investors. The prepaid accounts led to relationships, which led to friendships, which led to larger financial commitments. "So the prepaid accounts were a good way to test the waters," says Dunlap. "It allowed us to finance the new café with preexisting business and personal relationships, to bring in twenty people at a $5,000 investment each. That's what Cutting Edge Capital is helping with, now. The prepaid accounts still help—someone will put down $500 or $100 and that will make a big difference covering the expenses that come up with starting a business—but it's only a small piece of the $100,000 we're raising."

Dunlap is mindful that his business is running a café, not selling coupons: "It takes a lot of work to sell these prepaid coupons—communicating with our email list and customer base, and putting an offer out there in front of them. And as a small business, our time and energy are limited."

As of this writing, Dunlap has raised $60,000 of his needed $100,000 and feels confident about raising the rest. In case there's a delay—approval from the local health department and other agencies is pending—he has bought a mobile food cart to start selling coffee and food in front of the construction site. "We've been closed for a while and our customers are walking by, wondering when we're opening. The cart gives a little bit of our business to our customers. They can get a cup of coffee at least. It also might be a feeder for our fund-raising model. I might run into somebody who I know really well through the old café, someone who is committed to the redevelopment of downtown Oakland, and he might end up becoming one of our next $5,000 equity investors."

Dunlap sees ways of expanding into other Bay Area locations without betraying his local roots. "Before we opened our first café, we convened a kind of a town hall. We asked people what they would like in a café that serves the community. If we went into another community in the Bay Area, we'd ask that same question. 'Hey, we're new here! I don't know, what was here before? What'd you like? What can we do for you?'"

To Dunlap, the novel use of pre-selling and other kinds of local investment are important selling points of his business. "When you're investing in services and products and businesses that you'll use, you're saying, 'I want *this* in my community, I want *that* in my community.' You become the architect of your own Main Street."

Zero Returns

A second strategy local businesses are using to run the securities law gauntlet is to ask investors, including unaccredited ones, for money, property, exotic museum pieces—anything short of stolen goods—with no expectation of getting any return. Your motive might be pure: Perhaps you're looking to open the gates of heaven by distributing all your worldly possessions to the community's biggest-hearted entrepreneurs. Or your motive might be wickedly self-absorbed: You're praying that a great story about your generosity in the *Chronicle of Philanthropy* leads to sales at your own business doubling, or to thousands of new investors knocking at your door. All these motives are permissible, as long as you don't plan on making money directly.

One popular website seizing on the zero-return exception is Kiva.org. Established in 2005, Kiva has sought to become the global-electronic version of the Grameen Bank, the famous microcredit pioneer that earned its founder, Muhammad Yunus, a Nobel Peace Prize. Splashed across Kiva's home page, with thirty-three photos of promising developing-country entrepreneurs underneath, are the words: "Empower people around the world with a $25 loan." Another box says:

How it works:
1. Choose a borrower
2. Make a loan
3. Get repaid
4. Repeat!

Today a picture of an intense, half-smiling young woman in a black jacket, when clicked, brings you to a page with a thumbnail sketch of Veronica

Alexandra Tenesaca Bravo. We can learn about her region of Cuenca, Ecuador, her business, and her "ask." Two days a week, Veronica sells used clothing in a stall in the city market, and she is seeking a loan of $350 to purchase inventory—in her case, more used clothing. She has already raised 42 percent of the money and has $200 to go. Veronica promises to repay monthly over eight months. We can see profiles of the other lenders to Ms. Bravo and learn more about their history in the region. We can learn about her "field sponsor," Fundación ESPOIR, which has facilitated more than $2 million of loans to 4,533 Kiva entrepreneurs and has earned a "risk rating" of four out of five stars (that's good).

Because the $25 loan to Ms. Bravo is repaid without interest, it is arguably not a security under federal law (though some states might conclude otherwise under their own securities laws[2]). This has liberated Kiva from onerous SEC filings that have bedeviled other for-profit P2P sites like Prosper .com. Economists who teach that the only motive investors have is profit should take note: More than half a million people worldwide have made Kiva loans—currently totaling $216 million, through 133 field partners in sixty countries—without making a dime. The repayment rate is 98.75 percent. Even though the lender can't profit, the recipient certainly can.

A related kind of development has been the proliferation of websites inviting donations. Kickstarter.com, for example, is designed to support great projects in the fields of food, design, fashion, technology, games, comics, and journalism. People pitch their idea (often with a memorable video), lay out their financing goal, ask for contributions in small change, promise small gifts to patrons (T-shirt, record albums, books, special-events invitations), and if the goal is met in the targeted time, the deal consummates. Unlike Kiva, money is just given, not loaned. Because Kickstarter awards sponsors gifts of only token value, securities law is circumvented. After facilitating an eye-popping $15 million in sponsorships in its first year, Kickstarter now is raising more than $1 million every week.

Guideline 3 in Kickstarter's rules explicitly says "no business funding, projects only," but the fine print provides clever entrepreneurs with a map for circumvention:

> If your project hopes to make money, that's perfectly fine! Rather
> we're underlining that we only allow projects. A project is something

finite, with a clear beginning and end . . . Examples are making a film versus starting a film studio, or designing a new piece of apparel versus starting a fashion label.

Needless to say, hundreds of food businesses—er, projects—have gotten off the ground from these donations. Two Chicagoans raised $40,074 from 492 backers (the goal was $30,000) to launch Pipeworks Brewing, a new microbrewery. Their four backers at the $2,500 level were entitled to work with the brewmasters and have the final beer products named after them. Just Ripe, a worker-owned food collective selling local and regional foods, raised $12,920 ($12,000 goal) to open a storefront in Knoxville, Tennessee. The Get Fresh Express, a delivery company that aims to bring healthy food into urban food deserts, raised $10,968 ($10,000 goal) to buy a refrigerated truck.

It's not quite charity (the IRS won't let you take a gift deduction), but it's not equity, either. *Micropatronage* is the term Lewis Winter, a young graphic designer from Melbourne, uses to explain to *The New York Times* why he contributed to five projects. "If I was rich, I'd fund whole projects, but this allows me to fund as much or as little as I can afford."[3]

There are now dozens of new crowdfunding sites popping on the web, each with its own niche. IndieGoGo has an international flair. Cinema Reloaded allows you to be a co-producer of a film. Peerbackers doesn't monkey around with Kickstarter's caveats—it's specifically about crowdfunding new businesses. As I write, today's top offerings on that site are for an environmentally friendly carpet cleaning company in Lexington, Kentucky, looking to purchase a van, a Rotovac Powerwand, and other supplies; "three Brooklyn girls" wanting to move their cupcake-baking operation from a community kitchen into a rented storefront; and an inventor of a portable, encrypted key for computers eager to begin mass-volume manufacturing. Care to help?

LIONS in the Street

James Frazier of Port Townsend, Washington, may be the only investment adviser in the United States who graduated from Wharton, started a hedge fund, and highlights in the "background" section of his CV "permaculture and social justice."

Frazier helped set up the Local Investment Opportunities Network in 2008 to help local investors share and vet interesting local business-funding proposals with one another. Between periodic meetings involving his members, Frazier receives local-investment pitches, circulates them to members designated by the entrepreneurs as preexisting relationships, and then leaves it to individual investors and entrepreneurs to meet and strike their own deals. Unaccredited investors can participate, though it's up to each business to create a deal structure that allows their money (or not). Because LION is not selling any securities, or taking commissions or fees, it tiptoes around the SEC proscriptions against public solicitation.

To keep LION's relationships personal, Frazier does most of his organizing by word of mouth. He appreciates the publicity from local (and increasingly national) press, but he doesn't seek it out. "I would just say generally we do our best to keep it small, but we want people to be able to find us. So far, it has worked out well."

The need for more investment in Port Townsend, a community with 9,113 residents, is stark, says Frazier: "The recession has really created a huge demand for money. That's driven a lot of people to us—sometimes directly, and sometimes through the local small-business-development center, the local economic-development council, or the local college with entrepreneurship courses."

As a general rule, LION doesn't turn away any business proposal. Frazier dutifully circulates every pitch he receives to members with whom the local entrepreneurs designate as having preexisting relationships. "We don't pass judgment on any investment, we don't vet anything, we let our members decide. More than half our investing opportunities, I'm guessing, don't get much of a response. But there are also some very compelling proposals."

"People start getting creative when they're working with their neighbors, and, in our area, some of the businesses have really cool products: There's a cidery, a cheese maker, and a goat dairy. Some of our investors have taken some of their interest or dividend payments in kind. So they're getting not only dollars but cheese and cider. This is also a better deal for the businesses, too, because they usually are paying returns at market value, but it only takes their cost to produce. People just love the different kinds of returns they're getting."

Even without in-kind perks, the financial returns have been impressive. According to Frazier: "Businesses tend to have to pay local investors less than what they'd have to pay the bank, while investors are getting more from local businesses than what they'd be getting on their savings otherwise. People will meet in the middle, doing deals at 5, 6, 7, maybe 8 percent. Everybody loves that. Plus, all the dollars stay local."

Frazier wants LION to create a *culture* of local investment in Port Townsend: "There's now far more dialogue between business owners and the investors who are also their customers, their neighbors, and their mentors. People are working together on locally based economic development in general. And the results speak for themselves. We've got all sorts of businesses that are operating or have expanded or are thriving because of local investment. In turn, the local investors are thriving, too. They're not just getting a good financial return for their retirement or creating income for retirement— they're also getting the pleasure of supporting their community."

Frazier has been compiling data on all the investment activity in Port Townsend over the past five years, including several pre-LION years. He's tabulating what kinds of investments have occurred, how big, whether they were debt or equity, what were the terms, and so forth. His assessment is that LION has injected two million additional dollars into the local economy.

LION's roots go back to Frazier's Wall Street years, when he recalls feeling like an alien, or an imposter. He co-founded a hedge fund in 1999 but was uneasy about the absence of values in his work. Peers would ask if he was doing socially responsible investing (SRI), and he would respond, with a wee bit of shame, that he was just pursuing profit. "My only solace," says Frazier, "was that I was taking the money I made and buying organic food, living consciously, and supporting good causes. But it bothered me. I wanted to be making my money in a good way. So when I left the hedge fund world I had the opportunity to rededicate my practice to SRI, and to bring my economic and investment career more in line with my values."

Over time, Frazier's SRI mission expanded into local investing. "There's no better community to invest in than your own," he would tell his friends and clients. He would explain that local investing is actually the oldest form of investing on the planet. "Before there were global stocks and bonds to invest in, there was just helping your neighbor open up a hardware store or bank or whatever." He would also point out that because Port Townsend is a small, isolated community, every dollar of local investing has a particularly powerful multiplier impact on the entire economy.

Frazier turned up at a seminar I held in Port Townsend on local economy building in early 2009, and he stood out as the one guy in the room who wasn't going to wait around for permission to act. He also understood immediately that local investing required a fundamentally different kind of approach. "Local is really about the place and what the opportunities are there. It doesn't lend itself to large pools of money, unless those pools of money are distributed through locally focused groups."

Sure, Frazier sees the importance of national groups like Slow Money and RSF Social Finance promoting tools for local investing but thinks they will only succeed if community groups like LION are circulating and discussing their proposals. "It's going to take a local touch," he says, "to make anything really go."

At the outset, Frazier helped his members decide on two important rules about how LION should work: Anyone could participate. And all members had to make their own investment decisions. LION's founding members were committed to all kinds of people being in the network, including unaccredited investors. They felt that their presence would naturally attract the kind of local, small businesses that made up the fabric of their community. Frazier has tried to include lots of noninvestors as well, since they still could help spread the word. "I'm actually not invested locally, myself, at this time. My financial situation isn't such that I can really afford to lock my money up for any amount of time."

Making members responsible for their own investment decisions was a critical part of LION's legal design, but Frazier admits that this also means that the group isn't for everybody: "Since the law prohibits us from giving advice on which investments are good, all the members need to analyze the proposals for themselves. We encourage our members to hire an adviser if they feel like they need one, and I'd say most members do have financial advisers. But they're also very comfortable making decisions on their own. Our members have a strong sense of what they want their money to be doing."

The distinction between a permissible private solicitation and an impermissible public solicitation varies state by state, and Washington is more permissive than most. "If you just have a big, open membership and all sorts of businesses that don't necessarily know anyone in the group are submitting their investment opportunities to you, then it becomes more of a public offering."

Frazier acknowledges that LION's success could cause it to stray across that line. "When our group started out it was really small, and we already had personal relationships with the businesses we were connecting with. But as word has gotten out and the membership has grown, we've been getting investment opportunities from people I don't know and—I'm guessing— some of the other members don't know. The circles are widening, so we have become more careful. We now publish a list of our members for businesses, so that they can check the box on everyone they have a preexisting relationship with, and then we'll just send their materials to those people. I don't know how the membership will take it."

Today LION remains informal—so much so that it still doesn't have a budget. "The only thing we've ever done in terms of raising money was to hire a lawyer to look over our legal documents, but even then he wasn't a securities lawyer." Frazier also has informally consulted with Cutting Edge Capital and Slow Money to think through the legal details of what LION is doing and expects those collaborations to benefit the whole community-investing movement, which is growing.

Frazier is puzzling about how to transform LION into a more sustainable model. It really can't be scaled up, but perhaps it can be replicated, licensed, or even franchised. As word has spread, other local-investment groups around the country have asked Frazier to help them set up their own LION groups. One group that has already taken its first steps, including approved use of the *LION* name, is in Madison, Wisconsin. "It has kind of been overwhelming," admits Frazier. "My response has been to create a tool kit or blueprint for other communities to follow. We have revised our legal documents to reflect our actual experience. And we're in the process of relaunching our website. We're trying to create a one-stop shop for other people to do this.

"My dream is to have a huge network of these LION groups, local investing groups, all over the country. In every little town, every little place, there would be a core group of people who want to invest their money locally and help their neighbors, friends, and family pursue their economic dreams."

Following the Crowds

James Frazier and his fellow LION members weaved together LION through methodical, face-to-face network building. But is there any good reason why Internet-savvy investors couldn't do this virtually in towns across America?

That's the promise of the fast-spreading crowdfunding sites on the Internet. Take Prosper.com. By connecting a broader universe of lenders with a broader universe of borrowers through a very efficient platform that all but eliminates banking middlemen, Prosper provides both investors and borrowers with more options. Since launching in 2006, the site has facilitated nearly a quarter of a billion dollars of lending—all in chunks under $25,000. The home page currently claims that investors, who can lend money directly or purchase other Prosper debt notes, are averaging an annual return of 10.4 percent. They can bid on loans in increments as small as $25. For borrowers, the pitch is equally appealing:

No Hassles, No Hidden Fees

If you have good credit, you're a perfect candidate for finding a loan on Prosper. We connect you with individual investors and offer you low fixed rates without any of the hidden fees, red tape, and attitude associated with other types of loans. Signing up is a quick and easy process, and you'll have the opportunity to tell potential lenders as much (or as little) as you want about why you'd like to borrow money.

New crowdfunding sites are debuting on the web almost weekly. You can now do lending not only through Prosper but also through the Lending Club (based in the United States) and Zopa (United Kingdom). If you're an accredited investor, you can participate in crowd-sourced equity financing of promising start-ups through Crowdcube (UK), Seedmatch (Germany), and GrowVC (Hong Kong). Seedrs is opening up equity finance to unaccredited

British residents. CurrencyFair will allow you to play in the high-finance field of money swapping.

There's only one little problem with this burgeoning field: Where's the *local* investing? All these sites are matching investors and businesses from very different, very distant places. Every dollar invested thousands of miles away via crowdfunding is arguably a dollar that will not be invested locally. That the people involved are strangers means that there's a stronger need for intermediaries and policing. The more attenuated the ties between a business and an investor, the more there needs to be mechanized vetting, securitizing, and trading—the very things that got us into the global mess we're in today.

I'll concede that I'm excited about some crowdfunding initiatives that would be very hard to fund through purely local investing. Websites like Kickstarter let us throw a little change at that one-in-a-million project we think might be a global game changer. The Kivas of the world are essentially transforming long-standing foreign aid programs—which for years have reeked of political opportunism, bureaucratic waste, and multinational-business cronyism—into more efficient, personalized, and entrepreneurial microloans. Significantly, no one involved in these sites is trying to get rich. The recipients are being vetted by the crowd for quality, and the donors are not expecting to profit. At a site like Prosper, in contrast, lenders and borrowers from across the planet are trolling for deals just to make more money.

After trying and discarding other models of crowdfunding, Dana Mauriello of Profounder, a website that advises users on how to raise funds from friends and family, concluded that crowdfunding small investments for large chunks of change is a perilous activity. "When you put in $50, you might forget you ever did that, and move on with your life. It's a non-event."

Some would argue that anonymous lending facilitates privacy and objectivity. I worry that it facilitates fraud. Why shouldn't lenders and borrowers really know each other? An alternative approach is suggested by FundingCircle, a site in the United Kingdom dedicated to crowdsourcing business lending. There's a "community circle" option that allows you to create your own local-to-local (L2L) funding circles based on interest or place, and you can opt to be publicly visible to your circle or not. If you live in Brighton, Bristol, or the East Midlands, you can join a group like this today.

It's worth crediting all the P2P sites with two important accomplishments for local investment. They have demonstrated that it's possible to evaluate smaller borrowers, including small businesses, in a cost-effective way. For years, skeptics of local investing contended that the costs of doing due diligence on small businesses were just not worth the benefits. That argument is now history.

Second, these sites have really shaken up the pre-Internet thinking of the world's securities-regulatory establishments. In the autumn of 2008, while the U.S. economy was tanking and credit markets were contracting, the SEC decided it was time to take down one of the few viable sources of credit still operating, namely Prosper. It was no small irony that two weeks after issuing a "cease and desist" order to the site, it became public knowledge that the nitpicking regulators at the SEC somehow had missed the multibillion-dollar frauds of Bernie Madoff.

The crux of the SEC dispute was what kind of institution Prosper really is. Prosper's CEO argued that his services were essentially those of a bank: taking money from lenders and paying them interest; providing loans to borrowers and charging them interest; and taking small fees for mediating the transactions. From the SEC's standpoint, however, Prosper was selling unregistered securities. Guess who won? It took nine months and $4 million in legal bills for Prosper to reopen with SEC approval.

Now that this legal work has been done, community groups can deploy the tools of Prosper and similar sites for truly local investing. If these sites add community circle elements and make borrowers visible, I'm all in favor. Unaccredited investors will have another readily available tool for putting money into at least reasonably credit-worthy local businesses. Some of the community-development lenders described earlier, like Claudia Viek of the California Association for Micro Enterprise Opportunity, are talking with the P2P sites about how to facilitate more local lending to their clients.

How far can P2P sites go? Might it be possible for a Prosper-like site, with enough paperwork, to get SEC approval for microequity P2P platforms? Innovators on the web will undoubtedly press federal regulators on these and other questions in the years ahead.[4]

In the meantime, some of us have decided to petition the SEC to revisit some of its silliest rules. Two years ago, I wrote a piece for a journal of the San Francisco Federal Reserve arguing that the SEC should exempt all investments under $100 in microbusinesses (that is, with a stock valuation under $250,000).[5] It's hard to claim with a straight face that a $100 investment in a company carries more risk than, say, a bad dinner for two at a new restaurant. Yet allowing just this simple reform could open up billions of new dollars for capital-starved local businesses.

My Cutting Edge Capital colleague Jenny Kassan worked with the Sustainable Economies Law Center to prepare a memo to the SEC fleshing out this proposal.[6] They modified the exemption to apply only to stock issues below $100,000 and helpfully added that the offering had to come from individuals (to prevent the proliferation of misleading corporate shells), and then you could only float one offering at a time (to minimize the risk of fraudsters mass-producing these offerings). Nearly a thousand people wrote the SEC in support of this proposal, and by May 2011 the head of the SEC, Mary Schapiro, agreed to convene a top-to-bottom review of this and other crowdfunding proposals. Kassan is now petitioning for the $100 exception in Washington State. And she's preparing to do likewise in other states. But the initial reaction of much of the regulatory community has been predictably cool. Heath Abshure, Arkansas's securities commissioner, vented about our proposal to *The Wall Street Journal*, "First it's $100, then $200 and next thing you know they're risking thousands of dollars they can't afford."

Ultimately, however, regulators must follow the law, and lawmakers in both parties are proposing major overhauls. During the summer of 2011 a group of Tea Party Republicans in Congress, led by Darrell Issa of California, began proposing to deregulate much of "crowdfunding." Representative Patrick McHenry of North Carolina proposed a bill—which ultimately passed the House by a lopsided vote of 407 ayes to 17 nays (10 abstentions)—that companies be able to crowdfund up to $5 million from unaccredited investors, provided that no individual contributes more than $10,000 or 10 percent of his annual income. In September 2011, President Obama included more modest crowdfunding reforms in his second jobs-stimulus package. For the first time in three generations, the huge barriers facing unaccredited investors might finally might be torn down.

Going DPO

Meanwhile, in the absence of securities law changes, the final play for a local entrepreneur seeking unaccredited investors, including strangers, is to go public on the cheap. The term *direct public offering* has no special meaning among securities lawyers. It really is a colloquial description of a company selling its securities directly to individual investors. Most public offerings are from companies seeking at least $25 million through what's called an initial public offering, or IPO. (The median size of an IPO in 2009 was $140 million.) Because those securities are usually created and underwritten by a big investment bank and then pre-sold to its network of broker-dealers, the sales are not direct. A DPO, in contrast, is typically less than $5 million, and often under $1 million.

Several times every week, I'm reminded of the virtues of DPOs when my daughter, Rachel, insists on Annie's Homegrown organic macaroni and cheese. It's unbelievable to me that a nine-year-old can develop such deep brand loyalty, but given that the number of foods she likes to eat can be counted in the low two digits, who am I to question? In 1996, desperate for $1.5 million in capital to expand its manufacturing capacity, the company stuffed flyers offering $6 stock shares into every box. It was a home-run success.

That same year, 1996, Spring Street Brewing Company carried out one of the first Internet-based stock-selling campaigns. The proprietor, Andrew Klein, himself once a highly paid Wall Street attorney, advertised his Regulation A offering right on the beer bottle and directed enthusiastic drinkers to surf over to his website and download the prospectus. Even though he raised only $1.6 million of the $5 million he wanted, Klein unleashed a revolution of small companies nudging their customers to become owners. Other successful DPOs during the late 1990s came from Thanksgiving Coffee, Blue Fish Clothing, WoundFast Pharmaceuticals, Real Goods Trading, The Red Rose Collection, Zap Power Systems, and dozens of breweries and wineries. Some of these businesses flopped in the long term, but they did demonstrate the viability of the DPO as a capital-raising tool. Klein himself tried to create a cookie-cutter Internet sales process for small companies through a new company, Wit Capital, though the bursting of the tech bubble in the late 1990s and competition from established Wall Street players made it an impossibly hard slog.

One unappreciated fact about these DPOs is that almost none of them promoted local ownership. Most sold shares in multiple states. An interesting exception was Community Grocers in Mount Ayr, Iowa, created in 1996.[7] Frustrated when the 1,700-person town's only grocery store, part of the chain run by Hy-Vee, moved to the outskirts of town, Joe Murphy rallied 322 residents to buy up $640,460 worth of stock in a new community store. Almost half these investors only bought the minimum lot of $250, and three-quarters live within twenty-five miles of the store. The grocery opened debt-free and in the fifteen years since has tripled in size. Most remarkably it has paid its investors an average dividend of 5.25 percent—better than Wall Street.

Jeff Haugland, general manager of Community Grocers and its largest shareholder, says, "In the beginning, everybody felt proud about having a new facility in a small town. We're the poorest county in the state of Iowa. There were no automatic doors in any businesses in town. There's still not a stoplight in the community. We were twice the size of any business when we came in. It was a totally jaw-dropping deal."

For businesses seeking local investors, the DPO path with the most promise is the intrastate exemption. As the name suggests, it applies to companies whose business is primarily conducted within a single state and that only sell stock to investors in a single state. If even one share is offered, sold, or resold to an out-of-state resident within nine months of the initial offering, the entire exemption can be lost. To provide some guidance for a firm that wishes to use this exemption, the SEC has created a "safe harbor." If the following three guidelines are met, the SEC presumes that the law has been complied with:

1. Eighty percent of the firm's assets must be located in the home state.
2. Eighty percent of the firm's revenues must come from in-state purchasers.
3. Eighty percent of the offering must be used within the state.

The so-called 80–80–80 provision seems demanding, but it's really all about local business! It benefits a firm that resides locally, sells locally, and reinvests locally. If a company meets these criteria, the only remaining obstacles to a DPO are state laws. As noted earlier, some states are particularly demanding and insist that you put together an elaborate offering statement and jump through numerous other regulatory hoops. Some require expensive audits. In New Mexico, however, a short filing plus a $350 filing fee will do the trick.

There are a bunch of other rules, exceptions, and booby traps that are not worth dwelling on here. For example, a firm that wishes to sell a DPO in more than one state obviously can't rely on the intrastate exemption. Alternative routes, like Regulation A, will be needed for local businesses that operate near state borders or sell regionally. Small firms seeking to raise only $1 million or less could try to qualify under the 504 exemption in multiple states. A relatively simple form developed by the North American Securities Administrators Association called the Small Company Offering Registration can be filled out once and submitted to all the relevant states. In some regions, a single state will act as a coordinator for all the states in the region, making the process somewhat easier. The important bottom line, even for do-it-yourselfers, is you have to consult with a knowledgeable attorney.

It used to be that hiring an attorney for tasks like these required committing $50,000, $100,000, $200,000, or even more. And if you ask an attorney to take the lead in putting together all your basic documents (articles, bylaws, minutes, budgets), reviewing your financial statements, preparing your private placement memorandum, filling out your SCOR form, meeting with and making follow-up calls to the appropriate state securities regulators, your legal bill could be astronomical. Some local entrepreneurs respond by having a friend's uncle or an uncle's friend contribute assistance pro bono (free or heavily discounted). But beware: As Ari Derfel's tale suggested in chapter 6, attorneys without securities expertise are remarkably unaware of what they do not know and can make costly mistakes.

The better alternative is to take advantage of the small but expanding universe of securities specialists who are committed to keeping your bill low. They insist that you do most of the work, they show you how to transform your business plan into a PPM, they do a cursory review, and they point you in the right direction to do all the legwork with the regulators yourself. For now, the price for an entrepreneur seeking to do a DPO this way might be in the $25,000 to $30,000 range. Soon, however, it could be significantly lower.

Cookie-Cutter Offerings

An example of an attorney promoting this kind of bare-bones approach is Jenny Kassan. I first met Jenny in 1991, when she was a student intern working for me at the Institute for Policy Studies. Her very colloquial, laid-back, California demeanor betrayed the fact that she had nearly a photographic memory and an almost superhuman ability to rip through difficult materials. Despite my efforts to convince her not to go to law school—I regarded my own legal training as the most hellacious three years of my life—she proceeded to attend Yale Law School. She hated it. Like me, she was appalled that so many of her professors and colleagues, among the country's most brilliant thinkers, were throwing themselves at high-paying corporate clients rather than at those in society with the greatest needs. She completed her law degree and then went on to get a master's degree in urban planning from UC Berkeley. At that point, we saw that we were both very interested in finding new ways local businesses could be formed and capitalized to strengthen struggling communities. We teamed up on research papers and projects here and there over the past twenty years, and finally decided to join ourselves at the hip, along with John Katovich (whom I'll introduce in chapter 8), in a new business called Cutting Edge Capital.

Among Kassan's recent DPO clients has been Workers Diner, a venture in New York City that aspires to be a great eating hangout for the working class. Employees in the diner can build equity stakes in the company, and other locals have the opportunity to buy preferred shares. Kassan is using the SCOR form to help the diner's founder, Chris Michael, raise half a million dollars in New York, New Jersey, and Connecticut. Michael hopes to pay investors, who must purchase a minimum of $100 worth of stock (four shares), an annual dividend of 3.75 percent.

Once she completes a few more SCOR forms, Kassan plans to develop a software package that will greatly simplify the process. "Each state is different," she cautions, "so it's hard to predict how each state is going to react to a DPO application. Some states are very comfortable with the SCOR form and others may never have seen one before!" She's already done the drill in a couple of states and plans to create software that people can use to fill in the blanks online; it then spits out a filable SCOR form, a subscription agreement, and other legal documents.

Creating a greater flow of DPOs in particular states, Kassan argues, begins to make local stock markets possible. "Let's say you have ten DPOs in Washington State, or maybe twenty-five; you could then have a secondary trading market only open to Washington State residents. There may not be a lot of trading going on, but there would be an actual marketplace where people could sell their shares if they needed to. The only way there's ever going to be anything to trade on the local exchange is if a bunch of people do DPOs. DPOs aren't hard, but they are a mystery to people. If we get to the point where it's much easier, it's cheaper, and it's automated, I think it could really lead to an actual local stock exchange. It would be pretty amazing!"

Ken Priore, who periodically assists Kassan with preparing DPOs, argues that for California, which represents more than a tenth of the U.S. economy, the best way to speed up the DPO assembly line is to negotiate with state regulators through what's called *qualification by permit*: "Depending on the particulars of an offering, it allows suitability standards that are much lower than the federal accredited investor standards. It also allows direct advertising, it allows the use of the Internet, it really allows communication with the investors in a way that you don't have with your Regulation D private offering."

Priore currently has several clients using this qualification by permit process, each raising several million dollars. One advantage is that the state regulators do much of the work for you. Priore can quickly put together a submission with all the basics, and then the state lets him know exactly what sections need more detail. It's an iterative process, a lot of back and forth, but it can get done, inexpensively, in under six months.

Priore flew to Washington, DC, in November 2010 for the annual SEC gathering where small-business practitioners give frank feedback to regulators. "There's a reluctance to look at the DPOs and understand what's going on, because they're so busy trying to manage much larger stakeholders. They've really written off anything that's $5 million or less, and say, 'Let's just keep the regulations restrictive, because it's just going to be ripe for fraud.' And that's the end of the discussion.

"The challenge is that we now have technology making it easy for local businesses to go out and communicate with lots of people around them, build stakeholders, and raise a few million dollars. The regulations never conceived of this. It's a shame if five hundred people in the community get together, want to raise some money for a local business, and there's really no clear path. I also think of the developer of an iPhone app out there, who has thirty or forty thousand people using his application. He should be able to go out there and raise a hundred bucks from everybody. From a business standpoint, the regulators shouldn't get in the way. And from the regulators' standpoint, this is exactly the type of investor that they *shouldn't* be concerned about."

Scrapping Model-T Regulations

The examples in this chapter suggest ways businesses can involve unaccredited investors and still comply with federal and state securities laws. But the time has come for a top-to-bottom overhaul of this regulatory regime. Reform proposals from both the Obama Administration and Congress are steps in the right direction, but what's needed is a great leap. For eight decades Americans have endured a system that all but banned 98 percent of us from investing in the local half of the economy. Few of us even noticed, let alone judged it an abomination. Why did it matter that our life savings went exclusively into global business while our communities fell apart? Perhaps we were confident that if we diligently put our savings into corporate stocks and bonds, if we methodically grew our IRAs and 401(k)s, we would retire in relative comfort—communities be damned. What did it matter that the richest among us were getting wealthier faster and the poorest were descending into greater misery? Most of us were doing fine.

But the comfort, security, and smugness that underlay our acceptance of this grotesquely inequitable system has now crumbled. Millions of Americans have already lost their life savings to the speculators on Wall Street, and tens of millions more see a very real possibility that in weeks, hours, or seconds, the entire financial marketplace could collapse. This level of insecurity is likely to grow as oil prices rise, as environmental disasters (like the BP oil spill in the Gulf of Mexico) multiply, and our personal and national debts deepen.

The securities law system that was supposed to protect us from abuse has been, even on its own terms, a dismal failure. Many applaud the SEC and state counterparts since the financial crisis for tightening their oversight of the big-business marketplace, where the American public invests in half the economy. I do, too. But that does not excuse decades of neglect in the small-business marketplace. The wall cutting off 98 percent of the U.S. public from the other half of the economy needs to be torn down if we ever wish to restore economic vitality to our communities. There are at least three reasons why even the SEC should find it sensible to change these rules.

First, as we have seen, many of the SEC's rules do not accomplish the proffered objectives. What good reason can there possibly be for banning a potential investor from *talking* with any business at any time? Ham-fisted bans on communication have no place in a free-market democracy. Nor is there a coherent rationale for preventing every American from risking up to $100 on a new business. The danger—compared with, say, allowing any American with no spare income to lose his or her life's savings in one of a thousand casinos in the country with no questions asked—is modest. For investments greater than $100 in local small business, for stock exchanges trading these securities, and for investment pools exclusively involved with these securities, the SEC should devolve rule making to the states—because it *is* truly a local matter. We should press state legislatures to greatly simplify the rules and lighten the legal bills on honest small businesses. There are hundreds of ways this can be done—I've suggested only some of them. The point is to encourage a new era of experimentation and innovation in regulatory reform across the United States.

Second, the reforms above actually would *strengthen* the regulatory structure governing securities in the United States. The overreach of the current law is making the SEC a laughingstock and bringing its legitimate rules into disrepute. Like any regulatory agency in tough times, its budget, staff, and time are limited. Every hour spent combing through a corner grocer's offering document to make sure every penny is accounted for is an hour unavailable to find real fraud. When the SEC's shutdown of Prosper's tiny P2P loans coincided with revelations of its decades-long neglect of Bernie Madoff's abuses in the autumn of 2010, the evidence of its poor priorities and misallocation of resources could not have been more appalling.

Third, at the end of the day, securities regulators need to understand the evidence about what makes the economy tick. Their condescension toward local business—the *Why should we bother with small fish?* attitude—has become another reason the American economy remains stuck in a searing recession. There is overwhelming evidence that local small businesses are the only way out of the current doldrums (or future ones). Local entrepreneurs hold the keys to prosperity—to local income, wealth, jobs; to strong tax bases, infrastructure, and schools; to civil society and democratic participation. These are the only businesses that can help communities increase their resilience and insulate themselves from the coming storms. If we don't reform our marketplace for small securities, and soon, we will fast become a second-rate nation with a third-rate economy.

Local Exchanges

Most Americans' eyes glaze over when they hear a term like *liquidity*. But the concept goes to the very heart of what's broken with our investment system today. *Liquidity* refers to the ease with which an investor can convert a security to cash and vice versa. Investors value the ability to get out of bad deals and buy into good ones, or to cash out because they have pressing expenses like Junior going to college. Over the past century the most common places where the holders of securities can buy and sell securities quickly, and at low cost, have been stock exchanges. Without these exchanges, a security would be harder to buy and harder to sell.

Illiquidity means that investors who can't sell their securities risk losing significant value, and those who cannot buy securities risk missing the boat. Liquidity therefore gives securities more value. That's why investors are willing to pay a premium for it. How big a premium? One of the most watched indicators of the stock market is the ratio of a stock's price to its earnings (its PE ratio). In a very liquid market like the New York Stock Exchange, the PE ratio for listed companies is typically twenty to one. If the same company did not have publicly traded stock—if instead it had to meet the shareholders and negotiate sales personally—its stock price would be significantly lower.[1] The premium that investors are prepared to pay for liquidity may even be greater than the actual value of the underlying security!

Liquidity is also essential for the economy to operate efficiently. Every time buyers of a security have to spend more money on shopping for a security, they have less money to invest in one. Ditto for investors who have to waste time—and thus money—selling securities. A large marketplace, where it's easy and inexpensive for buyers and sellers of securities to find one another and make deals, means that there's more money that we as a society can invest in our businesses.

The securities market in the United States today is really two markets—one for Wall Street's giants and one for small businesses. The big-business marketplace today is almost perfectly liquid. Many of its companies are publicly traded on stock exchanges, open for buying and selling by every American adult. The owners of privately held companies accept less liquidity as a reasonable price for other goals like keeping the books and strategies private, avoiding scrutiny, or maintaining control. But privately held shares can be freely sold, at least initially, to accredited investors through websites, pools, exchanges, clubs, and societies.

The small-business marketplace, in contrast, is practically nonexistent. If it were any more illiquid, local business assets would be frozen solid. There are no stock exchanges for local companies, no places where most Americans can buy and sell shares of their favorite small Main Street firms. Almost none of these companies are publicly traded. And securities laws also prohibit 98 percent of Americans from buying or selling even privately held shares. If I owned 10 percent of my favorite local pharmacy, it would be illegal for me to sell those shares on the web, even on my own Facebook page. For unaccredited investors—and believe me, I'm one—there are also no websites, pools, exchanges, clubs, or societies to sell these shares. The best I can do might be to pitch to my friends and family, or suggest a purchase by investors in my local inner circle (maybe through my local LION group).

So we have a highly efficient, highly functional, highly liquid marketplace for big-business securities, and we have a totally inefficient, dysfunctional, illiquid marketplace for small-business securities. Given that the latter marketplace is what matters for real economic development and community vitality, we can begin to apprehend why the U.S. economy is in such deep trouble, and why it is so essential to create a dependable marketplace for investors in local business.

It was not always this way. For roughly the first 150 years of U.S. history, securities and their marketplaces were relatively unregulated. In the early 1900s there were dozens of stock exchanges scattered across the United States, most of them facilitating trading of local companies. Some of these exchanges were inefficient and did not do a very good job of preventing fraud or manipulation, but many were indispensable tools for local economic development.

No serious scholar blames these local exchanges for causing the Great Depression. Far more important was the fact that unregulated securities were being sold everywhere, with every dollar invested being able to leverage ten-plus dollars of borrowed stock. Once the system started to collapse, it was clear that financial promises everywhere were going to be broken. Other culprits responsible for the crash of 1929 were the unreliability of U.S. banks and the mercantilist policies that choked the global trading system. But there's no doubt that local stock exchanges were among the earliest casualties of one of the legislative remedies Congress enacted—the Exchange Act of 1934. Reviving these marketplaces for local companies is a critically important requirement for fixing our national economy today.

Resurrecting Regional Exchanges

John Katovich is an unlikely advocate for local stock markets. A decade ago he was general counsel of the Pacific Stock Exchange, which at that point was trading the same kinds of securities found on the national exchanges. When trading became more electronically automated, he presided over the closure of that exchange and later became general counsel of the Boston Stock Exchange. The Boston Exchange was then acquired by the NASDAQ, and became an all-electronic market run on the NASDAQ platform. Katovich, who was one of the top lawyers for one of the largest stock markets in the world—until he recently resigned—is convinced we need new regional exchanges focused on local businesses.

When Katovich was just six years out of law school, in 1985, he was approached to join the legal team overseeing the Pacific Stock Exchange in San Francisco. At that point, there were about a dozen regional exchanges operating alongside two national exchanges, the New York Stock Exchange (NYSE) and the American Exchange (AMEX). (The NASDAQ wasn't yet regarded as an exchange—it was an association of broker-dealers trading mostly small-cap stocks including new high-technology companies like Microsoft and Micron.) The Pacific Stock Exchange was mostly trading two things: shares of companies that were also listed on the NYSE and AMEX, and regional companies that were not listed in New York but nonetheless could be bought and sold nationally. The latter companies tended to be small and traded lightly, so brokers, dealers, and traders, all of whom earned a commission for each trade, were not very interested in dealing with these companies.

Katovich teaches capital markets to MBA candidates at the Presidio Graduate School, where he loves to revisit the overlooked history of stock exchanges in the United States. Since World War II, that history has been mostly about mergers, acquisition, and consolidation. The Pacific Stock Exchange, for example, was the result of a merger between the San Francisco and Los Angeles exchanges in the 1950s. At that time, Los Angeles focused on oil and gas stocks and San Francisco on mining stocks. The two exchanges figured out how to connect electronically, and once their traders could see all of their bids and offers, they concluded that they didn't need to operate in two separate locations anymore.

At that point regional exchanges had only two ways they could do business. One was to offer discounts or other special handling deals for shares listed in New York. The second was to offer unique, regional stocks unavailable on the other exchanges. The regional exchanges chose to focus on the first and gradually dropped the second.

"From the late 1970s on, once technology enabled high-speed interconnection among all of these exchanges," Katovich says, "traders began to migrate their business back to New York. If the New York specialist was trading in IBM, he or she—mainly he—had a book of buy orders and sell orders, and had to manage a fair and orderly market of trades. On the regional exchange, another specialist trading IBM was pretty much basing what he was doing off of what was going on in New York. He would be making deals, telling investors that they would get as good a price as they would have gotten on the New York exchange but with lower fees. By making those kinds of deals, regional dealers could do a tremendous amount of volume and make an eighth of a dollar on many transactions. Most of our regional specialists had a book that consisted 90 to 95 percent of New York–listed stocks, and then perhaps three or four locally listed stocks. Gradually, most of the specialists wouldn't even take on locally listed stocks anymore.

"For those regional specialists who continued to trade the smaller companies," Katovich continues professorially, "it was not only time consuming and expensive but also risky. They could wind up with a bunch of unfulfilled buy and sell orders of the local stocks, and they had no other exchange on which to dump them. Trading the New York stocks, in contrast, could be done in higher volumes, with greater assurance that ultimately every seller would find a buyer. They were making really good money back then on the New York stocks. Why bother with these locally listed companies?"

Electronic interconnection among the exchanges led to another factor that wound up undermining regional exchanges: brutal competition. Everyone, everywhere was competing for the same dollar flow. That meant that the only profits possible were with high volumes, which made trading low-volume regional stocks less attractive. Competition was intensified by changes in the calibration of trades. For many years, stocks were listed in dollars and eighths of a dollar. Then nickels. Then pennies. Once that happened, the transaction costs decreased to the point that regional specialists could no longer offer any discounts on the New York stocks whatsoever.

The march of technology now demands that trading companies pay millions for the privilege of locating their computers on the premises of exchanges so as not to lose that nanosecond edge. Legal "clearance" of trades, which used to take five business days, now takes three and soon may be immediate, as it is in many foreign markets today. The trading day, which used to run 9:30 AM to 4:00 PM Eastern, now bleeds into after-hours trading pools that run 24/7.

In principle, the regional exchanges could have made their business work had they returned to their roots and specialized in listing and trading local companies. But they couldn't figure out how to attract enough local businesses to list, enough broker-dealers to sponsor those businesses, and enough investors to trade them. The costs of keeping the buildings, the real estate, and the staff at these exchanges became too great. So one by one, the regional exchanges were dissolved or acquired. Today few stock exchanges remain in the United States besides the NYSE and NASDAQ consortiums: the National Stock Exchange (originally the Cincinnati Stock Exchange) was recently bought by the Chicago Board Options Exchange in an attempt to capture more stock transactions; and the Chicago Stock Exchange. Neither do much volume. They are mainly handling buy-sell completions for other trading firms and are struggling to stay alive.

"When I came out to work for the Boston Stock Exchange," Katovich explains, "I had an idea that if I could help it stay viable and competitive on a national level, we could develop a couple of other types of exchanges underneath, including a local stock exchange and a socially responsible stock exchange. For the latter, we might create good filtering process and apply it to the companies listed at NYSE or NASDAQ." But three months after Katovich moved east, the NASDAQ purchased the Boston exchange and made clear to Katovich that they were not interested in anything local or sustainable, unless it could turn a profit immediately. That pretty much killed the idea. Instead, they began using the Boston exchange for lower listing standards, in the hope that stocks that couldn't survive on the primary market might still have a home.

Katovich thinks we have two market failures today. One is the dysfunctional nature of the mainstream exchanges. "At NYSE and NASDAQ today, you have six to ten billion shares of stock trading every day, along with very complex derivatives and derivatives of derivatives. When you break it all down, you realize that probably less than 1 percent of all of that financial flow of capital actually gets to a nonfinancial company that develops products, services, research, and development. We need to get back to the original idea of a stock market, which was a place where a company could get capital so that it could operate and grow in a modest but viable way. Markets today are now a business unto themselves, with the original intent of providing needed capital mostly as an afterthought."

The second market failure is the complete absence of a place where local and regional companies can get capital. "I view a local exchange market as a fundamental component of how you develop redundant economic systems," says Katovich. "If we rely on only a national or global system, there's a lot of potential for spectacular failure. As we experience climate change, population shifts, and other strange things coming our way, we will need viable local regions to be interacting and supporting each other. I view local exchanges as a foundational building block for creating that redundancy and resilience."

To succeed, Katovich insists, local exchanges will need exceptional quality control. There actually are places where smaller companies can go public and be traded right now called the OTC (over the counter) and "pink sheet" markets. Few of these companies are local to any particular place, and many trade with each share worth only a couple of pennies. "They attract a lot of shady activity," says Katovich, "because there's this silly notion that every penny stock is ready to become the next ten-dollar stock, which means you should get it while it's hot. So you get a lot of abuse. These markets will take any company they can get to list on it, because it means more listing revenue."

Successful local exchanges need to embrace a fundamentally different philosophy. The emphasis has to be on quality, not quantity; on well-established local companies, not mysterious start-ups; on trusted CEOs, not messiahs nobody has ever heard of; on high quality and user-friendly information, not the piles of irrelevant data and legal boilerplate you find in most disclosure statements; on slower transactions that favor long-term investors, not short-term speculators.

On this last point, Katovich concedes that local investors themselves may need a different mind-set: "If you just have a bulletin board system in place with no intermediary, you'd have to convince investors that someday, if you were patient enough, you might be able to sell your stock. And comparing that to the markets today, where you have anywhere from six to ten billion shares trading daily and far more liquidity than you ever really need to make fair and orderly markets, the scenario I just described could look very scary to an investor." But perhaps it could look reassuring. The idea that shares might sit in someone's possession for months or years, rather than fractions of a second, could reorient investors to the long-term value of investing in real wealth. It also could relieve their fears of a repeat of the cataclysmic stock market drop of May 6, 2010, which, as we saw in the introduction, was exacerbated by short-term speculators.

The SEC will only permit local exchanges if they are exceedingly careful about the companies they recruit. "If you're out to rip someone off," Katovich points out, "you're not interested in having a full-fledged review of how you act. Whether you care about the environment, how you take care of your workers, and how well you govern the companies . . . None of those things are on the top of your list. By filtering for those good things, you can actually filter out bad companies, or at least those companies more prone to abuse."

Perhaps, Katovich speculates, a local exchange will have to start with accredited investors. "If we can create a viable operating marketplace and prove that it actually works well, I think we will have good arguments to come back to the SEC with and ask for more latitude toward allowing for non-accredited investors to participate. That's my ten-year goal."

Katovich follows the SEC's thinking on exchanges, in part because his job at the NASDAQ was to help it carve new niches, and in part because through his old law practice (which he has recently rejoined) he provides legal counsel to other companies thinking about creating their own local exchanges. Much of that practice, which had been run by Jenny Kassan after Katovich left California for Boston, is now being integrated into Cutting Edge Capital.

The legal opening for new local exchanges that Katovich sees emerging has its roots in 1997, when the SEC issued new rules on alternative trading systems (ATS). An ATS equipped with a broker-dealer license may be the magic combination for a viable local exchange. And the one company Katovich thinks will be the first to achieve this—a company he has provided legal counsel for through his law practice with Kassan—is Mission Markets in New York.

An Exchange with a Mission

The Mission Markets website provides a glimpse of what local stock exchanges in the future might ultimately look like. The core of the site contains several platforms on which users can find all kinds of securities related to triple-bottom-line businesses. The Impact Investment platform has private placements of debt, equity, and other kinds of securities from community-oriented companies, including cooperatives, microfinance companies, and economic-development agencies. It also has some direct public offerings. The Earth Exchange facilitates the trading of carbon credits, transferable development rights, fisheries catch shares, and water rights shares. Accredited investors can access all the transactions, while unaccredited investors can participate in only some of them. Investors find securities listed for set prices and then can click to learn more about them and buy them. The user experience is more akin to eBay than E*Trade.

The founder and CEO of Mission Markets is Michael Van Patten, a twenty-year Wall Street veteran who co-founded the NYPPEX, a successful exchange for high-dollar private placements. Several years back, Van Patten decided that making big bucks was not enough. He wanted to apply his expertise on securities laws, capital markets, and investment to businesses with deeper social and environmental objectives. "Traditional capital-market participants, broker-dealers, gatekeepers, and financial advisers may not be fully aware of what these social and environmental markets are," says Van Patten. "They may not really care that much. We try to convince them, from a business perspective, that they need to be paying attention to this expanding area. And we also try to convince socially responsible businesses that you're not going to get enough capital without engaging the mainstream investment community."

Mission Markets was incorporated in late 2009 but did not launch its website until the summer of 2010. The core of its business today is the sale of socially responsible securities (few of them local) to accredited investors—mostly the kinds of private offerings and Community Development Financial Institution opportunities discussed in chapter 5. Investors across the country can register with the site, shop online, and purchase specialty securities they are unlikely to find on any other site on the web. Where else, for example, might you buy credits for wetland mitigation or water quality? Mission Markets aims to be the go-to place for raising capital for sustainable agriculture, organic food, renewable energy, pollution prevention, or green manufacturing.

In its first year Mission Markets signed up nearly two hundred companies. "That means," clarifies Van Patten, "that businesses seeking capital have started the process of creating their own presence on our online platform and meeting the minimum listing requirements. Once they register, they have to fill out all their information, upload lots of documentation, and go through a vetting process, which takes anywhere from a couple weeks to several months. Right now, we only have twenty-seven or twenty-eight live offerings, with a value of about $340 million. It's a process that takes time. We also have a subsidiary, an advisory service, that helps companies put together their documentation for a fee.

"We're not really an exchange," Van Patten insists, in case federal regulators ever read this chapter. "To be considered a true exchange, you have to be approved by the SEC as an exchange, and that's not something we care to do. We are a private marketplace. No secondary trading has occurred on the site yet."

Yet. The activity thus far has been a dress rehearsal for what everyone knows is coming. Van Patten has become a fixture at social-investment conferences recruiting more offerings, a wider range of securities, more issuers, and more investors. Sooner or later, Mission Markets would like to become a full-service exchange or, more precisely, an ATS.

Mission Markets has focused thus far on private offerings above $100,000. For smaller offerings for unaccredited investors, Van Patten is banking on "community portals," where investors and businesses in particular places can make one-on-one deals with one another—essentially an Internet version of James Frazier's Local Investment Opportunities Network, described in the last chapter. Mission Markets would relieve a local portal operator of the onerous burdens of making special filings with the SEC.

"Our virtual marketplace," says Van Patten, "allows us to create portals for a region, a city, a state. Any locale, or any group in a locale, could create its own virtual investment exchange. A portal would allow each group to oversee its own investments, membership, and be as discreet or open as they want. But it would enable them to do this in the context of regulated capital markets and securities-compliant infrastructure, which provides standardization of offerings, documentation, settlement of investment moneys, monitoring of the investors in general, and the ability to communicate and share due diligence and information. That is an area we think is going to grow tremendously."

Van Patten argues that one of Mission Market's competitive advantage is that it is FINRA-regulated. FINRA stands for the Financial Industry Regulatory Authority, a private organization run for and by key players in the securities industry—such as broker-dealers, their agents, and investment advisers—to keep quality-control standards high. "The fact that we are affiliated with a broker-dealer, have registered reps, and comply with securities regulations gives us a lot of power and strength."

As local-investment pioneers around the country become excited about selling and exchanging local securities, Van Patten has been eager to help. On the Hawaiian island of Maui, for example, David Fisher, the director of the local Small Business Development Center, has been spearheading a campaign to create a statewide stock exchange. In May 2011, when the state legislature was debating a bill mandating a study of the concept, Van Patten provided testimony in favor.

A skeptic might argue that for groups like LION, the Mission Markets platform just adds electronic bells and whistles to preexisting relationships. But Van Patten counters that he helps groups "do much more, in a much more organized fashion. The Mission Markets platform allows them to communicate their message and to attract many more participants and many more users within their community. Right now, they are doing everything in a kind of one-off, unstructured way. Our infrastructure provides a place for documentation, where people communicate, where deals and due diligence can be done. There also is a minimal listing requirement, which means that companies being traded on there have at least been somewhat vetted. It allows investors to focus on what's important: the opportunity."

Van Patten keeps returning to the issue of quality control, as Katovich did, even for groups like LION. "It's one thing to have community investment, but it's another thing to make sure that those investments are secure, that there's no fraud going on." And the logic for carefully vetting companies gets stronger as a network gets larger.

A critical service the Mission Markets platform already provides for traders is reliable measurement of each business's bottom lines. "If a company says it's sustainable," asks Van Patten, "what does that actually mean? Bring third-party metrics in, so if a company says it's sustainable, it can prove it! Be transparent. That's how we're looking at this. In my opinion every company going forward is going to have to have some type of sustainability measurement."

To provide these metrics, Van Patten has decided to partner with B Corp, which, as described in chapter 2, helps companies benchmark and score their progress on various social and environmental criteria. In fact, Mission Markets itself is a certified B Corp. But as with everything, Mission Markets embraces diversification. So there are other metric tools being incorporated as well. True Cost provides environmental metrics. Paul Herman's HIP method combines "human impact" with "profit." Users of the Mission Markets site can decide which metrics are best suited to their objectives.

"Additionally," says Van Patten, "we've created our own broad-based metric called MI4, which stands for mission and four key impacts: financial, environmental, social, and governance. And we've done this because we feel that if an investor or an issuer has more choices about how to measure sustainability, it's going to benefit them. Let's just say you're using the True Cost metric, and that metric is very heavy on the environment side, but you care more about the social side. MI4 allows our users to place more weight on the preferences most important to them."

Mission Markets of course will continue to provide metrics on the traditional bottom line. "I think one of the biggest challenges of these markets is that there is not a long track record of returns. A marketplace like ours will provide more transparency about what the returns are over a period of years. That's what every sector or asset class needs, a history of returns investors can point to."

Van Patten hopes to persuade local-investment innovators that it's better to deploy a platform of trading quickly and inexpensively with Mission Markets than to build one from scratch. "If the Hawaii Stock Exchange decided they wanted to create all their own technology and do everything else, it might cost them maybe half a million dollars and take them a year or longer to develop it. Using a community portal or a private portal within Mission Markets costs them $40,000 or $50,000 and could be up and running in 120 days."

Van Patten is not yet persuaded that Hawaii or any region should try to start a local exchange just yet: "Here's the thing: You need to involve the financial gatekeepers, sponsors, brokers, and financial advisers. To get just one platform in just one state up and running is very challenging. How many companies are going to qualify as public companies in the state of Hawaii? Who knows? But there are clearly private companies that need capital that could eventually become public. What you need is an infrastructure that provides capital formation all the way through what you might call the private–public company continuum."

He's right, of course. It will take time for any community to have enough direct public offerings to justify a local exchange. But maybe it's years, not decades. That's why Van Patten talks now about creating hundreds of different portals, each containing a slightly different network and complying with SEC rules. Brokers might have password-protected access to some sites, and unaccredited investors might only be permitted to visit some portals but not others. Access also might be limited by residency, so only Hawaiians could go to their state portal. These portals also might be linked with local chapters of national organizations like Slow Money. "Over the course of the next year or two, by adding these community portals and these organizations interested in using our platform, we'll be able to expand our investor member base by thousands. And we expect to attract broker-dealers who have hundreds or thousands of clients on their own. Once you have that kind of critical mass, you're going to see a lot more transactions occurring."

Fifty in Five

When my last book, *The Small-Mart Revolution*, was published in 2006, I began traveling almost nonstop to nearly every state in the United States and most of the provinces of Canada to promote strategies of economic development rooted in locally owned businesses. And the one idea I sketched that consistently drew the greatest interest was the creation of local stock exchanges. From the most conservative states of Utah and Idaho to the liberal bastions of Oregon and Vermont, audiences were excited by the possibility of ditching Wall Street and investing in their own community markets. Lots of people came up to me after these talks and asked for advice on how to begin, but only one individual that I'm aware of actually has tried to do it. Meet Trexler Proffitt, a business professor at Franklin and Marshall College in Lancaster, Pennsylvania. After my speech I told him that getting SEC approval for an exchange, as Michael Van Patten noted above, might cost upward of a million dollars in legal fees. Proffitt set out to prove me wrong.

"So I began researching through 2008," recalls Proffitt. "I received a grant to do surveys in the local communities. I thought that if I could contribute anything to this discussion, it would be a template for local organizing and maybe a little bit of intellectual overhead. But by fall of 2008, I was convinced that local exchanges were feasible, although they would have to be done in a new and interesting way. And that's when I set about trying to put all the pieces in place that would make it normal and easy for people to log on to a website run by their local community and invest in local firms."

Two years later, Proffitt's odyssey to create the LanX, the Lancaster Stock Exchange, continues. The financial crisis deepened his conviction about the *why* for the project and the *where*, but he is still tinkering with the *how*.

Proffitt is one of the very few scholars in the United States to study the economic impact of the early stock exchanges. In a recent working paper, he found that regions with their own stock exchanges had experienced double the rate of economic growth over the comparable national growth rate. Proffitt concedes his research is still at an early stage. Histories about stock exchanges in the United States are hard to find, and archives of original documents from these operations are almost nonexistent. But by using U.S. Census data, he compared a region's economic performance for the years before and after its exchange was founded. The conclusion: A well-designed local exchange could stimulate significant economic growth in the region.

Proffitt has several theories that explain his findings. His most basic, and interesting, is that while banks allocate capital to successful enterprises, exchanges allocate capital to promising entrepreneurs of early-stage enterprises and growing firms. "Exchanges are all about valuing the future. Banking, in my view, is about where you stand at the present. It's a very backward-looking way of giving people money. The already successful enterprises have no trouble getting bank loans. Also, during the nineteenth century, banks were a little bit shady. Nobody trusted them. So having a stock exchange was actually a pretty significant development. While it might seem riskier to us, it's ultimately about transferring that risk quickly to other people. Those who can afford to take the risk, bear it. And those who can't afford it, stay out. That's how, I would argue, a local exchange can facilitate economic growth."

Proffitt accepts that the four currently remaining stock exchanges, far from promoting economic development, are largely facilitating speculation. "And yet, everyone would agree that some degree of risk management is required to make markets work efficiently. That's where the Wall Street services of today are really making a huge difference: It's getting the market to go from 90 to 100 percent efficiency. But in local community economies, an improvement from 0 percent efficiency to 20 percent efficiency would be a huge help. Right now, there's practically no liquidity in my local market to speak of. Pieces of companies are being bought and sold, but it's so far below the radar, so private, and so low-volume that we really don't see it. So maybe what these local exchanges will do is take us from 10 to 80 percent efficiency."

Like John Katovich, Proffitt sees significant capital-market gaps that remain now that all the exchanges have merged together. "There's no way that we're going to have a thriving community economy unless there's more financing in that gap—particularly for companies looking for between about $500,000 to $10 million. Unless you are at the $250 million level, the New York Stock Exchange doesn't even want to talk with you. I'd say that hole is a market opportunity for the rest of us. I don't know if there's a lot of money to support Wall Street–style fees, but I do know there's a need. And anytime there's a need, somebody will be willing to pay."

But is Lancaster the right place to launch this kind of experiment? The region is anchored by four small cities: Reading, York, Lancaster, and Harrisburg. Culturally, says Proffitt, "it's a fairly conservative region. The cities are heavily Democratic, but many counties are heavily Republican. James Carville once said Pennsylvania is Philadelphia and Pittsburgh with Alabama in between. At the same time, a significant number of folks are interested in what I'd call back-to-basics relationships. The idea is to use your leisure time for civic engagement. Community and family are all-important. Who do you trust? You trust your neighbors. What's neat about our local exchange effort is that we have both ends of the political spectrum uniting around it. If we could create institutions locally that would facilitate trust, particularly in people's financial lives, we can resonate with people of all political stripes."

At least ten businesses in the Lancaster area have indicated that they could use the exchange to raise capital right now. Sure, the area has its share of local banks and revolving loan funds. The Community First Fund serves a ten-county region, including the four cities, and it gives out low-interest, subsidized, or packaged loans (often with other lenders) up to about $400,000. But for capital greater than that, there's no obvious source. Proffitt believes "there's a lot of money here waiting to be invested. Plus, we would open the door to the rest of the state as well."

The big questions are how: How can the LanX get started? How can it stimulate the issuance of more direct public offerings and other securities? How can it facilitate the trading of those securities without running the risk of fraud?

One obvious possibility would be to hire Mission Markets to build a LanX-branded portal. "What's great about what Michael Van Patten has done is that he really emphasizes the information flow, as opposed to the transaction flow, and that's what we prefer, too." But Proffitt believes he can do most of what Mission Markets does with simpler, off-the-shelf technology, and by deploying a platform locally, his information about listed companies will be locally grounded, locally managed, and locally trusted. He suspects that if LanX keeps developing its own ideas, other platform developers out there might even donate technology to the project. "We're going to be very cautious about the technology. We want to proceed in stages and show that each stage of the implementation will work. We don't want to jump ahead of where folks are."

The technology, however, is just a small part of the uphill journey. It's the legal bells and whistles, the relationships with broker-dealers, the information available on traded companies—all the working parts of a local exchange. But even here, Proffitt remains convinced there are low-cost solutions. He is communicating regularly with other grassroots groups, exploring how they are handling the legal and administrative challenges. In Toronto, for example, there's an initiative under way to create an exchange for social enterprises like housing developments for poor people.

By sharing everything he has learned with colleagues in Canada, Hawaii, and elsewhere, Proffitt hopes that each new local exchange "won't need four years to get where we are. They can just do it in six months or less. Our goal is to share what we discover with anyone who wants to organize at their local level. Each of us takes some of the work and pursues our own local thing. In Hawaii, they've advanced their legislation to create a working group with the state securities regulators—and then there'll be a precedent for state-level change we can implement here. We're finding here, several years in, that there may be many ways of doing this without any change in regulation, or with a few safe and simple exemptions."

Securities lawyers go nuts when Proffitt talks like this. John Katovich, who's sympathetic, sees hundreds of thousands of dollars of filings needed to make the LanX operational. Michael Van Patten has spent more than that already to get all the legal approvals for his platforms. Yet everyone understands that the regulators hold the keys to the kingdom. State regulators *could* give their blessing to a low-tech LanX as an experimental prototype, and then ask federal regulators for a waiver on the grounds that intrastate securities being traded intrastate are no one's business but Pennsylvania's. But will they?

Proffitt approaches the legal questions with disarming simplicity: "2008 was the first time I started talking to regulators in Pennsylvania. They said, 'Look. We don't really care what you do with your exchange—that's a federal matter. But if there's fraud, we're going to go after you. So you better be sure that nobody's using your exchange for fraud.' And it's that simple. If the exchange is designed well, and you have checks and balances built in to monitor everything, produce an auditable trail of your activities, and maintain transparency, then regulators have nothing to fear. I think you get into problems when everything is so secret, hidden behind the scenes, with too many intermediaries you can't see into. That's where it gets murky. And so a lot of our decisions locally have been around mitigating that kind of fraud risk."

One way Proffitt thinks he can accomplish this is by keeping start-up companies out of the LanX. "We want firms that have a stake in the community. We want to see the firm be five years old before we list anything that they offer. Sure, there will be a procedure for exceptions, but generally speaking, we want to assure the public that they're buying into an established business, they're buying into the third generation of something where the employees and customers can vouch for it, and where the CEO is still there and can vouch for it."

Proffitt's obsession with a low-cost approach is a point of pride. He and his colleagues are all volunteers right now, working on the LanX in their spare time. They are mindful that several big-dollar efforts have stumbled. One example is Invest BX, a huge undertaking by the West Midlands regional government in the United Kingdom to create a local stock exchange. The project currently employs five full-time staff, with a government grant of five million pounds. "I spent some time with them to learn more about what they were doing, and how they were doing it. Everyone was very generous in sharing their concept and experiences. They were really sharp and experienced people—the platform should be extremely popular. They had five years to show results, but I fear now that they won't have much to show as a securities market." After four years Invest BX is listing just three securities—and only two of them are real companies. There's practically no trading. While the registered buyers and sellers of Invest BX are regional, the exchange decided to outsource trading to a London-based broker, which in turn charges high fees. Since then, the staff have shifted their work to more conventional subsidized loan programs for small and medium business finance.

Skeptics of local exchanges will undoubtedly point to the Invest BX and say, You see, there's no deal flow! Proffitt would counter that there was no deal *creation*. "We look around our area, and see tons of need for capital among the local firms. We just had dinner last week with execs from six of our local firms, and brought them together to discuss their stories. We went around the table, and as each described their business, their future, and their experience with financing, the others would nod with understanding and lean in toward one another, seeing the common interest in creating new alternatives that could help them obtain millions of dollars they all desperately need." Wolfgang Candy needs to add production capacity to meet large orders from national retailers; Kimberton Whole Foods wants to launch its fifth local grocery store; and York Water wants to raise funds to upgrade distribution equipment. "In the end it's about financing the future sooner. That translates into jobs, tax base, stability, and a better local economy."

The lesson Proffitt learned from Invest BX is that mobilizing a critical mass of companies to participate is more important than the exchange itself. So his focus right now is recruitment, and getting recruited companies comfortable with disclosure. "Our first stage in implementation is to put up an information-sharing site where we wouldn't actually supervise any trades at all. For the local community, that's important. It's not expensive. It just tests the willingness of the businesses to disclose. We'll put them through the wringer and say, 'Are you willing to share this? Are you willing to share that?'"

It's effectively a test run for the LanX. It will hopefully prove to local companies in the region that disclosure can be done easily. It will prove to Pennsylvania regulators that a small exchange can avoid fraud. It will prove to the public that the top locally owned companies need their money. And it will prove to investors that there are serious local-investment opportunities. Any transactions would happen offline.

Even in this first stage, Proffitt sees the makings of a business model. Investors might find it valuable to browse companies that have gone through the LanX process, with listed information duly verified. Companies in the region might find it valuable to get a LanX seal of approval. "Even if no transactions happen or only a few transactions happen offline, we can then interview participants and ask them, 'How did this go? Did you see any value in this? Do you want a trading capability?'"

The second stage might be limited trading, where LanX promotes and records the transactions between listed companies and accredited investors (including institutions). An outside broker might carry out these transactions, but to avoid the Birmingham problem, the broker would have to be local and charge modest fees.

"The last stage is our ultimate test, which means involving the retail investor, the person on the street investing in the restaurant they've just eaten at. If we can get to that stage—and I'm not totally sure we can, because that's where all of the federal and state fraud protections kick in—then we'll be in good shape."

Proffitt returns to his efforts to woo state regulators. "The way I think we're going to get there is by having a successful stage one and stage two. We won't get there if we don't go through this process somewhere in this country. Someone has to go first—to show the regulators, to show the local public, 'So, here's our incidence of fraud. Here's how we caught it, here's what we did about it.' If the pilot local exchange is successful, then we're going to see a massive proliferation down the road. And that's our real goal. We need to imagine having fifty local exchanges in five years."

The most urgent need for the LanX right now is funding, to hire the staff who can solve the remaining issues. Proffitt wants state agencies to consider underwriting local exchanges across Pennsylvania in the name of economic development. "We're talking about such a small amount of money that most states can find it in their budget just by not repaving a bridge. And because the exchange generates its own fees from participants, the initial grant is really just start-up money."

Another way to launch the LanX might be to mobilize the region to own the exchange. It could be a cooperative. It could be a nonprofit, as the New York Stock Exchange was until recently. "We might issue shares to those investors in the community who have a long-term view, who think they'll be here forever. It could be the community foundations. It might be local institutions like hospitals and colleges. It might be private companies. And it might be wealthy individuals who have made a home here. Our reasoning now is that, within our eight-county region—four big cities—if we make our pitch right, we should be able to find between ten and twenty investors who hold this long-term, community-improvement mind-set."

Whatever the ultimate structure of the LanX, Proffitt intends to hold it to the same standards that he will impose on listed companies. For now, he is setting it up as a for-profit B Corporation. He also wants the exchange to have enough business to return something to investors. "I think these days, a 1 to 3 percent return is what's welcomed by mission-oriented institutional investors. Hopefully we could do better, but we don't want to overpromise. What's for sure is that your money will be working for the community."

Forty Thousand Exchanges

On the opposite side of the country, in California, is a self-educated investment impresario named Michael Sauvante with another vision of a local exchange. A retired veteran, he pursues securities reform with the single-minded intensity of a commando. He presents key articles, well organized, on his various websites for interested members of the public and has outlined half a dozen fascinating innovations. One of them is called the Universal Exchange, or UNIEX. The basic idea is to create a website that just lists public companies—preferably DPOs trading only intrastate; users then would buy and sell shares directly with one another. Like Michael Van Patten, Sauvante avoids uttering the words *stock exchange*.

"There's one particular feature you will find on stock exchanges," says Sauvante. "If you do not have it, according to the SEC's own website, then you are not considered a stock exchange. And that one feature is whether you actually are conducting the primary and secondary trades."

He draws an analogy to the portals on Yahoo! and Google dealing with finance. They post all kinds of information about companies that investors use to decide in which to invest, and they even point users to the places where they can buy and sell stock in these companies. All of this is unregulated. "But once you start doing the matchmaking," says Sauvante, "bringing together a seller who wants to sell some shares and a buyer who wants to buy them, and you oversee the actual exchange of funds for stock between those two parties, you will be considered by the SEC to be an exchange, or at minimum a broker that must be regulated. The SEC also says that if you take those matched parties and redirect them to somebody else, like a broker who's legally entitled to manage the transaction, then you are not a stock exchange." Sauvante is more comfortable calling UNIEX an information portal, where users can find high-quality information about small companies and then are directed to other places where they can buy and sell the securities.

Like Trexler Proffitt, Sauvante thinks that the first goal of a successful local exchange is mobilizing enough companies. Part of his evangelism, therefore, is to convince companies that DPOs are easy. One of Sauvante's websites, CommonwealthGroup.net, nicely lays out the specifics of how to get a DPO approved. Another approach to making DPOs cheaper might be for a U.S. state to do what the United Kingdom did in the 1990s. The regulators there recognized that the London Stock Market was not addressing the needs of smaller businesses, so they allowed the creation of an Alternative Investment Market, or AIM, which currently has thirteen hundred companies listed on it. At the heart of the AIM is a streamlined merit review run not by regulators but by qualified businesspeople. "They created a program that calls for the presence of a Nomad, which I think is one of the best in the world. *Nomad* stands for 'NOMinated ADvisers.' Nominated Advisers are essentially sponsors that are typically either law firms or large accounting firms, which any company wanting to list on AIM must engage. These Nomads wear two hats. They step into the shoes of the government regulators and make sure that the company is in compliance with all of the regulatory issues. They also wear a second hat on the business side. They're responsible for making sure that the business fundamentals are there, that the business plan is sound, and they wind up coaching these companies on both sides of that equation."

Not everyone thinks the Nomad system has been tough enough in its scrutiny of participating British businesses. But Sauvante counters it has worked reasonably well in preventing fraud. "The United States needs something like that at the national level, though I think that we could begin on a state-by-state basis. If we could convince legislatures that another group is better qualified to oversee the process of companies going public than their bureaucrats, then you would have a more streamlined process for issuing DPOs."

Even if reform begins at the state level, federal regulators can and should encourage it. In late 2010, along with John Nelson of Wall Street Without Walls (an advocacy group trying, among other things, to involve more mainstream investors in CDFIs), Sauvante proposed that the SEC simply embrace a federalist approach and declare that purely intrastate investment activity be left to the states. If a company is 100 percent owned by residents of a state, why should the SEC care at all about the regulatory questions surrounding its offerings? Ditto for in-state investment companies with portfolios exclusively made up of such local companies, and in-state exchanges trading exclusively their securities. The SEC has broad authority to grant waivers and exceptions to encourage innovation and experimentation.

Sauvante has gotten indications of interest from SEC insiders, ranging from polite "yeah, we'll look at it" to tactical recommendations about how to recruit the White House. He has been talking with the Startup America Partnership, co-chaired by Steve Case, founder of AOL, and Carl Schramm, CEO of the Kauffman Foundation, which has President Barack Obama's blessing to recommend regulatory reforms that benefit small business—including changes at the SEC. No one, however, expects the SEC will voluntarily adopt Sauvante's proposals anytime soon—least of all Sauvante himself. He and others are pushing for congressional action to force the SEC and FINRA to consider creating a new self-regulatory organization (SRO) that would assume regulatory oversight over small-business capital markets, leaving FINRA to regulate Wall Street and big business. The SRO would include a broad cross section of representatives from the small business community, including entrepreneurs, investors, lawyers, economic developers, regulators, and the like. If successful, this new SRO could radically alter the whole landscape for local exchanges, DPOs, crowdfunding.

In the meantime, Sauvante is continuing to press his Nomad idea in a couple of states. Perhaps FINRA would be willing to become the designated approval body. Or perhaps an organization like BALLE could step in. The basic idea is that, like the Nomad system, "when this group puts its seal of approval on a company, the public should be able to trust that it's legal and not a scam."

Returning to UNIEX, the Universal Exchange, Sauvante explains, "We're exploring a launch here in California. And it best can be described, out the gate, as a specialized investing firm *and* a specialized investment banking firm focusing on small and medium-sized enterprises. We'll be working with smaller companies to do all the Nomad stuff, to help them get cleaned up. The first stage would be evaluation. Are they viable enough to even go forward? Is it worth it for us to spend time on them and for them to spend money on us? If that's a yes, then we'll get the company in good shape to make it attractive to investors, clean up all its governance issues and so on. We will help them apply to the state to do a DPO. And then we will go out and help them to actually raise the funds. Since it would be a California-approved intrastate DPO, we would be allowed to publicly advertise for investors who live in California. This then brings us full-circle back to the UNIEX concept, which would be where we will advertise and promote our clients."

What about secondary trading? "We want to help companies to get to the point where their stockholders are in a position to freely sell their shares without restrictions. SEC Rule 144 lays out certain steps a small company can take that are not very complex. If you are a small company and your investors have held their stock for more than a year, if you can get an opinion letter from an attorney acknowledging those shareholders satisfy SEC Rule 144 holding period, you can then convert all or most of your shares from restricted to unrestricted or control-restricted. And at that point, those shareholders would be able to buy and sell their shares with the help of UNIEX and a broker." UNIEX would still not transact the actual purchases and trades. Those could take place in many other places, perhaps the simplest being on the listed company's website.

But if UNIEX encouraged local businesses to issue shares that then became unrestricted and resellable anywhere in the world, wouldn't that destroy their local ownership? "Actually," explains Sauvante, "most of the constituent companies we're focused on are just serving local markets. I'm a mom-and-pop shop doing something locally, and I'm only of interest to my local community. The web allows you to create a multilayered system. At its base UNIEX would provide information about your local companies. But if a company starts expanding beyond a single, local market, UNIEX will allow other investors to see the opportunity. So the market and the investors will go hand in hand.

"There's something like forty thousand cities, towns, and counties in the country, and they all have companies. These companies would become part of a database, and you could layer it for easy access by the viewers. So even though I may be mostly concerned with Silver Spring, Maryland, I might want to see all of the solar energy companies in Maryland. As we build up UNIEX, we will get the database populated and you, the user, will be able to sort based on all kinds of different parameters. It's the Burger King concept: 'Have it your way!'"

Unlike Mission Markets, which was founded with millions in start-up capital to deploy a state-of-the-art website, Sauvante sees UNIEX as a scrappy, low-budget upstart. "Our whole approach is to really grow it organically. It may be an extremely rapid growth, but we can't jump in the deep end of the pool. We've got to start from the wading pool."

The Prize

Sooner or later, someone will crack the legal obstacles that have all but prevented a capital marketplace for the small-business half of the economy. It might be the sophisticated Mission Markets platform. Or perhaps it will be the upstarts like the LanX or UNIEX. No doubt that, once the concept is proven, copycats will appear specializing in particular communities, particular kinds of companies, or particular kinds of securities. And once that happens, the $15 trillion shift will be well under way.

Not everyone in the local-economy movement, it needs to be said, is excited about local stock exchanges. David Korten, author of *When Corporations Rule the World* and, like me, a founding board member of BALLE, worries about local businesses being turned into just one more commodity traded by speculators interested only in instant profits. "Local equity investing should be slow and stable. Folks who place a premium on the liquidity of equity shares are speculators, not investors."

Korten points out that "the public trading of equity shares introduces absentee ownership into the local economy. The shareholders, if they invest through a fund, may not know what business they own. All they know is what financial return their investment is generating. Likewise the entrepreneur who founded and operates the business no longer has control and may not even know who his or her owners are. He or she must operate the business to maximize financial return to the owners or suffer the consequences as absentee owners unload the company's stock in favor of 'higher performers.'

"One of the foundational concepts of BALLE is that ownership should be rooted in the community in the hands of local people who know and trust each other, and who have a shared interest in the well-being of their community and its natural environment. The widespread trading of shares in local companies could be the death of the local economy movement."

Korten is more comfortable with lending than with equity investment. "Equity investors can take over the firm at will. Lenders cannot. Folks who want to invest locally through an intermediary that assures an acceptable degree of liquidity should put their money in a local credit union or community bank that loans to local businesses."

Korten is not against equity investment per se, but he believes it should be based on a personal relationship between the entrepreneur and the investor. "Potential equity investors might form or join a local cooperative, for example. A cooperative mechanism is more stable and you know exactly what you belong to and what the enterprise is doing. And the trading of shares is controlled by that organization. Once you're into public trading, then that generally implies that there is no control, that anybody can buy and sell shares. It is an invitation to abuse, as Wall Street Daily demonstrates."

As we've seen, the pioneers of local stock exchanges are sensitive to many of these concerns. John Katovich, Michael Van Patten, Trexler Proffitt, and Michael Sauvante all want to promote slow trading of companies, and to ensure that traders have excellent information about the companies they're trading. They are mindful that disclosures highlight not just the profitability of traded companies but their triple-bottom-line performance. They would restrict participation in local exchanges to locally owned companies and local residents, so that they really know one another and place long-term local ownership restrictions on traded stock (that's what Sauvante meant by the term *control-restricted stock*). Those who remain worried that their local stock exchanges are not local enough still could invest individually in or through local credit unions or cooperatives, as Korten prefers, though even they may need more liquidity to justify investing more of their life savings locally. Does liquidity necessarily lead to speculation? Maybe. But it's instructive that a locally owned company like Equal Exchange sees value in making some of their securities tradable on Mission Markets' platform. Ultimately, local exchanges will only be as sound, financially and philosophically, as the entrepreneurs who run them and as the companies and investors who use them. Korten's worries that local investment tools, in the wrong hands, can be corrupted should be heeded, but not only with respect to local stock exchanges. Even the cooperatives and small loan funds that Korten likes could be corrupted (recall that many practitioners of nonprofit microlending deplore the entry of usurious for-profits in the field). Whatever tools are chosen, local living economy advocates have no choice but to be vigilant that each is truly serving community prosperity.

In one respect, the debate about the virtues of local exchanges is academic. There's no doubt that some of these exchanges will start operating in the very near future. Most of the innovations described in this chapter could occur without any changes in existing securities law. They just require money. Mission Markets is ready to create many parts of a local exchange, as soon as a local client signs up. The SEC has also said, through several widely publicized no-action letters, that a company that has completed a DPO can allow buying and selling of its own securities on its website.[2] A tool like the UNIEX is essentially a bulletin board for local investors to find companies of interest, go to their websites, and trade accordingly. This is, of course, slow and clunky. Visionary broker-dealers naturally will step in to simplify and speed up these transactions. One can imagine a broker-dealer from Toledo or Albuquerque declaring herself as the local-stock specialist for her community members.

At that point, the difference between a broker-dealer manually handling local deals and an electronic exchange doing so seems a mere formality—and silly. Perhaps this would prompt the SEC to revisit its rules for exchanges. Perhaps it will take up Michael Sauvante's proposal that strictly intrastate trades of local securities be left to state regulators. And then, perhaps, a few states will prototype their own local exchanges.

"I often hear people ask, when they first hear about local investing, 'Well, what is there to invest in, in your area?' That reveals our blindness," reflects Trexler Proffitt. "There's a whole stratum of our economy—these small and medium-sized businesses, family-owned businesses, small mom-and-pops, start-ups, you name it—that's dark, that no one knows about, can value, or can invest in."

Every day we are inundated by statistics about the Fortune 500 economy. The nightly news lets us know how the New York Stock Exchange and the NASDAQ performed that day, as if they were proxies for the entire economy. In fact, they represent only the phantom economy rife with speculation and fraud. The real economy is in our backyards.

"The trick," says Trexler Proffitt, "is to make our local businesses investable—to help business owners tell their story better, to a larger audience. I can tell you the story of the actual local businesses that need your money. Do you have time to hear all those stories? Probably not. But I can collect them in a nice compendium called an online trading platform, and then you go look at them at your leisure.

"Every statistic you can imagine will show that there's more growth potential—more high-risk, high-reward potential—in the smaller companies growing. It does not matter really if they are ultra-small, if we can temper the risk. And that's all a local exchange does through its policies and procedures. What it does is light up this dark part of our world that isn't visible to investors right now.

"The investment world is responsible for trillions of dollars of transfer per year. If we are able to show the value of those local firms, and put that value in front of the right people, money will start to shift. And it doesn't have to be a lot for it to make a big difference. Once the lights start going on, a few places here and there, people will realize that the darkness doesn't have to remain dark. Then you can light up all of it. And I think that's going to be a very powerful movement, and one that might happen in a very short amount of time once we get it going."

Everybody into the Pool!

As local, state, and regional stock markets become commonplace, all kinds of creative local-investment funds will pop up to take advantage of proliferating local securities. Residents of Butte, Montana, might have a Silver Bow Local Investment Fund with a broad assortment of local stocks and bonds. Oregonians could choose between the Salem Food Business Fund and the Eugene Renewable Energy Fund. Some funds might focus on particular types of company—perhaps a Durham Cooperative Fund in North Carolina or an Austin B Corp Fund in Texas. And for those investors still worried about the risks of geographic concentration, there could be something like America's Local-Manufacturing Fund of Funds or a Midwest CDFI Fund.

Standing in the way of all these intriguing pools of money is—surprise!—the SEC and a supertanker of rules around investment companies. Generally speaking, compliance with the elaborate rules governing "investment companies," enacted in 1940, can cost funds hundreds of thousands of dollars. Funds with one hundred or more investors must comply. And the participation of even a single unaccredited investor in a fund significantly raises the legal expense.

The options for unaccredited investors who wish to invest intelligently in a diversified pool—and not just make risky, one-off investments in their favorite businesses—are therefore limited. This chapter explores half a dozen remaining options: revolving loan funds at various scales; a local mutual fund; a local stock investment club; and a relatively unfamiliar kind of company called a BIDCO.

School Notes

The initials *RSF* stand for Rudolf Steiner Foundation, which promotes Steiner's "anthroposophical" philosophy of learning and living. RSF set up a Social Investment Fund in 1984 to support its network of Waldorf Schools for private primary and secondary education. It expanded lending to mission-oriented for-profits in 2006. RSF has another fund focusing on mezzanine debt investment in promising triple-bottom-line (TBL) companies, only open to accredited investors. A third fund reinvests charitable accounts of socially minded clients in all kinds of "impact investments."

Administering RSF's Social Investment Fund today is Esther Park, who previously had done small-business lending at ShoreBank with clients ranging from microbusinesses in U.S. inner cities to mega-banks in former communist countries. Park became disenchanted with the CDFI world and began looking for new approaches to finance small business. "I was interested in bigger issues like environmental protection and food systems. Even though these issues have strong impacts on low-income communities, they cross-cut a lot of other demographics." She also wanted to return to the West Coast, where she was born, and RSF, based in San Francisco, fit the bill.

Every business loan RSF gives out must pass three tests. It must fall within one of its mission areas: food and agriculture, education and the arts, or ecological stewardship. Second, the enterprise must have strong TBL features. "We probably put for-profit companies through a more rigorous test than our nonprofit companies, but it's essentially the same. So we look at an organization's product, production, and supply chain. We want to see that social and environmental values are being imbued throughout every aspect of the business." Third, the financials have to pen out. Park chuckles, "We want to lend to good borrowers who will pay us back."

RSF's bias is toward companies that have been around for at least two years and have a clear sales record. Loans must be collateralized by their assets or other guarantees. "We also," adds Park, "focus on folks that are pre-bankable, who don't quite qualify for bank financing. Although we certainly have people come to us who are completely ready for bank financing but specifically want to work with a mission-aligned lender. We won't turn those folks away."

About a thousand investors have their money in RSF's Social Investment

Fund. Park estimates that 80 percent are unaccredited, but 80 percent of the Fund's money probably comes from the 20 percent who are accredited.

Does a local loan fund have to get federal and state approval to become an investment company? Probably not, since small loans and industrial banking are exempt.[1] Still, for unaccredited investors to provide capital for such funds, the securities issued by the fund must be registered with the SEC. A few ambitious loan funds have decided to pay the huge legal bills to allow unaccredited investors to purchase their "notes."

The decision to include all kinds of investors, accredited and unaccredited, flows naturally from Rudolf Steiner's thinking. "It just sort of started out that way," says Park, "and it has become kind of a hallmark for us. We believe it's incredibly important to provide opportunities for unaccredited folks to invest with their values. And so we've gone through a pretty hefty registration process. We have to create a prospectus each year, and then we have to register that with the appropriate department in each state. We do a blue-sky, state-by-state strategy, where we have registered our securities with each of the states, and then we essentially update our offering every year."

The fund, technically based in California, has registered its notes in thirty-eight states. It is not registered in states where the rules are too complicated and the legal work is too expensive. "There are just some states," says Park, "where they wish that the terms of our note were longer or they don't like that their returns automatically roll over if you don't redeem them—just a variety of structural things that they've raised flags on."

While the fund historically has not tried to connect its business borrowers with investors in specific places, community building has always been a central goal. "When we were doing a lot of school lending," explains Park, "we would essentially do an assessment of each school's community, to see how well that community could support its project. We also often asked schools to raise investment for their loan from the parents. It wouldn't have to be the full amount of the loan, but it was a symbolic contribution, in recognition of the fact that there's not some magic endowment somewhere where we have hundreds of millions of dollars and that it takes real people to provide the funds for us to lend."

RSF currently sets the interest rate on its loans—RSF Prime—based not on market rates but on a negotiation between representative investors and borrowers. "We are trying to provide opportunities for investors and borrowers in the same region to meet each other and have a meaningful conversation about their financial transaction. That said, we have over a thousand investors across the country and many don't live anywhere near any of our borrowers, and we only have about seventy-five borrowers. So that's still a challenge. But we're definitely moving more toward a local model, for sure."

In recent years RSF has explored setting up a national exchange for its loans, so that investors could more easily target their loans to businesses in their own state. A bunch of models have been explored, but nothing has been decided on yet.

Another big challenge, which the managers of RSF Social Finance are wrapping their minds around, is moving from loan to equity investments. "A couple of our entrepreneurs," Park reports, "have told us they have customers who would love to invest in their business. Unfortunately, there's just not a great vehicle to make that happen today."

But the potential, Park believes, is huge. "Too many times I've heard, 'I invited venture capital to the table and it almost killed the company!' I've also heard about businesses wanting angel investment, but wondering, 'Where the heck do I find these angels?' Getting small amounts of equity for small businesses is a big challenge right now. If you get enough of these people together, you could actually come up with a large amount of capital. It's just a totally untapped resource out there."

Pawnshop Progeny

If RSF can register notes for its revolving loan fund in thirty-eight states, then surely persistent organizers can register notes for a local fund within just one state. That's the backstory of the New Hampshire Loan Fund and the Biz Mountain Fund in North Carolina. These funds, in turn, have inspired Steve Fireman, a former business attorney, to bring unaccredited investors into his revolving loan fund in Columbus, Ohio, based at the Economic and Community Development Institute (ECDI).

ECDI was started by Inna Kinney, the daughter of Russian immigrants. When Kinney's parents first came to Columbus, they were highly skilled professionals who couldn't speak English very well and whose credentials in the motherland didn't count for much in America. Like millions of other immigrants before and since, the family had to scramble entrepreneurially to make ends meet. They created a regional chain of what you might call the original recycling facilities: pawnshops.

Fireman sat on the board of a nonprofit called Jewish Family Services, where Inna Kinney ran a division on business and asset development that trained new immigrants, particularly refugees and asylum recipients, to start their own businesses. She was especially concerned that immigrants, lacking a local credit record, could not get capital. Kinney and Fireman were so successful at raising grants for this work that the decision was made to spin off the work into a new nonprofit. ECDI was born in 2004.

ECDI received a license from the Small Business Administration to operate as a microloan intermediary and continued to grow. In 2007, Fireman came to work there as the entity's vice president and general counsel. Now he's president, overseeing fourteen different loan funds with $7.5 million in assets. "In 2004, '05, and '06," he recalls, "ECDI served a lot of the low- to moderate-income people with specific loan funds focused on them. We also had unrestricted funds that we could use for any type of small business. With the banks not lending and the housing bubble bursting, we started getting referrals from banks for business banking customers. The 'unbanked' became pretty much everybody who wanted to start a small business. Today, business-loan requests are just pouring into us. We're the place people go! If you have a cool concept to open a bakery or a restaurant, or to revive a famous old-fashioned community movie house, you don't even bother going to the bank anymore."

Until recently, most of the money for these loans came from the usual suspects for community development: foundations, government agencies, and commercial banks. But Fireman realized that, given the magnitude of the current financial crisis, these sources were falling far short. "It became apparent to me," says Fireman, "that this business creation could not just be something ECDI or other CDFIs do. It also wasn't just something for the government to do. Ordinary people needed to participate. We decided to brand and market ECDI to invite people in Central Ohio to invest in their own economic community."

Fireman studied other funds around the country that allow unaccredited investors to participate. "Everybody was very open and very helpful, because obviously their locale is not competing with my locale. That kind of inspired me. If they could do it, we could do it, too."

Fireman decided that investors should get a return, though not a huge one. Those who keep their money in the fund for three years get 2 percent per year. A five-year commitment gets 3 percent per year. "I was motivated," recalls Fireman, "by other fund managers who said, 'It doesn't matter. You're paying something.' The real pay is what they're doing for their community, and the fact that you're not just asking for a donation."

To find his way through the securities laws, Fireman had a board member who was a partner at a prestigious local law firm. The legal work wasn't free, but it wasn't outrageously expensive, either. "We ended up having to file under a very specific Ohio securities statute. It turned out to be relatively new ground for the regulators, which was kind of cool."

Anyone interested in investing receives an offering memorandum, a subscription agreement note, and audited financials. If you're interested in investing, you then have to return the subscription agreement, signed to acknowledge that you understand the documents. Even though unaccredited investors can participate, the state required unusual boilerplate in subscription agreements that placed some demands that they have a minimum level of wealth. Clause 7, for example, states: "I have adequate means for providing for my current needs and personal contingencies and have no need for liquidity in this investment. My overall commitment to investments which are not readily marketable is not disproportionate to my net worth; and my investment in the Note does not exceed ten percent (10%) of my liquid net worth . . ." Another requires subscribers to aver that they have "knowledge and experience in financial and business matters." That's a lower standard than the SEC's for a sophisticated investor, but it still demands something.

ECDI completes the process by preparing a physical note for the investor. Technically, there's a mini-closing, though the investor doesn't need to be physically present for it.

"As you can see," Fireman explains, "it's not like you go onto the website, fill out the documents, and sign up. It's not as easy as going to Prosper or the

Lending Club, although we're working with a potential partner to automate a lot of this process."

In just a few months, Fireman has attracted several $10,000-plus investors and more than a dozen $1,000 investors. His goal for this initial offering was $1 million, and he's optimistic about achieving it. "People really get it and want to help us. There's a lot of buzz about our offering."

Another hoped-for partner is a mainstream economic development group in town called Columbus 2020, run by the fourteen Fortune 500 companies based locally. While most of their attention focuses on old-style corporate attraction and retention, they are also committed to accelerating small-business creation. "And that's where we plug in," says Fireman.

Fireman also plans to market his fund to younger professionals, who might be interested in $1,000 to $5,000 investments. A number of local officials have become champions, which could translate into corporations and charitable foundations putting larger sums into his fund. Fireman acknowledges this is all new for Columbus. "It's not like Philadelphia or Chicago or Cleveland, where there's this history of CDFIs like us serving the underserved. Columbus has always been this kind of white-collar, government, Ohio State, Battelle, semi-high-tech, low-heavy-industry type of area. We have to brand and sell ourselves. But the good news is that, after this recession, people here really understand the need to invest local."

And not just invest. After you put money into the fund, Fireman sends you a discount card that's usable at any of the three hundred businesses being assisted by ECDI's fourteen loan funds. A for-profit company called Small Business Beanstalk, which ECDI supports, runs the program.

To maximize his leverage, Fireman insists that every ECDI loan be matched, dollar for dollar, by a loan from another source. It could be the Small Business Administration or the City of Columbus. Fireman also is trying to pry open lending participation from banks in the region.

Once this loan fund closes, Fireman has big plans for expansion. "I'd like to raise money for a Women's Business Loan Fund. I can see setting up funds for different communities, where the actual neighborhood or municipality or suburb helps us as well. As the technology gets better, I can see having more of peer-to-business lending, and then people can invest in the exact businesses they like. And I can see us doing this in the other cities in Ohio. For instance, we're starting to look to do some work in Cleveland and Cincinnati. All of this work is challenging—and gratifying!"

Coast-to-Coast Intermediation

As noted at the beginning of this chapter, some local investors may want to hedge their risk with geographic diversification. An early glimpse of how they might accomplish this can be found in the Community Investment Notes of the Calvert Foundation. Recall from earlier chapters that Calvert started as a mutual fund specializing in government bonds and gradually diversified into other socially responsible business products, catering primarily to accredited investors. The Community Investment Notes, begun fifteen years ago, are open to everybody.

"The proceeds from the notes," explains its prospectus, "are placed as direct investments in community development financial organizations with missions that include low-income housing, economic development and business development in urban and rural communities. The funds are lent to these domestic and international groups at slightly below-market rates. Borrowers are selected on the basis of their ability to contribute to growing local economies and to provide low-income communities with avenues to economic self-sufficiency."

The Calvert Foundation Community Investment Notes is effectively a national fund of local CDFI funds. Investors find terms from three months to ten years, with annual interest rates as high as 2 percent for the longest holders. Investors who buy directly from the Calvert Foundation must buy at least $1,000 of notes. But many of Calvert's eight thousand investors are now buying notes over the Internet for as little as $25.

Jesse Chancellor—president of Community Investment Partners, a wholly owned subsidiary of the Calvert Foundation—explains that all of the funds within the Calvert Foundation prioritize affordable housing, CDFIs, community loan funds, microfinance funds (domestic and international), and fair-trade businesses. "Retail investors tend to like our note's stability, the impact, the diversification of it; they often deal with us for a long, long time. They like our overall mix of microfinance and housing and banks."

They also like its track record. "Because our note has been so stable for so long, both in terms of the social impact we've delivered, as well as the quality and safety—no investor has ever lost a dime of money with us—it has become in many ways a gold standard," says Chancellor. "It really is for many people a safe and sound investment, even though there's no rating behind it. We think that by offering it to individuals in such small denominations, we allow younger investors in and make them aware of the potential of the broader world of impact investing."

Calvert's impact investing is not quite local, but it's moving in that direction. "The foundation is not yet connecting investors in one place to investments in the same locale," Chancellor says, "but money does ultimately flow largely to the places where the investors reside. Many of our investors seek some level of local targeting. It's one of the considerations we use when we make investments. The portfolio is about $180 million, the last time I looked, so there's a lot of investments we're tracking locally, especially in the community facilities and the small-business lending side."

The Calvert Foundation has followed the legal path of RSF Finance and has registered its notes in forty-nine states—every state except Pennsylvania (RSF, again, is registered in thirty-eight). It then distributes the relevant prospectus to interested investors residing in those states. Until 2005, the Calvert central office, not far from my home in Maryland, issued paper notes, but then through the magic of a "trust indenture," the notes became electronically transferrable and holdable in any brokerage account in the country. Another distribution channel is MicroPlace, which is an eBay company that specializes in small-dollar microfinance.

"Our role and goal in the future," says Chancellor, "will be to continue to demonstrate at greater scale, and in broader and deeper markets." He sees Calvert's niche as being a great prototyper. "When we started investing in microfinance, very few people were investing in microfinance. When we started making loans directly to CDFIs here in the U.S., it was an unknown asset class for people. Now both of those are being thought of as premier ways to solve problems in their particular arenas."

So what's next? Chancellor and his colleagues are thinking hard about how to tap retirement funds for impact investing. And how to increase their note holders' ability to target investing in their own community. "We'll probably have local funds, specifically geared toward economic development for certain parts of the country. The first step for us will be creating more local products on the money-out side. So when investors buy the Calvert Foundation Community Investment Note, they will see, in addition to these national and international activities, a set of specific local or regional initiatives."

Chancellor has seen demand for local investing grow exponentially, but the challenge is how to create a sufficiently diversified pool that's safe for the investor. "We have to maintain the integrity of our portfolio." The answer is clearly not Wall Street. Chancellor contends that today's capital markets fail the needs of community economies. "A lot of local knowledge was lost in the rush to create bigger pools of capital. Efficiency is not necessarily the be-all and end-all goal. If we lose the ability to connect that capital locally, then we've essentially failed."

Mutually Assured Absence

Americans today can choose to invest their pensions or other long-term savings in more than seventy-five hundred mutual funds. If, for example, you have your retirement savings in TIAA-CREF, you have two dozen options from which to choose. Once you wade through all the reassuring fund names like High Yield Bonds, Mid-Cap Value, and Large-Cap Growth, you quickly realize that every single one of them contains primarily nonlocal, publicly traded stocks and bonds. True, you can find municipal bonds in a few of these funds, but not a single fund focuses on an identifiable community. Shop around the Internet and you can find newfangled funds for oddball securities representing pools of foreign currencies, commodities like wheat and oil, and precious metals like gold and silver—but no mutual fund specializes in local small business.

Mutual funds must comply with myriad federal regulations under the Investment Company Act of 1940, but two of the rules heighten the challenge of going local. The first is that they must be "open ended." The term refers to the ability of an unlimited number of investors to put money into the fund or withdraw it as they wish. The total number of dollars in an open-ended fund can expand or contract like an accordion. A mutual fund manager has some criteria—big-company stocks, computer stocks, a mix of 60 percent stocks and 40 percent bonds, socially responsible stocks, and so forth—by which she invests the pool and then exercises her best judgment about how to maximize the rate of return. When you invest $1,000 into an open-ended fund, the manager adds your money to the pool and continues to invest by the declared criteria. When you want to take $1,000 out, the manager has to sell $1,000 of the pool's securities evenly, consistent with the criteria. A "closed end" fund, in contrast, is a fixed pool of money; once its shares are sold, you cannot enter unless an existing shareholder sells to you. The manager of a closed pool, of course, has to make ongoing judgment calls about which securities to buy and sell, but the kitty remains closed.

The second important rule governing mutual funds, implied by their open-ended character, is that they must be liquid. (There's that term again, *liquidity*.) By law, a mutual fund manager must be prepared at any moment to honor an investor's decision to exit. Within seven days, the manager must be able to pay cash for the investor's shares at their value, more or less, when the sell order is given. If a mutual fund were made up entirely of stocks that could not be resold for months or years, this would be impossible. The legal mandate of a mutual fund manager is that no more than 15 percent of the fund can be illiquid.

Practically speaking, therefore, local-investment innovation must unfold in a certain order. A community first needs to have a critical mass of local securities. Then a local exchange is needed to give these securities liquidity. Then and only then—when many local stocks are tradable—can a community justify creating a local mutual fund. It would be hard to get the required liquidity without a local exchange. And it would absurd to have a local exchange without local securities.

That said, I *could* set up a Maryland Investment Fund tomorrow, if I wanted to. The estimates of the legal expenses I've gotten range from $50,000 to $500,000. I could dedicate my fund to holding exclusively state and local bonds, which are all fairly liquid. I could use up to 15 percent of my customers' money to buy difficult-to-trade private shares of local businesses. Or I could use that 15 percent to buy notes in Maryland CDFIs or loans in cooperatives. *Yet no mutual fund like this exists in the United States today.* Municipal bond funds do exist, but even these tend to be state-specific rather than local.[2]

A couple of mutual funds have taken baby steps in the local direction. The Bullfinch Greater Western New York Fund was founded in 1997 by Christopher Carosa to give New Yorkers living in the fourteen westernmost counties—from Rochester and Syracuse down to Pennsylvania—the ability to invest in the region's top companies. Carosa's regional design has outperformed index funds over the past five years. The fund contains big companies operating upstate: Paychex, a national payroll processor based in Rochester; Graham Corporation, a designer and manufacturer of vacuum and heat-transfer equipment, headquartered in Batavia; and Corning, Inc., one of the world's leading glass manufacturers. All of these firms are major regional employers. All are traded publicly on the New York stock exchanges. None, however, is locally owned.

Slightly more local is Everence Community Investments, which manages high-social-impact investments for Everence Financial (formerly Mennonite Mutual Aid). Launched in 2000 by the financial services arm of the Mennonite Church, Everence Community Investments makes loans to CDFIs, including credit unions like Self-Help in North Carolina and specialized microloan funds like those of ACCION International and Coastal Enterprises of Maine. These community investments are spread across the country and therefore not really place-based, concedes Mark Regier, director of stewardship investing, though they are "closer to the ground. So, for instance, we invest in low-income housing programs in specific areas, international microfinance, church construction in underserved communities, environmental business initiatives, and community development credit unions." This part of Everence, however, is a tiny, $10 million sliver of the whole fund. Unaccredited investors typically will put their money into the Praxis Mutual Funds, which in turn only places about 1 percent of its capital in Everence Community Investments. Most of the Praxis money goes into publicly traded companies, albeit ones carefully screened to be socially responsible.

Everence Community Investments wants to do more locally. It recently partnered with the Calvert Foundation to bring its Community Investment Note to Everence's network of investors and financial advisers. Called the OneWorld Community Investment Program, this product allows individuals to direct their investments to international microfinance, faith-based domestic community-development organizations, or a combination of the two.

Everence Community Investment also plans to offer its own community investment security to its retail investors in the near future.

In summary, the United States has two mutual funds, run by Calvert and Praxis, that seek to include community-development investments as part of their investment portfolios, but both have a national shareholder base and neither focuses on a particular geographic locality or region. That's it! Why are there no genuine examples of local mutual funds? I put that question to Laura Anne Corsell, a Philadelphia attorney and expert on structuring investment funds. She sees growing investor interest in community-development investments and in funds that include securities issued by locally based companies.

"The mutual fund framework," Corsell says, "is much more flexible than is necessarily reflected by the types of offerings that are out there—there's no legal impediment to a mutual fund being a socially responsible or locally focused organization." In fact, a mutual fund adviser can deploy any investment strategy that she reasonably believes will generate a good rate of return. Corsell sees no regulatory prohibition to investing up to 15 percent of a fund's assets in community investments like local securities, as long as there's proper disclosure. The idea, for a fund adviser, is: "Sure, we could invest exclusively in traditional companies, but we choose to commit a piece of the funds' money to local business to serve certain social goals that are important to us. If you're going to invest in our fund, you should share those hopes and dreams."

Still, Corsell cautions that anyone setting up a local mutual fund will not find it easy. Just the challenge of scale is daunting: "Mutual funds have to hold their assets and account for them in a particular way, so if they've got a lot of very small positions, the administrative burdens can get very expensive, very quickly." To cover start-up fees, ongoing legal and accounting costs, advertising, care and feeding of members, and so forth, a bare-bones mutual fund probably needs assets of at least $25 to $50 million. That's a tall order for a start-up.

After you've got $25 to $50 million in hand, there's the issue of diversification. For a mutual fund to receive the special tax treatment afforded to registered investment companies, it must diversify its holdings.[3] "Imagine a fund with $25 million in assets under management that is designed to invest substantially all of its assets in companies with substantial ties to the Philadelphia region and one-half of its assets in small, local companies," Corsell hypothesizes. "Such a fund might hold, for example, a 10 percent position (or $2.5 million) in each of five publicly traded companies with significant ties to the Philadelphia area. To satisfy the 5 percent investment ceiling for the remaining half of the fund's assets, the fund's manager would have to limit investments in any single company to $1.25 million. Finding at least ten attractive investment opportunities among local businesses, however, that can absorb $1.25 million in investor dollars could take some doing." Which underscores why a local stock exchange is needed before a local mutual fund makes much sense.

Even when local mutual funds exist, moving retirement funds into them will not necessarily follow. Most of us don't invest in these funds ourselves but depend on intermediaries. If you work for a large company, a labor union, or for the government, your pension fund choices must be stamped for approval by an army of investment experts. These "custodians" have a number of fiduciary duties imposed on them under a federal law called the Employee Retirement Income Security Act (ERISA). Some of these duties are straightforward. No stealing. No self-dealing. Report your every investment action often and honestly. More limiting is the duty to exercise a standard of care, skill, prudence, and diligence. Not a few employee fiduciaries have taken the position that this standard demands that they give their pensioners the options of stocks or bonds—period. Choose between Tweedledum and Tweedledee. Friends of mine who are college professors, whose funds are overseen by the financial services nonprofit TIAA-CREF and who have asked for more regional or local options, are consistently given a polite brush-off, with the explanation that such options would be inconsistent with the fund's fiduciary duties. Compared with the abysmal performance of Wall Street? Please.

For now, the absence of actual local mutual funds makes such lobbying premature. Once a few of these funds are around, employees can then begin demanding that their fiduciaries include them on their 401(k) menus. To me, the argument is simple: How can you possibly claim to be my fiduciary if you insist on investing my money, against my wishes, in destructive global businesses rather than in the local businesses I care about? You are *my* fiduciary, buddy, not Wall Street's!

A few large state employee pension funds have also made some small, prototyping local investments. Since 1999, the New York State Common Retirement Fund has targeted more than $800 million into in-state investments, including $271 million in 107 companies based in New York.[4] In 2008 the Michigan Retirement System committed $300 million to Invest Michigan!, which contains two funds that support promising companies based in state.[5] Similar investments can be found from public employee pension funds in Ohio, Indiana, North Carolina, and New Jersey. CalPERS, the California state pension fund, created a Green Development Fund to support promising businesses in the state and also has invested in California real estate projects. Steve Dubb of the Democracy Collaborative at the University of Maryland, and an expert on innovative public-investment strategies, is especially impressed with Alabama: "They've used their pension fund to invest in a whole network of golf courses, which has been an economic-development boon to the state and created a tourist industry that didn't exist."

These "economically targeted investments" have been criticized for their relatively poor performance, but the blame hardly belongs on their "local" character.[6] As is the case with most economic-development subsidies, almost all these investments have gone into global companies with some superficial ties to the state like the site of a headquarters. Pension fund investment in truly locally owned businesses has yet to be tried.

No Small Potatoes

In his famous field report on the United States in the early 1800s, Alexis de Tocqueville noted the extraordinary prevalence of voluntary associations. This continues today in the form of modern political parties, Kiwanis Clubs, Parent–Teacher Associations, and bridge clubs. That Americans would come together to improve their community through investing clubs seems only natural. And simple! So simple that a group of older women in Beardstown, Illinois, wrote a best-selling book, *The Beardstown Ladies' Common-Sense Investment Guide* (1996), promoting the group's practical way of evaluating and investing in stocks, which enabled them to achieve a whopping 23.4 percent annual rate of return between 1983 and 1994. Well, that was the hype. Long after they cashed their royalty checks, the ladies' numbers withered under careful scrutiny (in reality, they probably underperformed the S&P 500). But their legend lives on in stock clubs across America, nearly all of which invest 100 percent in nonlocal securities.

The SEC has given a pass for investment clubs to operate without formal approval, on one big condition: *Every single member must be actively involved in every single investment decision.* If that criterion is met, a club can pool money from its members, invest in any securities it wishes, make profits, and provide its members with a nice check at the end of each year. As soon as even a single member becomes passive and starts relying on the investment advice of others in the club, legal alarms get tripped. Clubs must have fewer than one hundred members and, practically speaking, to adhere to the active-investor rule, they probably should have fewer than thirty.[7]

Maine has recently green-lighted one creative spin on investment clubs: No Small Potatoes Investment Club, an offshoot of Slow Money Maine. The president of No Small Potatoes, Linzee Weld, is no investment guru. She's a nonprofit gal who had helped her town's land trust preserve a local farm. "I had gotten involved with some farmers who needed financing to build infrastructure on their farms," she says, "and became aware of the hurdles farmers face getting financing. Woody Tasch's book *Slow Money*, about investing in local farms and food businesses, opened doors for me on how to strengthen the local farm economy."

At a Slow Money gathering in Maine, Weld met Marada Cook, who owns an organic food distribution company called Crown O' Maine. Her business picks up produce and value-added food goods from farms and small businesses all over the state and then distributes them to groceries, natural food stores, and buying clubs. In 2009 Cook started extending credit to some of her vendors who couldn't keep up with the demand for their local products because they lacked money to buy ingredients, or containers, or on-farm storage space. These loans had a business purpose: to increase sales for her suppliers and improve Crown O'Maine's bottom line.

At the next Slow Money Maine meeting Cook presented a list of nine farms and fishermen's co-ops she thought could use microloans. She suggested microloans to help a yogurt maker buy another pallet of jars; to help a potato farmer get more seed; and to help a blueberry grower buy a freezer and store increased quantities of bagged blueberries. The group was aware of a few other microloan funds in the state: One was run by Coastal Enterprises (described in chapter 5), and another was run by the nonprofit Maine Organic Farmers and Gardeners Association (MOFGA), both of which tended to make loans $5,000 and higher.

As Slow Money Maine continued to showcase farmers who could benefit from small loans, attendees got motivated to act. Several people began making loans personally to food producers, until they could figure out a way to pool their money. "The advantage of pooling your money is that you're spreading the risk." The group explored setting up a microloan fund with MOFGA to make smaller loans, until Chris Hallweaver, a software and food business entrepreneur in the Slow Money Maine network, suggested the group create an investment club to serve the microloan niche. "We went with the investment club model, because it allowed investors to connect directly with borrowers without an intermediary." And they decided to name the club No Small Potatoes (NSP).

After the group studied the SEC's rules and got approval from state regulators, it started with ten members, each chipping in $5,000. They envision growing the club to twenty members, with a fund of $100,000. They considered having a lower buy-in threshold, but it didn't seem worth it. "If you have twenty people putting in $1,000," explains Weld, "you've only got $20,000 to loan out. We wanted a bigger pool of money to work with. And we also wanted a group that wasn't too big."

NSP welcomes all kinds of investors, accredited and unaccredited. This is not surprising—most of the Beardstown ladies were certainly not accredited! In fact, Weld herself is unsure which of her colleagues meet the SEC's income and wealth standards for being accredited—the question has never arisen. It probably helped that the Maine securities department decided that the potential economic-development benefits outweighed any concerns about legal snafus. When newcomers hand over their $5,000 check, they sign an agreement with the usual acknowledgment that they might lose everything. "We are very clear with potential new members that their investment in the club is at risk."

Attracting members to the club has not been difficult. Flyers about the club circulated at various Slow Money events, and word got out by word of mouth. Eleanor Kinney, one of the club's founders, noted, "A growing number of people want to do something different with their money that benefits their community. No Small Potatoes is an entry point for people to engage financially in the local farm sector."

The club now has thirteen members who have each invested $5,000. Actually, one member has put in $10,000 already, and others are considering upping their ante. The rules of NSP stipulate, however, that no one can contribute more than 25 percent of the total pot. None of the members of the club to date is a banker or professional lender, but they support one another through face-to-face meetings and through an online social network. They've also organized workshops to train themselves on certain basic financial skills, such as how to read financial statements.

To ensure active participation of club members and to comply with SEC rules, the operating agreement of No Small Potatoes requires that a majority of all members must approve each loan. (Everyone's participation in every investment decision, mind you, does not require everyone's agreement with every decision.) Members in small groups personally interview potential borrowers, and then the group votes on whether or not to approve a loan based on the application and interview.

Entrepreneurs looking for loans have to fill out an application and provide trade, bank, and personal references. They must describe their business, their financial situation, and their projections for the coming year. "We ask for a fair amount of financial information for a relatively small loan," explains Weld. "But we figure that a borrower would have to go through this process anyway to get money from the bank. We really want to get satisfactory answers to two questions: Does it look like this is a financially viable operation, so we'll get our money back? And do the plans for growth look realistic based on prior experience? We also check credit and trade references."

Another consideration for NSP is the networks the farmer belongs to—MOFGA, the Crown O' Maine distribution system, or a farmers' market, for example. "Maine is a small state, and we want to lend to people who are connected to existing networks. The more people are connected, the more incentive they have to repay a loan."

For the moment, the application process is free. That could change if the number of applicants escalates. The club is also considering a pre-application process to screen out candidates with the lowest likelihood of approval.

The club plans three lending rounds per year: one in February before the growing season starts, one in the summer, and one in the autumn. In its first lending round, in April 2011, NSP made six loans, all $5,000 or less, to farmers and food businesses in six different counties. "We loaned money to a goat cheese maker, a butcher, a farmer who is getting into the composting business, several vegetable farms, and a farmer who wanted to improve his software for online marketing" says Weld. "Two of the borrowers were certified organic farmers; two had apprenticed with MOFGA, and a couple farms were conventional. It felt like a good mix."

NSP is interested in making loans that grow Maine's food economy. "We want to help individual farmers succeed. But we're also interested in helping businesses that help farmers reach new markets. A couple of the businesses we lent to in our first loan round aggregate goods from several farms and then sell them to larger or higher-volume customers. They are creating new markets."

The repayment rates on the loans vary between eight months and three years. The interest rate is 5 percent. "We thought about whether or not to go lower, and decided not to. We figured 5 percent would help us cover our annual legal or accounting costs and begin to build a loan loss reserve."

The club's members intend, however, to do better than break even. After covering expenses, they're hoping for a 2 to 3 percent annual return. Weld does the math: "You earn $5,000, you have $2,000 in expenses, and you split the remaining $3,000 between twenty club members. This isn't a formula for getting rich, but it also isn't philanthropy."

Even if the profits turn out to be small, the other rewards are huge. "It's fun!" insists Weld. "What we saw in our first round of lending was that a small loan, between $2,000 and $5,000, can make a significant difference in a small business. It can help a farmer or entrepreneur grow a revenue stream that will positively affect the bottom line. We lent one woman the working capital to farm this season, and if we hadn't lent it, I don't know where she would have gotten it. Another woman was able to buy a van to bring more produce to market: as her farm revenues grow, she can cut back her off-farm work hours."

"I think our microloan fund is about establishing connections between people in the community. I can go to a farmers' market in Portland now and buy produce from one of the people we lent money to. One of our borrowers said, 'We wanted to start with a loan less than $5,000 to get to know you, and if it works, build a relationship with you as lenders in the future.'" Those kinds of connections are, in a small way, growing the capacity to grow food locally in Maine—which, as Marada Cook can tell you, helps farms, distributors, and markets up and down the supply chain.

Given the scale at which the club operates, isn't all of this, well, small potatoes? "On the one hand, a small group of us are making small loans to a small group of farmers," Weld says. "However, there is real power in connecting individuals financially to their local food producers. If this ball gets rolling, it can have impact on a larger scale." Maybe it will inspire a lot of other clubs to form in the state or nationally. Maybe it will convince other financial institutions about the promise of microloans, especially to farmers and local food businesses. Maybe the club, and others like it, will start putting their money into local CDFIs like Coastal Enterprises or the Vermont Sustainable Jobs Fund. Maybe there will be an online lending program, such as Kiva, connecting individuals online to local farms and food businesses. Weld thinks the day will come when an abundance of microloan funds makes clubs like No Small Potatoes obsolete.

BIDCOs

Another pool that unaccredited investors might use to support local business comes from the Small Business Investment Incentive Act of 1980. Called business-development companies or BIDCOs, these entities need not register as investment companies. This vehicle has been thoroughly exploited by Wall Street professionals but largely overlooked by local-business developers.

Congress understood that private pools of money can contribute to economic development, especially if the public purpose of assisting small business is front and center. A BIDCO is essentially a venture fund for small businesses. The BIDCO must provide beneficiaries not only capital but also managerial and technical assistance. And while unaccredited investors cannot invest in any BIDCO, if a BIDCO goes public through an intrastate offering like any other company, they then can participate. One could imagine, for example, No Small Potatoes organizing a BIDCO involving perhaps twenty-five local food businesses in Maine, taking the BIDCO public, and then inviting residents throughout the state to support the diversified pool.

Among the tiny number of securities attorneys familiar with BIDCOs is Ken Priore, who works with Cutting Edge Capital in Oakland and whom we met in chapter 7. "I started becoming involved with them back in 1999, during what I call 'Dot-Com 1.0' or 'Bubble 1.0.' Even though it's an investment vehicle that's perfectly suited to the tech community, no one was interested back then. At the time there was probably enough money in the pipeline for more traditional private equity plays. No one wanted to go through the additional regulatory burden associated with being a public business-development company."

But Priore and his colleagues at MVC Capital were intent on doing something different. "Our tagline then was 'Democratizing Venture Capital.' We were new to the VC field, I was twenty-nine years old, and we saw BIDCOs as a fresh approach. Here, we thought, is an asset class that people have been locked out of, because they were not accredited investors, yet we could help them have it as part of their investment portfolio. They could invest a percentage of their portfolio directly in technology companies, and it would still be in the context of a diversified fund."

MVC Capital is still traded on the New York Stock Exchange but looks a lot different than it did a decade ago. "The fund unfortunately got caught in the backdraft of the market correction," says Priore. "A new group of outside interests decided to file suit against the management of the fund for taking excessive fees, a new management team was installed, and the fund relocated from the Bay Area to New York City. Its investment strategy is no longer focused purely on early-stage technology companies. It still trades and you don't have to be an accredited investor to invest into it, but it has moved away from its roots."

BIDCOs have proliferated in the years since, particularly on the East Coast, but they do not look anything like what the Small Business Incentive Act intended. "In 2008 in particular we started to see more BIDCOs out of New York," says Priore, "where investment-banker types became interested—but not so much because of the innate attributes of a BIDCO. A number of people who were used to playing with the 1940 Investment Company Act looked at this and said, 'Well, why don't we start using this vehicle? We won't have to submit to the same regulatory regime that we would as a full-blown investment company.'"

While Priore and his colleagues were not focused on local businesses per se, they certainly didn't treat their BIDCO as just a regulatory dodge. They set up a rigorous infrastructure to monitor and manage their portfolio companies. "We required every company in which we made an investment to give us an active board seat. We created private networks where the management of Company A could meet the management of Company B, and they could share ideas and we could answer questions for the group. You could say we basically created a social network for ourselves. We really wanted to create an entrepreneurial ecosystem so that a portfolio company knew that when we took them on they were getting more than just our money—they were getting our active engagement."

Some of this diligence was aimed at improving the performance of the companies, but it also was what the law required. "We didn't know how the regulators were going to enforce the requirement of active managerial assistance, so we decided, if nothing else . . . document, document, document! If it ever happened that we had to prove our compliance to the regulators, we had a whole, transparent system in place."

The structure was attractive to some start-ups, but not to everyone. "I definitely know," says Priore, "that we lost out on investing on some deals because ultimately the executives involved didn't like that we were a publicly traded company. They worried that we were going to have to disclose information they would rather keep private." But worries about privacy are just not as great as they used to be. "What's different from ten years ago is that now there are more and more people who are used to sharing information immediately. In fact, they now want everything to be public, because it engages their stakeholders more directly and completely."

The companies MVC Capital focused on, again, were not what most people consider local businesses. These were high-risk, high-growth, high-tech start-ups like some of the first voice-over-the-Internet telephone companies—the kind that could start anywhere and easily could be relocated to somewhere else. Because these businesses were small, they technically qualified for BIDCO involvement.

The possibility for BIDCOs to invest locally, however, clearly remains. Priore believes that moving BIDCOs into local investment actually vindicates the original intent of Congress. The very reason BIDCOs were given an exemption from the Investment Company Act was, in Priore's estimation, to "aggregate their resources for a greater good, to fund some sort of collective action in a single community."

With the growing national interest in local investing, Priore sees more start-up businesses not just willing but eager to have exactly the kind of managerial assistance a BIDCO might offer. "When I go to a community bank, it's not the same as going to some guy in New York and asking him to invest a million dollars in my business. The community banker is going to call me every month, sit on my board meetings, and be active in my business. He's going to become a stakeholder, not just in terms of the money he has invested but in terms of the amount of effort he's willing to expend. He's doing this not just because he wants to get back his money plus more, but because he has to drive past my building every day. Maybe he knows someone who works for me. Managerial assistance is really part of community building."

Priore recently recommended the BIDCO structure for clients proposing an enterprise called the Food Commons. The principal architects of this idea are Jim Cochran, the strawberry grower running Swanton Berry Farms discussed in chapter 2, and Larry Yee, a retired agricultural professor from the University of California. They want to create regional incubators for local food businesses across the country, while enabling residents to invest in a diversified fund to support them. The BIDCO concept fits, hand in glove. Given the long time it may take for local mutual funds to materialize, BIDCOs constitute one of the best options residents of any given community might have for creating diversified portfolios of local businesses.

The World of the Possible

In Stanley Kubrick's cinematic masterpiece, *2001: A Space Odyssey*, a turning point for human history is when man-apes discover that sticks can be used as tools and weapons. (Pump up the musical score—*Also Sprach Zarathustra*.)

Local sapiens has now reached a similar moment. Properly using the newfound local investing tools of banks, cooperatives, CDFIs, local stock, and stock exchanges, we can finally direct our money to flow into local businesses. We also can begin to deploy new tools for creating diversified pools of local investments, such as local loan funds, stock clubs, BIDCOs, and mutual funds. But there's still one more option that may be the most promising local investment strategy of all: investing in yourself.

Investing in Yourself

Is it possible to beat Wall Street's 5 percent long-term performance by investing in your community? If you've read this far, you know the answer is a resounding *yes*! Co-op members who lent to the Weaver Street Market in North Carolina and to the Seward Co-op in Minneapolis earned well over 5 percent per year. Many outside investors who bought preferred shares of the Coulee Region Organic Producers Pool, a co-op of organic farmers, are still receiving an annual dividend of 6 percent. Equal Exchange has paid a dividend to its preferred shareholders averaging above 5 percent for twenty-two years. Investors who participate in New Markets Tax Credits automatically get a tax credit equal to 5 percent of their capital for each of the first three years and 6 percent for the next four—even if the investment generates no real return whatsoever. Burt Chojnowski's returns have been good enough to convince outside investors to put more than $300 million into his local companies and projects over twenty-five years in Fairfield, Iowa. Most of LION's deals in Port Townsend, Washington, are paying between 5 and 8 percent returns per year. Microlenders on Prosper.com are averaging an annual return of 10.4 percent. Jeff Haugland has paid the local shareholders of Community Grocers in Mount Ayr, Iowa, an annual dividend of 5.25 percent.

All of these profitable initiatives proceeded within existing securities laws. If, however, national or state governments were to implement sensible, simple, zero-cost reforms, the number, variety, and promise of local-investment opportunities could expand dramatically. The many examples in this book— and the thousands of others out there, some of which may be happening in your community right now—suggest that the universe of local investment is expanding faster than financial astronomers like myself can possibly keep track of it.

Not every local company, of course, will beat the 5 percent rate of return from existing markets. Betting on any one or two businesses, just like betting on any one of two NASDAQ stocks, is very risky. No one should read this book as suggesting that we each should pull all our money out of the stock market and put it all into our neighborhood diners or bookstores. As models for local investment proliferate, the focus will shift to the quality of each investment and the quality of your local-investment portfolio. The country is about to travel up a steep learning curve to discern the best local businesses from the fraudsters and grifters, and how to build a local-economy infrastructure in our communities—replete with local purchasing, entrepreneurship programs, local business alliances, and public policy reforms—that will increase the probability of local businesses succeeding and local investments paying off. One modest step might be to move 5 percent of your money from Wall Street to Main Street each year. By the time you get to 100 percent in twenty years, the nation should have a thriving network of regional stock exchanges and local mutual funds.

But another vexing question about local investment I puzzle over is this: Does it make sense to invest in anyone else's business, bank, project, or fund until I have thoroughly invested in . . . *myself?* Might I get a better than 5 percent annual rate of return investing in my own bank account, my home, my own energy-efficiency measures, and my education? Most of us ultimately have a significant portion of our wealth in these intimately close items. Getting these investments right might be the single best way to invest locally.

To beat Wall Street, investments in yourself must achieve not a 5 percent annual rate of return but a 7 percent rate. That's because most of the options could not qualify for tax-deferred IRA or 401(k) investments, and the extra 2 percent, as we saw in chapter 1, approximates the lifetime benefit of tax deferral. Remarkably, though, the 7 percent goal is achievable—and in so many ways that many Americans, perhaps most, might never need to think about retirement accounts again.

Become Your Own Banker

There is one absolutely guaranteed place where you can get a rate of return well over 7 percent —in fact, often over 15 percent or 20 percent. Pay off the damn credit cards and stay out of debt! As the Sage of Omaha, Warren Buffett, says, "Nobody ever goes broke that doesn't owe money."[1] Besides being expensive and self-destructive, credit card debt winds up sucking money out of your community and into the hands of distant banks, back offices, and collection agencies. Yes, you know this, and yet you, like most Americans (and like me, too, as I'll elaborate shortly), have probably gotten hooked on easy credit.

Here are some sobering facts about Americans' relationship with credit cards. In 1990, the average American household had about $3,000 in credit card debt. It has since more than quintupled to $15,300. By the end of 2010, total credit card debt was expected to exceed $1.1 trillion. According to a recent survey by *Consumer Reports*, a third of Americans don't have credit cards at all, but most of these folks are poor and therefore vulnerable to even worse depredations from payday lenders and loan sharks.[2] About half the population pays its cards off every month. The rest of us have a problem—albeit one that can easily be fixed in a way consistent with the goals of a local living economy.

Recall Sam the Saver, whom we met in chapter 1 and who is our model citizen investor and financial planner. The few of us who rise to the laudable standards of Sam and never accumulate credit card debts nevertheless must borrow periodically for big-ticket expenditures such as a car, kitchen appliances, college tuition, and so forth. (We'll discuss the biggest ticket item, your house, shortly.) The interest rates we pay on these loans are less usurious than credit cards but almost always are well over 7 percent (government-guaranteed student loans sometimes might be a notable exception).

In chapter 1 we asked whether Sam should put $5,000 into his IRA each year, and we pointed out the benefits of his doing so because of tax deferral. But Sam actually would have been wiser to put his first ten years of after-tax savings, $3,500 per year, not in an IRA, but into a savings account that he might call the Bank of Sam. Mindful of his local economy, Sam would put his money in a local bank or credit union. As big purchases arose, Sam could negotiate a deal with Bank of Sam about how to pay back his own loan. Because Sam is nice to himself, he would probably charge himself no interest and no fees. Isn't that the kind of bank we all really want?

If his credit card interest rates ran 7 percent or lower, then Sam might agonize about creating his own bank. For every dollar he borrowed from himself, he would be gaining a small amount of avoided credit card interest

THE CASE FOR THE BANK OF SAM

What are the advantages of Sam creating his own bank over ten years rather than putting money into a retirement account? In the first option, Sam puts $5,000 per year into his own bank, accumulating $50,000 over ten years. He keeps his money in low-risk CDs that pay 2 percent per year. In ten years he has accumulated $4,750 of interest beyond his principal of $50,000.

To understand what happens if Sam puts his money into a tax-deferred retirement account, we'll change the payback to 7 percent —5 percent from Wall Street plus 2 percent bonus on tax deferral.[3] In this scenario, he earns about $19,100 beyond his principal of $50,000. He gets $14,350 richer over a decade than he would in the first scenario. This is effectively what Sam gives up by creating his bank.

To justify creating his bank, Sam has to avoid $1,435 in interest charges per year ($14,350 divided by ten). As noted in the text, the average American household now has $15,300 in credit card debt. According to the website CreditCards.com, the average APR on new credit cards is 14.8 percent. The typical household is therefore paying $2,265 in interest to credit card companies per year—and would be smart to create its own bank.

The justification, moreover, is stronger for those who are younger. Most of us tend to borrow more in earlier years—to buy a car or basic appliances, for example. Young people also tend to default more and therefore get sacked with much greater APRs. Additionally, young people need their own banks to save up a down payment for their home, which, as we will soon see, itself carries huge financial benefits.

but losing a bigger gain from his retirement account. But we all know that actual credit card rates today are usually two, three, even four times higher! So unless Sam were a Buddhist monk renouncing all worldly possessions, this is a no-brainer. For those of you who like numbers, I make the case for the Bank of Sam in the adjacent box.

Sure, there are optimistic scenarios where Sam might not need his bank and might lose money by not investing in his IRA. But a smart financial thinker like Sam will give the pessimistic scenarios just a little more weight. He might keep in mind that he could find himself, at some point in his life, in some kind of emergency where he suddenly needed $50,000 or $100,000. He could lose his job. He could get cancer. He could be sued by an obnoxious neighbor. He could be robbed.

Another consideration underscoring the value of keeping a modest reserve of cash is that we are entering turbulent times. In the last few years, both the stock market and the housing market have tanked and many serious analysts fear that both could crash again, perhaps even more catastrophically. Some predict a perilous period of deflation ahead, where falling prices convince consumers to delay spending and trigger deep recessions. Others fear inflation, given the enormous size of the U.S. deficit and rising oil prices. In either case risk-averse lenders might cut off loans or credit cards, raise rates, or both. Since Sam doesn't like to gamble, he will create a hedge against uncertainty through his own federally insured bank account.

This proposal is hardly original. Listeners to AM talk shows may have heard about a similar scheme, called "Bank on Yourself," which encourages you to invest in a specialty life insurance policy that also can serve as your low-risk bank. Frankly, since your savings have to live somewhere, whether it's under your mattress, in a money market account, or embedded in a gold stockpile, these options are all worth considering. But given the importance of keeping your money close to home and supporting local businesses, you should probably put your cushion in a locally owned bank or credit union, not a distant insurance company.

The bottom line is this: If you create a slightly larger cushion than you think you'll need, you'll never need to worry about credit cards or consumer loans again. What wouldn't millions of Americans (including me!) give to redo their early years with this kind of approach. At some point, you then could move into the next level of investing. That would not be going into the global stock market. It would be buying your own home.

Become Your Own Landlord

Investing in your own home strengthens your community. While the evidence has been debated in recent years, the degree of homeownership in a neighborhood does seem to correlate with many other quality-of-life indicators, such as educational achievement, low crime, civic participation, public health, and property values. This led recent presidents as diverse as Bill Clinton and George W. Bush to push for "an ownership revolution" in the housing market. And if you are diligent about getting your mortgage through a local bank or credit union, where you'll find the most competitive rates anyway, you can rest assured that your interest payments will be recycled through your community through additional local loans.

A home purchase really delivers two different kinds of valuable rewards. One is that you've got a place to live. Hey, you have to live somewhere! Instead of paying a landlord every month, you effectively become your own landlord. Yes, you enter a debt with your mortgage (hopefully, again, with your local bank), but as you pay it down, you grow an asset that ultimately eliminates rent payments for the rest of your life. The second reward is that you now have an asset that you can draw upon for your retirement. At some point, if you need the cash, you can sell your home and move into a smaller one. Or you can enter a "reverse mortgage" with a local bank that pays you an income stream and gradually works you out of ownership. The reality is that most Americans use their homes as their piggy banks for retirement anyway.

Now, some of you may be thinking: Buy real estate? Are you crazy? After housing values across the country have plummeted in recent years and forced millions of owners into default? But consider all the following:

- The best time to buy any asset is after a bubble involving that asset has burst. Right now there are many future millionaires buying up cheap abandoned or foreclosed properties by the dozens.
- I appreciate that the financial crisis has left a significant percentage of Americans unable to sell their existing home, let alone buy a new one. Many of us have no choice but to go back to basics, pay down our debts, and build our own banks before we

can consider buying a home again. If you're in this predicament, you'll have to wait before you invest in anything else, including your home.

THE CASE FOR HOMEOWNERSHIP

Suppose Sam decides, after creating his own bank, to buy a $100,000 home. Since the financial crisis, most lenders would require Sam to put 20 percent down (10 percent was possible during the freewheeling days of the housing boom but now is harder to do). Where will Sam find $20,000 for the down payment? The Bank of Sam, of course.

Right now, as I write, interest rates for a mortgage are at a record low, but let's assume that interest rates rise to a more challenging level of 7 percent. Sam gets a thirty-year fixed mortgage that results in a monthly payment of $532 per month. Over the thirty-year lifetime of the loan, Sam winds up paying his bank a total of $191,607: $80,000 for the equity (that is, the principal on the loan) and $111,607 in interest.

Let's compare Sam deciding, instead, to rent for thirty years. Just to make it simple, let's assume Sam's monthly rental is exactly the same as his mortgage might be—$532 per month. Sam the Renter is now free to use his $20,000 down payment as an investment in his IRA. Let's grow it for thirty years at 5 percent per year in the stock market to $86,440, which is an appreciation of $66,440. (In this case we use 5 percent instead of 7 percent, because we actually will measure the exact impacts of the tax deferral.)

Now add the homeowner's tax deduction. Sam the Homeowner can deduct his interest from his taxes over the lifetime of the loan, which amounts to savings of $33,482. Sam the Renter cannot deduct anything.

Before taxes, Sam the Homeowner comes out nearly $47,000 ahead! As a renter, Sam pays rent over thirty years and ultimately winds up with no asset to show for it. As a homeowner, Sam pays the same "rent" but in the form of mortgage payments, enjoys the exact same amenities—a good place to live—and has a $100,000 asset (assuming zero appreciation) at the end.

- A consequence of these recent crashes is that banks have raised
  their standards for new mortgages. The days of no-money-down
  loans or no-proof-of-income approvals are gone. Frankly, this is

As a renter/investor, Sam will ultimately have to pay taxes on the income he takes from his IRA. As a homeowner, Sam will not have to pay taxes on his home upon sale. Sam could enjoy up to $250,000 tax-free. Hence Sam the Homeowner comes out $67,000 ahead.

Sam the Homeowner gets another bonus, too: Immediately after the mortgage is paid in year thirty, he gets to continue to live in his own house for free, saving $6,000 in avoided rent each year. In contrast, chances are very good that Sam the Renter's rent, after inflation, would have risen over the years.

The bottom line is clear: *Using a chunk of savings to buy a home will generate a far better return than placing that chunk into a retirement account.*

The skeptical reader might quibble with some my assumptions. If housing values plummet and stocks skyrocket, these numbers will be all wrong.[4] Historically, however, according to Robert Shiller of Yale, real estate appreciates at just under 2 percent per year. And again, after a bubble bursts, as is the case for the housing market today, zero appreciation may be an overly conservative assumption.[5]

Table 2. Sam's Balance Sheet		
	Renter	Homeowner
Interest Rate	n/a	7%
Rent	(191,607)	n/a
Mortgage Payment	n/a	(191,607)
Starting Asset	20,000	20,000
Asset Appreciation	66,440	80,000
Income Tax Savings	0	33,482
Net Gain at Year 30	(105,167)	(58,125)
Taxes at Year 30	(19,932)	0
Final Gain	(125,099)	(58,125)

actually good news. Shoring up the standards of homeowner-ship protects the rest of us who wish to invest seriously in our homes.

- Renting is not a risk-free alternative. Remember that both the stock market and the housing market crashed more or less simultane-ously. Nothing is a sure thing anymore.

- If you become a homeowner and fall on hard times, you can always rent out a room or the basement. Or you can rent out the entire house and move into a small apartment until you get your finances back in order.

The lessons for a cautious person like Sam are simple: Keep relatively more in your bank before you become a homeowner. When you do become an owner, buy what you need, not what you want. And consider lower-cost ownership options such as buying a condominium, joining a co-housing group, or purchasing a house from a community land trust.

Once you've saved enough for a down payment, investing in your local home is unquestionably a smarter investment than investing in the nonlocal stock market. Working in your favor is the quirky federal tax code, which allows you to claim a tax deduction for interest on your mortgage. If your federal tax rate is 21 percent, then every dollar of interest you pay can be discounted by 21 percent.[6] This especially helps you in the early years of a mortgage, when nearly all your payments are interest. In other words, your rent is effectively 21 percent lower per year, in addition to the benefits of growing an asset. Check out the adjacent box if you want to see the numbers. The example shows that for a house *with zero appreciation* over thirty years, the case for putting money into a home rather than a 401(k) is rock solid.

But Sam, like many homeowners we know, can make his monthly payments *and* still put some money into his 401(k). Wouldn't it make sense for him to do that? To answer this question, let's introduce another option: Rather than putting money into his 401(k), Sam decides to pay down his mortgage faster. As the sidebar "The Case for Paying Down Your Mortgage Faster" shows, this also proves to be more lucrative than a nonlocal retirement account.

Home investment gives a local investor one huge, indisputable advan-tage. As the custodian of your home and as a participating member of your community, you actually have the ability to increase the probability of your investments succeeding. You can improve your house through repairs, additions, and tender loving care. You can help create a fabulous neighborhood spirit. You can contribute to the success of your public schools. And once you own your home, free and clear, no knuckleheaded politician or CEO can take it away from you. Being an active investor, holding a real deed to real property, means you're less vulnerable to the next generation of Bernie Madoff–like fraudsters. In contrast, when you place your retirement money on Wall Street, you can only watch and pray.

Is there a limit to how far you can extend the logic of investing in local real estate for your retirement? At some point, the mortgage is paid. Wouldn't it make sense to invest in your 401(k) *then?* Nope. You could then trade in your house for a more valuable new home or invest in home improvements. As far as the IRS is concerned, you can write off up to $1 million of mortgage interest payments on your taxes. A million-dollar local investment in a house, again, is three or four times what the average American household has in wealth. This strategy therefore provides most American households with an ample opportunity to amass a realistic nest egg for retirement.

If you do not want to move, you could continue to build your nest egg by investing in a second home and taking the mortgage interest deduction for that. (If you start renting it, however, you lose the deduction.) From the standpoint of a local living economy, buying a second home might seem frivolous. Getting a second home arguably means using more energy, and it's environmentally destructive if the second home is built on previously undeveloped land. But you could buy a second home that's more energy-efficient, has a splendid greenhouse, and is sited in an existing, smart-growth neighborhood. Once your first home is paid off, you turn that into a rental, move into this eco-home, continue to grow your nest egg, and thereby lighten your environmental footprint. The point is that there are many creative ways to organize your investment in your homes without becoming an eco-villain.

If you have all the real estate you need, you might proceed to invest in houses you give or bequeath to your kids or grandkids. Invest in your family before you invest in Walmart.

Even if you believe you've saturated the opportunities for growing wealth

THE CASE FOR PAYING DOWN
YOUR MORTGAGE FASTER

To understand the rationale for Sam paying down his mortgage faster, rather than contributing to his nonlocal IRA, let's use as our baseline the assumptions from the previous box. Sam has taken out a thirty-year fixed mortgage on a $100,000 house, with $20,000 down. Based on an interest rate of 7 percent, his mortgage payments are $532 per month.

Sam decides he can save an extra $5,000 each year and wonders whether to put that money into his home or his IRA. If he uses it to make additional payments on his mortgage, he will have to pay $1,500 in income taxes at the end of each year. Spread over twelve months, $3,500 net amounts to an extra monthly payment of about $292. This additional payment allows Sam to pay off his mortgage in twelve years instead of thirty. He reduces his interest payments by a spectacular $73,362, and can begin enjoying the benefits of free rent in year thirteen instead of year thirty-one.

Sam's other option would be to put the $5,000 each year into a tax-deferred retirement account. By the middle of year thirteen, Sam's $5,000-per-year IRA contribution with 5 percent annual growth in

through your own bank and your own home, there's still more you can do to invest in yourself before dabbling in the risky world of Wall Street.

Become Your Own Utility

The typical U.S. household is spending about $3,500 per year on electricity, fuels, and water. If you're trying to get a 7 percent return on investment or better, you could spend $1,000 on dozens of kinds of efficiency measures that would save you more than $70 on your energy bill each year. You could use your $1,000 to buy a new high-efficiency refrigerator, oven, or washer the stock market yields $88,565. (Again, we use 5 percent instead of 7 percent, because we actually are measuring the ultimate tax impacts.)

What appears to be a small gain for Sam the Investor actually is wiped out by taxes. The gains from mortgage interest payment reduction come with no additional taxes, while the gains from the retirement account ultimately are taxed. His net from his retirement account is reduced to $61,996. When the mortgage is paid off, Sam the Owner comes out more than $11,000 ahead. And again, by paying down his mortgage faster, Sam can start accruing the benefits of being rent-free in year thirteen.

There is one wild card in all these calculations: interest rates. Over the past century, long-term interest rates have varied between 15.3 percent (in 1981) and 1 percent (today). Higher interest rates make buying a home a less attractive proposition. The reason why interest rates were high in the late 1970s and early 1980s, however, was galloping inflation. High inflation means that nominally attractive returns from all other alternative investments, like the stock market, must be heavily discounted as well. But high interest rates also make the potential payoffs from accelerating payment of the mortgage significantly greater. So some invest-in-yourself options look worse with higher interest rates, some better.

and dryer—plus you get the bonus of a brand-new appliance. Indeed, you probably can do much better than a 7 percent return. According to the U.S. Environmental Protection Agency, customers participating in many utility- or state-sponsored efficiency programs are saving 10 to 20 percent of their energy bills.[7] If Americans took full advantage of the more efficient appliances and took steps to improve the efficiency of their homes and buildings, they could cost-effectively save 10 to 30 percent on their energy bills per year.[8]

According to energy-efficiency expert Greg Pahl (author of another book in this series, on local renewable energy and efficiency), "Home energy efficiency retrofits are probably the best returns on investment you're going to get, as opposed to putting a windmill in your backyard. The home energy efficiency retrofits can pay for themselves, depending on where you happen to live and what the credits/incentives may be, in just a couple of years. Dramatic savings are realized very quickly. The money that you will be saving on your energy costs from these retrofits will make any further renewable energy system installations much more effective, and much more cost-effective."[9]

Of course, not every $1,000 investment in energy-efficiency equipment will make your house $1,000 more valuable upon resale—you may not be able to preserve all the principal invested. Some investments, like those in greater insulation, will increase your home value, while others, like appliances with a limited lifetime, won't. Economists sometimes call the latter a "wasting asset," which means it loses value over time, perhaps even immediately.

The entire discourse about energy-expenditure savings is oddly disconnected from that of long-term investment for retirement. Household efficiency measures are spoken of in terms of *years of payback*, with the investment *assumed* to contribute nothing to the long-term value of your house. If you install a thermal blanket around your hot-water heater that costs $200 and saves you $100 per year, it is said to have a two-year payback. Many regard paybacks beyond, say, five years as farther out on a limb than consumers are willing to go. A payback of six, seven, or ten years is too uncertain, too unreal, to be taken seriously. Yet in the world of 401(k)s, we are essentially asked to prioritize investing in a *forty-four-year payback*.[10]

For the remainder of this chapter, let's talk about "wasting assets" that nevertheless pay off for at least ten years. An investment of $1,000 in the stock market with a 5 percent return will be worth $1,629 at the end of year ten.[11] So if I invest $1,000 instead for triple-glazed, highly insulated windows in my house and those windows don't increase my house value by a penny, I will want an energy-bill reduction of at least $163 per year for ten years. Roughly speaking, then, for any wasting asset I need an investment in myself to pay off about 16 percent per year to beat the stock market.

The McKinsey Global Institute (part of McKinsey & Company, one of the nation's most respected business consulting firms) estimates that, worldwide, there's $170 billion of energy-efficiency investments possible by 2020 that could each generate an internal rate of return of at least 10 percent.[12] The *average* rate of return of all these investments, McKinsey believes, would be 17 percent.

Here's how someone like Sam the Saver should think about it: If his electricity bill is $2,000 per year, he would be smarter to apply the $5,000 he was going to put into his retirement savings into energy efficiency, as long as this meant he'd be able to reduce his energy bill by at least $800 (that's the 16 percent annual return). He could invest up to $12,250 if he could bring his entire energy bill down to zero. Of course, as electricity prices rise in the years ahead, Sam will be justified in investing significantly more.

If consumers had to make all these replacements themselves, even slam-dunk investment opportunities might be difficult to take advantage of. Who has time to study the options, shop for energy-efficiency devices, and make all these complicated calculations? But across the United States are private and public institutions ready to help.[13] New Jersey residents participating in the statewide program to replace inefficient heaters and air conditioners are saving $63 per year.[14] Pennsylvania is weatherizing the homes of low-income families and saving them $300 per year. New York State offers homeowners rebates on their investments in more efficient appliances, typically saving them $600 per year. And according to Energy Trust of Oregon, customers participating in its programs have collectively saved nearly $800 million on their energy bills.

Let's apply this thinking to an automobile: Suppose you drive fifteen thousand miles per year in an old, inefficient jalopy. If your clunker now gets fifteen miles per gallon, you're paying $4,000 for gasoline each year (assuming gas is $4 per gallon). Tripling your fuel efficiency to forty-five miles per gallon will save you about $2,150 per year. Let's assume that car will last for ten years. I could justify spending nearly $13,500 over those ten years on a more fuel-efficient car to get annual savings of $2,150 (16 percent return). With various federal and state tax credits for the purchase of high-efficiency automobiles, your payout could be significantly greater. And your high-efficiency car is likely to retain much of its value.

As was true for becoming your own landlord, you bump into limits on this investment strategy. Once you've become super-efficient, you again need to look for another place to put your money. Since the typical American household is spending $3,500 per year on utilities and $2,700 on gasoline, it will hit this ceiling once it invests $38,750 to become energy self-reliant.[15]

But there may be ways to go beyond this $38,750. Right now, many U.S.

utilities pay you to generate electricity for the grid. Put up your own wind-electric machine or photovoltaic array, and the utility will pay you for the surplus you sell back. Subdivisions and neighborhoods that work collectively to get themselves off the grid and get into the power-generation business may find themselves having a nice income supplement every month. The catch on this, for the moment, is that most utilities will allow you to run your meter back to zero but not negative. Many European governments, in contrast, have mandated "feed-in tariffs," where the utility not only must buy back your surplus but do so at a higher rate than your electricity bill. This has created a huge incentive for households, neighborhoods, and small businesses to get into the energy-production business. If U.S. states start to reform their utilities in this way, there may be no practical limit to how much you can invest in simple, renewable energy technology that easily will last as long as your house.

The logic of seizing every invest-in-yourself option that delivers better than a 16 percent rate of return can of course extend to other kinds of expenditures. It's worth investing $1,000 in water-efficiency measures, if you can bring down your annual water costs by $160. Or $1,000 in a home-based greenhouse, if you can bring down your food expenditures $160 per year. Or $1,000 in a great bicycle, if it reduces your driving costs by $160 per year. Or $1,000 in an Italian espresso maker, if it shrinks your Starbucks habit by $3.08 per week. But why stop there?

Invest in Your Potential

Warren Buffett says, "Generally speaking, investing in yourself is the best thing you can do—anything that improves your own talents. Nobody can take it away from you. They can run up huge deficits and the dollar could become worth far less, you're gonna have all kinds of things happen. But if you've got talent yourself and you've maximized your talent, you've got a terrific asset."[16]

Think of how many educational courses you could take, how many new skills you could acquire, or how many new degrees you could complete that would increase your earning power. Forget about enrolling in an expensive private university. Suppose you spend $10,000 per year over three years taking a bunch of classes to broaden your skills. If that $30,000 investment generates more than $4,800 in additional pretax income, your education will generate the needed 16 percent rate of return to do better than your tax-deferred IRA. Adrianne McVeigh, a management consultant and clinical psychologist in Atlanta, tells her clients that "the most successful executives and managers invest time and energy in their own self-development."[17]

Even if you're not prepared to change careers, there may be subtle tweaks of your lifestyle that could generate better than a 16 percent rate of return. Everyone knows that prevention of health problems is more cost-effective than treatment. The assumptions required to work out the cost–benefit numbers are admittedly rife with speculation, but there are plenty of low-cost ways most of us would agree would save us more than 16 percent per year. If you're a smoker, for example, investing several thousand uninsured dollars to quit can pay off in years of longer life with fewer maladies and health-care costs, as well as immediate savings by eliminating hundreds of dollars of cigarette purchases each year. There are similar, if perhaps less dramatic, payoffs by investing in whatever it takes—nutrition classes, exercise programs, spending more cooking healthy meals—to reap the myriad benefits of a healthier you.

Hey, Wait a Minute!

Have I gone too far with these arguments? I can imagine two objections. The first is something I've hinted at throughout this chapter—that smart investors will do everything on my list, *plus* save funds in their tax-deferred retirement accounts.

But I hope I've made it clear how far you can go before you should even think about a retirement account. Let's review: $50,000 to $100,000 for your own bank, $1 million for real estate, $38,750 for energy efficiency, who knows how much for your own education and earning potential—this is well beyond what 90 percent of American families ever dream about saving for their retirement. The average American household has an after-tax income of just over $46,000, and few will retire with anything approaching $1 million to their name.

The second objection might be that I'm comparing apples and oranges. Money saved is not the same as money invested—and ultimately, you do need cash or some kind of income-paying asset to live on when you retire. Your reduced electricity bill will not pay your grocery bill after you turn sixty-five. To make this analysis work, you have to be committed to capturing your savings and placing them into some kind of savings account or asset that ultimately pays you an income stream. But, again, there's no reason that asset cannot be your home. And each year, you can take your savings and plow them back into home improvements. When you're ready to retire, sell the home, move into more modest digs, and then place your savings into very safe, low-risk, local securities.

Whatever you think of strategies of investing in yourself, there's one overarching advantage to them over every other local-investment strategy discussed thus far: *You* are the person principally responsible for whether or not the investments pay off. You have the ability to improve your home, to tweak your energy-efficiency systems, and to upgrade your own personal earning power through the right class. You can bring down the risks of your investments going sour. You are the star of your own investment firm.

And it's in this spirit that I present one final tool to consider, what's effectively the secret weapon of local investors—namely, the self-directed IRA. Even though the tool is mainstream enough that a *For Dummies* guidebook has been written on it, 99 percent of Americans—even 99 percent of sophisticated investors—appear to be unaware of it.

DIY Retirement Funds

Tom Anderson is the founder of PENSCO, one of the largest providers of self-directed IRAs in the country, and until he recently retired he served as its CEO. "After twenty-two years of operation I'm proud that PENSCO has an A+ rating from the Better Business Bureau," he boasts, "and we've got $3.5 billion under administration. From a customer satisfaction standpoint, we're performing better than some of the top banks in the country."

Anderson is also the president of the Retirement Industry Trust Association (RITA). "We almost exclusively handle self-directed IRAs and retirement accounts as custodians, which means we provide the means to hold IRA and individual pension plans under the laws governed by the Internal Revenue Service. We hold their assets in custody, execute our clients' investment instructions, and report the value of their holdings—on an annual basis to the IRS and on a monthly basis to our clients. We also provide all the other traditional services, including Internet access to your account, and your ability to do all kinds of transactions, purchases, sales, transfers, and distributions. Basically we do everything that's required to keep your plan compliant with the law. And that's about it!"

The difference, of course, is *what* you can invest in. "Unlike broker-dealers or traditional banks, we're dealing with myriad asset types those institutions don't handle. For example, a broker-dealer like Schwab or Merrill Lynch generally will just handle traded assets like stocks, bonds, and mutual funds, and those assets are essentially processed electronically these days. Our systems and personnel are very specialized as every transaction is unique— sort of like a handmade shoe.

"We can do anything that is not prohibited by law," Anderson asserts confidently, "from buying forty head of cattle and putting ear tags on them in the name of your IRA, to buying a property underwater off the coast of Miami. There are only three asset types that a self-directed IRA can't buy: collectibles (antiques, artwork, a 1957 Corvette, alcoholic beverages, et cetera), life insurance, and the stock of subchapter S corporations. So, for example, we have bought fishing rights in the state of Alaska, really just a map of the ocean that allows somebody to fish—in this case for black cod—over a period of time. We then rent out these rights to smaller fishermen. We have helped start thousands of traditional businesses through early-stage capital, either at the very beginning like start-ups or with mezzanine financing. At this time there's very little credit out there for new-business innovation, and service providers like us are stepping into the gap."

You could use a self-directed IRA to put tax-deferred dollars into almost every local-investment option discussed in this book. The one prohibition is on personal use of the funds. You can't invest in your daughter's house, for example, or a business in which your spouse has greater than 50 percent ownership. But you can invest in almost every other type of local investment discussed in this book. That means that you can support a friend or neighbor's personal project. You even can invest in your neighbor's house. In Canada, where the rules around self-directed retirement funds are very similar to those here, a company in Calgary is being formed to enable groups of neighbors to invest in one another's homes, enjoy the tax benefits of mortgages, and avoid the high interest charges of mortgage banks.

Suppose you know someone who wants to borrow money to buy furniture or put her kids through college. You know she has plenty of assets, but they're tied up in the house or in a typical pension fund, so you're confident about getting paid back. You could use a self-directed IRA to loan her the money at, say, 5 percent annual interest—or whatever interest rate you preferred. And taxes on your gains would be entirely deferred.

What about the risks? Anderson isn't worried: "Harry Markowitz devised modern portfolio theory and got a Nobel Prize in economics for it. He found that if you diversify broadly into noncorrelated assets, you're going to significantly reduce risk to your portfolio and optimize it for possible gain. A self-directed IRA does this, because it gets away from having exclusively one asset class—stocks and mutual funds, which are sort of the same and both subject to systemic risk. When the market goes down, all these typical pension assets will go down accordingly. If you spread your chips around the table, you have a much better chance of not losing them all."

Anderson wishes that more Americans knew about self-directed IRAs. He believes that most retirement accounts are dangerously undiversified. In fact, according to most current statistics available from Investment Company Institute (ICI), more than 95 percent of all IRA assets are invested in the markets in one fashion or another. "These are an individual's most valuable portfolios due to their tax-deferred or tax-free status, and if any portfolio should be diversified it should be your retirement account."

On the flip side, self-directed IRAs provide a great source of investment capital and support innovation through the launch of new businesses. "The most significant success we had at PENSCO," recalls Anderson, "involved a group of entrepreneurs who came into our office in 1999 and wanted to start a business on the Internet. They were going to use a traditional IRA, but I suggested they use Roth IRAs because the gains would be tax-free. So they started this company, and the lead investor put in $1,800, because he didn't have any more. The limit at the time was $2,000. The others put in a certain amount, most of them the maximum contribution amount. Approximately three years later they sold the company to a national firm, and the CEO, the guy who put the $1,800 in, now had multiple millions in his Roth IRA. Then he took those millions in his Roth and became a lead investor in a whole bunch of other start-ups, which grew his IRA to hundreds of millions. All from his $1,800 investment!"

So why don't more people use this technique? Anderson thinks most Americans don't believe they are capable of handling their own finances. "People are accustomed to the normal contributory IRA. They get a solicitation from their bank in April just before tax time to take a deduction, they fill out a little form, and put $2,000 or $4,000 into an account, and it just sort of sits there. They don't pay a whole lot of attention to it. The whole process is relatively passive."

The custodian of a self-directed IRA, in contrast, cannot be the decision maker. That's what *self-directed* means: It's up to you. "I'm not allowed by law and contract to give advice to my own clients under our charter," says Anderson. "So if you want to invest in rental property in Idaho, you need to find a broker, you need to pick a property, you've got to evaluate it. Then you instruct the custodian to execute the deal. What we can do as a custodian, though, is provide a lot of information and education."

Because self-directed custodians cannot provide investment advice, those who use self-directed IRAs need to be financially literate, or work with a qualified adviser. "The kinds of customers we typically get are people who have been working for many years, who accumulate assets for ten or twenty years, and who are either retiring or changing jobs. When they change jobs, they have the ability to access their account pension plan and then roll it to an IRA. That inspires them. They think they can do better. They're generally people who know how investing works. Many are people who are successful, who have accumulated a good amount of money, and who are used to being decision makers. So they have the characteristics that are really helpful for being successful in a self-directed IRA."

One of Anderson's unrealized visions is to see the advent of an investment vehicle that would help his clients invest in public charities. "United Catholic Charities has hundreds of thousands of constituents. They might say in their newsletter that in addition to donating, you can make loans with us through your IRA, and we'll use that money for income-producing schools or other investment projects. I always thought this kind of program would take off like wildfire, because the money is just sitting there. There's $4 trillion in IRAs—more money than there is in defined contribution plans like 401(k)s. Nobody is championing this idea."

Anderson is confident that, sooner or later, someone will. "If you can light a fire under the whole idea—let's face it, all charities are hurting right now, they're not getting their traditional levels of donations because of the economy—all that money sitting in IRAs could be really helpful."

In the meantime, Anderson is using his new time in "retirement" to educate influential politicians, government officials, and regulators about the importance of growing the self-directed IRA industry. "Many in Washington take the view that people aren't capable of handling a self-directed account—this social-democratic attitude that we've got to take care of everybody, and that the government can do a better job managing your savings than you can. In light of the issues with Social Security and Medicare, one might be skeptical. Some have even proposed to make IRAs like pension plans, which would essentially lock everybody into the stock markets and virtually eliminate other investment options. I have to tell you that there's still a whole lot of naïveté in the government about investment and retirement issues. Many don't realize that the problem [causing the recent financial meltdown] wasn't the 401(k)s; it was that people were locked into them and they couldn't get out of their mutual funds fast enough."

A Personal Confession

Up until this point, I've been mum about my own personal investment strategy. Most authors in the investment field brag about their own brilliance and self-made wealth. Not me. To be honest, this book is a reflection on the many things I have done wrong in my investment life—and the beginning of my own rehabilitation. I never created a Bank of Michael. I didn't prioritize buying a home until I turned forty, instead unwisely pouring my extra money into the retirement ratholes hawked at my workplaces. My then-wife and I consistently spent well beyond our means—mostly on two private school tuitions—and foolishly racked up tens of thousands of dollars of credit card debt to underwrite this defensible but financially punishing choice. Periodically, we refinanced our home to pay off the credit cards, a technique that came screeching to a halt during the financial crisis. Like a perfect storm, Wall Street collapsed and the housing bubble burst when we decided to part ways, which forced us to raid our much-diminished assets to split our properties and pay off our debts.

Having just turned fifty-five, I'm now in the unenviable position of essentially starting from scratch. But I've learned some important lessons—about living within my means, about creating a cushion of savings, and about no longer getting snookered by the stock market or relying on a housing bubble again. Clearly I'm not alone. This past week a report appeared saying that 38 percent of all homes in America with second mortgages—mostly people, like myself, who took out home equity lines to pay off credit cards—were "under water," a euphemism for the home being worthless (or worse, since the debt on the home is greater than its value). Despite my Stanford education, my degrees in economics and law, my well-above-average income over many years, I fell into exactly the same traps as most Americans have. So one reason I wrote this book was to suggest for all Americans that another way, with less risk and more reward, is possible. And urgently necessary.

A personal presence throughout this project has been my dad, Jack J. Shuman, who died in December 2010 at the age of eighty-nine after a short, awful bout with amyloidosis. His life, his final days, and now his memories have swirled around me as I wrote (hence the dedication). In the basement of his house in Chesterfield, Missouri, are budget books kept throughout his adult life, where he meticulously recorded every penny of expenditure from 1948 on. Through methodical planning and modest spending habits that would have impressed even Sam the Saver, my parents were able to squirrel away enough of their middle-class salaries to own their home, pay for their kids' college educations, and live off my dad's telephone company pension comfortably for almost thirty years of retirement. My dad never did well in the stock market, and never expected to. The core of his wealth was his home and his family, and their primary investment strategy was a careful, modest lifestyle. Dad knew what mattered.

Today all of us in America are being similarly called upon to rethink our financial lives. We came to embrace the illusions sold to us by Wall Street that our stock portfolios and our houses would continue to grow by 10, 20, even 50 percent per year, and we spent like drunken sailors on that assumption. We used our homes as money machines in the conviction that their prices would escalate forever. Our political representatives did the same thing, with conservatives returning surpluses because "it's your money" and liberals upping entitlement benefits because "you earned it." The entire country is now in receivership, and the party is over.

We now have to clean up the mess left behind, both personally and as patriots. The core message of this book is we all need to return to basics, to realize that the secret to our wealth and financial security isn't in the casino of the global economy. We need to invest in our savings accounts so we stay out of debt. We need to invest in ourselves—our families, our talents, our own homes—and enjoy the rewards. And then, if we still have extra dollars, we need to invest in local businesses we know and we trust, so that our families, our neighbors, and our communities become our true sources of wealth.

The unappreciated treasure in our own backyards is the theme of Jean-Françoise Dumont's children's book *A Blue So Blue*. A boy who loves to paint the color blue is haunted by his inability to find the one shade of blue that has mesmerized him in his dreams.[18] He goes on a search around the world to find that blue—to the ocean, to the tropics, to a Mississippi blues bar—and yet he can't seem to find it. He travels to the desert where a mystical chief with a blue turban offers a clue: What he is searching for "may never have been far away." And suddenly the boy realizes where he has seen that magical shade of blue. It was right at home, in his mother's eyes.

Introduction

1. Graham Bowley, "Dow Falls 1,000, Then Rebounds, Shaking Market," *New York Times*, 7 May 2010.
2. Federal Reserve, "Flow of Funds Accounts of the United States," 4th Quarter 2010, 10 March 2011.
3. William E. Rees, "Thinking 'Resilience,'" in Richard Heinberg and Daniel Lerch, eds., *The Post Carbon Reader: Managing the 21st Century's Sustainability Crises* (Healdsburg, CA: Watershed Media, 2010), p. 27.

Chapter 1. A Living Rate of Return

1. Ric Edelman, *The Truth About Money* (Washington, DC: Georgetown University Press, 1996), pp. 215–17 (emphasis in original). I don't mean to pick on Ric Edelman personally, because in the dark universe of stock hawkers, he's one of the more personable, astute, and honest ones. But his rhetorical tricks are emblematic of the entire profession.
2. Ibid., p. 114.
3. At the start of 2010, a U.S. Social Investment Forum study showed $3.07 trillion of professionally managed assets in SRI funds. See U.S. SIF's "2010 Trends Report" (www.ussif.org/resources/pubs/trends).
4. "Sell Your Stocks, MIT Sloan Professor Urges Small Investors Saving for Retirement," States News Service, 12 March 2009.
5. This and subsequent market calculations use data developed by Robert Shiller of Yale University, which are available for download at www.econ.yale.edu/~shiller/data.htm. I calculate monthly returns for the S&P by subtracting each month's real price from the preceding month's real price, and then I add one-twelfth of the real dividends (each month's dividend listing is an annualized number). Shiller removes inflation by adjusting nominal numbers by the consumer price index.
6. Edelman, *Truth About Money*, p. 254.
7. Treasury Department Series I Savings Bonds return rates are set every May and November, and historical rates can be found online here: www.treasurydirect.gov/indiv/research/indepth/ibonds/res_ibonds_iratesandterms.htm.
8. Elizabeth Warren, interview by Lowell Bergman, "Secret History of the Credit Card," *Frontline*, PBS and *The New York Times*, November, 2004, http://www.pbs.org/wgbh/pages/frontline/shows/credit/view/#rest.
9. Anne Colamosca and William Wolman, *The Great 401(k) Hoax* (Cambridge, MA: Perseus Books, 2002).
10. Sam could retire at fifty-nine and a half and begin taking money from IRA and 401(k) accounts then. He also could contribute to both, if he chose, until he turned seventy and a half. If he were a true workaholic, he could continue putting money in a Roth IRA until

he turned eighty-five! The assumption that Sam retires at sixty-five is to model what most Americans would regard as a typical retirement scenario.

11. The federal tax rate for the average U.S. household, according to the Congressional Budget Office, was 20.4 percent in 2007. Catherine Rampell, "How Much Americans Actually Pay in Taxes," *New York Times*, 8 April 2009. Households in the top 20 percent of income paid 25.8 percent, and in the top 1 percent about 33 percent. The average household expenditure on state and local taxes was slightly below 10 percent in 2009. Blake Ellis, "Tax Burden Falls for First Time in Decade," *USA Today*, 23 February 2011. We assume, in our calculations, a total tax rate of 30 percent. States vary on how they treat retirement accounts, but for purposes of our calculations we'll assume that retirement accounts are fully sheltered when the savings are made and fully taxed when they are withdrawn.

12. Here are the details: 4 percent of $529,000 is about $20,000. Taking out 30 percent in taxes leaves $14,000. On a monthly basis that's $1,167.

13. Stephen Gandel, "Why It's Time to Retire the 401(k)," *Time*, 9 October 2009.

14. Ibid.

15. Ibid.

Chapter 2. Zero-Cost Stimulus

1. Edward L. Glaeser and William R. Kerr, "The Secret to Job Growth: Think Small," *Harvard Business Review*, July–August 2010.

2. David A. Fleming and Stephan J. Goetz, "Does Local Firm Ownership Matter?" *Economic Development Quarterly*, August 2011, pp. 277-81.

3. The NETS database, based on Dun & Bradstreet data mining, is available at www .youreconomy.org.

4. The Austin study is "Economic Impact Analysis: A Case Study," monograph (Austin, TX: Civic Economics, December 2002). It can be found at www.civiceconomics.com.

5. Most of these studies were conducted by Civic Economics and can be downloaded at www.civiceconomics.com. The Maine study is "The Economic Impact of Locally Owned Businesses vs. Chains: A Case Study in Midcoast Maine," monograph (Minneapolis: Institute for Local Self-Reliance, September 2003). The Toledo study is Gbenga Ajilore, "Toledo–Lucas County Merchant Study," monograph (Toledo: Urban Affairs Center, 21 June 2004). The Iowa study is David Swenson, "The Economic Impact of Ethanol Production in Iowa," monograph (Ames: Iowa State University, January 2008).

6. See, for example, IHS Global Insight, "The Economic Impact of Wal-Mart," November 2005.

7. Stacy Mitchell, "Localism Index," 1 March 2011 (www.newrules.org/retail/news/ localism-index).

8. Manufacturers, given their slightly larger average economies of scale, are slightly less likely to be locally owned.

9. Matissa N. Hollister, "Does Firm Size Matter Anymore? The New Economy and Firm Size Wage Effects," *American Sociological Review* 69 (October 2004), pp. 659–76.

10. See generally Thomas Michael Power, *Environmental Protection and Economic Well-Being* (Armonk, NY: M. A. Sharpe, 1996).

11. Don Grant, et al., "Are Subsidiaries More Prone to Pollute?," *Social Science Quarterly*, 84:1 (March 2003), pp. 162-173.

12. Alan Peters and Peter Fisher, "The Failures of Economic Development Incentives," *Journal of the American Planning Association* 70:1 (Winter 2004), p. 28.

13. Sherri Buri McDonald and Christian Wihtol, "Small Businesses: The Success Story," (Eugene, OR) *Register-Guard*, 10 August 2003.

14. This is on a gross-jobs basis—the total number of nonlocal jobs created versus the total number of local jobs created. Remember, however, that many of the nonlocal jobs did not stay. On a net-jobs basis (after the big departures), nonlocal jobs were thirty-three times more expensive.

15. Michael H. Shuman, *The Small-Mart Revolution: How Local Businesses Are Beating the Global Competition* (San Francisco: Berrett-Koehler, 2006), pp. 202–208.

16. Richard Florida, *The Rise of the Creative Class* (New York: Basic Books, 2002).

17. C. Wright Mills and Melville Ulmer, "Small Business and Civic Welfare," in *Report of the Smaller War Plants Corporation to the Special Committee to Study Problems of American Small Business*, Document 135, U.S. Senate, 79th Congress, 2nd session, February 13 (Washington, DC: U.S. Government Printing Office, 1946).

18. Thomas A. Lyson, "Big Business and Community Welfare: Revisiting a Classic Study," monograph (Ithaca, NY: Cornell University Department of Rural Sociology, 2001), p. 3.

19. Ibid., 14.

20. Robert Putnam, *Making Democracy Work* (Princeton, NJ: Princeton University Press, 1993).

21. Thad Williamson, David Imbroscio, and Gar Alperovitz, *Making a Place for Community: Local Democracy in a Global Era* (New York: Routledge, 2003), p. 8.

22. Judith D. Schwartz, "Buying Local: How It Boosts the Economy," *Time*, 11 June 2009.

23. Available from the Library of Economics and Liberty, at www.econlib.org/library/Columns/y2011/LuskNorwoodlocavore.html.

24. Allison Arieff, "The Future of Manufacturing Is Local," *New York Times*, 27 March 2011.

25. This statement is true whether one uses the Small Business Administration's threshold for small business (five hundred employees or fewer), or a more demanding threshold (one hundred employees or fewer).

26. See www.goodjobsfirst.org/states/south-carolina.

27. U.S. Census Bureau, *Form FT900, U.S. Trade in Goods and Services*, Current Release: July 2011.

28. U.S. Census Bureau, *Statistical Abstract 2009*, table 722, p. 483. The data cited are from 2005.

29. Shuman, *Small-Mart Revolution*, pp.65–66.

30. The International Energy Agency, in its "World Energy Outlook 2010" report, says that peak (conventional) oil production was reached in 2006 and forecasts a need for new alternative energy sources. For a primer on peak oil issues, the Post Carbon Institute's *Energy Bulletin* is a good starting point (www.energybulletin.net/primer.php).

31. There is disagreement about how far efficiency and renewables can go. An optimistic view is Amory B. Lovins, et al., *Winning the Oil Endgame: Innovation for Profits, Jobs, and Security* (Snowmass, CO: Rocky Mountain Institute, 2004). A more pessimistic view is Richard Heinberg, "Searching for a Miracle: Net Energy Limits & the Fate of Industrial Society" (www.postcarbon.org/report/44377-searching-for-a-miracle).

32. See, for example, Jane Jacobs, *The Economy of Cities* (New York: Vintage, 1969) and Jane Jacobs, *Cities and the Wealth of Nations* (New York: Vintage, 1985), pp. 99–101.

33. Jonathan Tirone, "'Dead-End' Austrian Town Blossoms with Green Energy," *International Herald Tribune*, 28 August 2007.

34. Marian Burros, "Uniting Around Food to Save an Ailing Town," *New York Times*, 8 October 2008.

35. Michael H. Shuman, "TINA vs. LOIS: The Small-Mart Revolution," *Sockeye Magazine* 12:1 (Autumn 2007), pp. 22–23.

36. Jeff Faux, "How NAFTA Failed Mexico: Immigration Is Not a Development Policy," *The American Prospect*, July–August 2003, pp. 35–37.

37. Ibid.

38. A government study found that while decreased maquiladora employment could be a result of the U.S. economic cycles, "industry sources and other experts noted that Mexico's maquiladoras also face increased global competition in the U.S. market, particularly from China, Central America and the Caribbean" (www.gao.gov/new.items/d03891.pdf).

39. *Now with Bill Moyers*, PBS, 19 December 2003 (www.pbs.org/now/transcript/transcript247_full.html). A good summary of current Walmart research can be found here: www.walmartmovie.com/facts.php.

40. Allan Chernoff, "Boycott BP Movement," CNNMoney, May 26, 2010 (http://money.cnn.com/2010/05/26/news/companies/boycott_BP/index.htm); Rich Blake, "Boycotting

BP: Who Gets Hurt?" ABC News, 2 June 2010 (http://abcnews.go.com/Business/bp-boycotts-spreading-frustration-oil-spill-boils/story?id=10800309).

41. Differentiating one's product through higher labor standards is just one of more than a dozen strategies that local food businesses are using worldwide to compete effectively against multinationals. For an in-depth review, see Michael H. Shuman, et al., *Community Food Enterprise: Local Success in a Global Marketplace* (Arlington, VA: Winrock International, 2010), available for free download at www.communityfoodenterprise.org.

42. Milton Friedman, "The Social Responsibility of Business Is to Increase Its Profits," *New York Times*, Magazine Section, 13 September 1970, p. 125.

43. Thanks to Laury Hammel for this amusing phrase.

44. For deeper exploration of these opportunities, see Michael H. Shuman and Kate Poole, *Growing Local Living Economies: A Grassroots Approach to Economic Development* (Bellingham, WA: BALLE, 2011).

Chapter 3. The Hidden Power of Cooperatives

1. Steven Deller, Ann Hoyt, Brent Hueth, and Reka Sundaram-Stukel, "Research on the Economic Impact of Cooperatives" (Madison: University of Wisconsin Center for Cooperatives, 19 June 2009).

2. Joe Folsom, "Measuring the Economic Impact of Cooperatives in Minnesota," *RBS Research Report 200* (Washington, DC: USDA Rural Business Cooperative Service, December 2003).

3. Co-ops do actually appear in the Affordable Care Act, as a recent Internal Revenue Service request for public comment points out: "Section 1322 of the Affordable Care Act requires the Department of Health and Human Services (HHS) to establish the Consumer Operated and Oriented Plan program (CO-OP program). The purpose of the CO-OP program is to foster the creation of qualified nonprofit health insurance issuers to offer qualified health plans in individual and small group markets. The CO-OP program will make available to qualified nonprofit health insurance issuers loans to provide assistance in meeting start-up costs and/or repayable grants to provide assistance in meeting any state solvency requirements."

4. General Accounting Office, "The Cooperative Model as a Potential Component of Structural Reform Options for Fannie Mae and Freddie Mac: Briefing to Congress," GAO-11-33R (Washington, DC: GAO, November 2010).

5. Safeway recently moved its corporate headquarters from Oakland to Pleasanton, California.

6. The Rochdale Principles can be read here: www.ica.coop/coop/principles.html.

7. Driven largely by the special tax treatment given to cooperatives under Subchapter T of the Internal Revenue Code, *patronage* is a term of art in the cooperative context. For consumer cooperatives, patronage refers to retail purchases. At worker co-ops, the term refers to labor inputs. For agricultural marketing co-ops like Sunkist and Organic Valley, patronage equals the commodities that member-farmers provide the cooperative for processing and resale.

8. Small consumer co-ops, however, may lose some of this pricing advantage because of their sub-optimal scale.

9. "Alternative Co-ops Are Taking Root," *Daily Yonder* (www.dailyyonder.com), 21 August 2010.

10. John Pencavel, *Worker Participation: Lessons from Worker Co-ops of the Pacific Northwest* (New York: Russell Sage Foundation, 2001).

11. Henry M. Levin, "Worker Democracy and Worker Productivity," *Social Justice Research* 19:1 (January 2006), p. 9.

12. "Alternative Co-ops," *Daily Yonder*.

13. Ibid.

14. 421 U.S. 837.

15. See www.foodcoopinitiative.coop.

16. See, for example, David Thompson, "Remember the Member: Co-ops Are in a Capital Revolution," *Cooperative Grocer*, January–February 2009.

17. Section 529 of the Internal Revenue Service Code.
18. Thompson, "Remember the Member," p. 8.
19. Gar Alperovitz, Ted Howard, and Thad Williamson, "The Cleveland Model," *The Nation*, 11 February 2010.
20. Erbin Crowell, "Mondragon and the United Steelworkers: New Opportunity for the Co-op and Labor Movements," *Cooperative Grocer*, January–February 2010, p. 8.

Chapter 4. Institutional Lending

1. Charles Ou and Victoria Williams, "Lending to Small Businesses by Financial Institutions in the United States," in *A Compendium of Research by the Small Business Administration's Office of Advocacy* (Washington, DC: SBA, July 2009), p. 28.
2. Stacy Mitchell, "Banks and Small Business Lending," *Huffington Post*, 9 February 2010.
3. Ibid.
4. Stacy Mitchell, "Credit Unions Hang Tough, See Surge in Deposits," *Huffington Post*, 22 June 2010.
5. Thomas Hoenig, Field Hearing Before the Subcommittee on Oversight and Investigations of the Committee on Financial Services, U.S. House of Representatives, 111th Congress, 23 August 2010, Serial No. 111-151.
6. Ibid.
7. Susan Witt, "Testimony of SHARE," given to the House Select Committee on Hunger, 14 April 1988.
8. Ibid.
9. The majority of shareholders now are unaccredited, though redemptions could change this.
10. See at www.sustainlane.com.
11. Brad Masi, Leslie Schaller, and Michael H. Shuman, "The 25% Shift: The Benefits of Food Localization for Northeast Ohio and How to Realize Them," monograph (Cleveland: ParkWorks, December 2010). Using IMPLAN, an input–output economic model, the study analyzed the degree to which local food businesses were meeting local demand in every food-business category, and in most they were below 100 percent. The 25 percent shift measured the impact of growing local businesses in every category one-quarter of the way toward 100 percent.
12. Ellen Brown, "The Mysterious CAFRs: How Stagnant Pools of Government Money Could Help Save the Economy," *Huffington Post*, 21 May 2010 (www.huffingtonpost.com/ellen-brown/the-mysterious-cafrs-how_b_585011.html).
13. Rob Garver, "Reluctant Role Model," *U.S. Banker*, April 2011.
14. "Oregon State Bank Analysis—Revised," monograph (Madison, WI: Center for State Innovation, December 2010).

Chapter 5. Anti-Poverty Investing

1. Gal Alperovitz, Steve Dubb, and Ted Howard, "Rebuilding America's Communities: A Comprehensive Community Wealth Building Federal Policy Proposal," monograph (College Park, MD: The Democracy Collaborative, 2010), p. 11.
2. Ibid.
3. Rich Cohen, "A Call for Mission-Based Investing by America's Private Foundations," monograph (Washington, DC: National Center for Responsive Philanthropy, September 2005).
4. See the broad critique of foundation investment practices from Mark Dowie in *American Foundations: An Investigative History* (Cambridge, MA: MIT Press, 2002).
5. According to the Internal Revenue Service, the total assets of private foundations is about half a trillion dollars. The Foundation Center reports that in 2006–2007 foundations gave $734 million in PRIs. Steven Lawrence, "Doing Good with Foundation Assets," from *PRI Directory* (New York: Foundation Center, 2010).
6. "Faith, Hope, and Capital," broadcast by PBS. Interview by Lynn Adler and Jim Mayer.

7. Vermont Sustainable Jobs Fund, "Farm to Plate Strategic Plan," monograph (Montpelier: Vermont Sustainable Jobs Fund, July 2011), available at www.vsjf.org/project-details/5/farm-to-plate-initiative.

Chapter 6. If I Were a Rich Man . . .

1. There are other exemptions that we discuss elsewhere in this book, like the federal exemption for agricultural cooperatives used by Organic Valley. For a complete list of exemptions, see the resources of the Sustainable Economy Law Center (www.theselc.org).

Chapter 7. Unaccredited Investing in SEC-Land

1. While prepaid discount cards do not trigger federal securities law, they could trigger securities laws in some states that apply the "risk capital test."
2. Thus far, the Kiva model has not been challenged in any state.
3. Jenna Wortham, "A Few Dollars at a Time, Patrons Support Artists on the Web," *New York Times*, 25 August 2009.
4. I wonder, for example, about the transnational implications of P2P activities. Seedrs, the UK equity site, allows all kinds of investors to support local business. What's the implication of a crazy quilt of national securities laws that allow Americans to make equity investments in small businesses in Great Britain but not the United States? How long will it take before a web-savvy entrepreneur sets up—in, say, Liberia—an "Invest-in-da-Bronx" website that creates a Bronx-only equity portfolio and accepts investment only from Bronx residents? Would the SEC really put pressure on Liberia to stop it?
5. Michael H. Shuman, "Local Stock Exchanges & National Stimulus," *Community Development Investment Review* 5:2 (2009), pp. 81–84.
6. Sustainable Economies Law Center, Letter to Elizabeth Murphy, "RE: Petition for Rulemaking: Exempt Securities Offerings Up to $100,000 with $100 Maximum Per Investor from Registration," 1 July 2010.
7. Denise Edgington, "From Steak Holders to Stakeholders," *Inc.*, 1 March 1997.

Chapter 8. Local Exchanges

1. The numbers vary enormously, by industry and by situation, but the academic literature estimates at least a 25 percent discount for illiquidity, and anecdotally, business owners cite much steeper discounts. See "Estimating the Liquidity Discount" (pages.stern.nyu.edu/~adamodar/pdfiles/eqnotes/pvt.pdf). For an anecdotal account, also see Loraine MacDonald, "Valuation of Private vs. Public Firms" (www.entrepreneur.com/growyourbusiness/sellingyourbusiness/article41972.html).
2. See the SEC response to Real Goods (www.sec.gov/divisions/investment/noaction/1996/realgoods062496.pdf).

Chapter 9. Everybody into the Pool!

1. Among the exemptions the Investment Act says are not included in its coverage of investment companies are: "(4) Any person substantially all of whose business is confined to making small loans, industrial banking, or similar business. (5) Any person who is not engaged in the business of issuing redeemable securities, face-amount certificates of the installment type or periodic payment plan certificates, and who is primarily engaged in one or more of the following businesses: (A) Purchasing or otherwise acquiring notes, drafts, acceptances, open accounts receivable, and other obligations representing part or all of the sales price of merchandise, insurance, and services; (B) making loans to manufacturers, wholesalers, and retailers of, and to prospective purchasers of, specified merchandise, insurance, and services; and (C) purchasing or otherwise acquiring mortgages and other liens on and interest in real estate."
2. Many choose to invest in state-specific municipal bond funds because of tax breaks (see

information on tax breaks for state bonds at personal.vanguard.com/us/insights/taxcenter/state-specific-tax).

3. Corsell elaborates: "For a mutual fund—a fund that sells and redeems its shares every business day—to receive the special tax treatment afforded to registered investment companies under the federal tax laws, at least 50 percent of the assets of the fund must be invested so that no company represents more than 5 percent of the fund's assets. Additionally, no more than 25 percent of the fund's assets may be invested in any single company."

4. "Taking Action on Job Creation: Invest Michigan! Fund," *Dispatch, Progressive States Network*, 21 November 2008 (www.progressivestates.org/news/dispatch/taking-action-on-job-creation-invest-michigan-fund).

5. Ibid.

6. See, for example, Edward Glaeser, "Local Pension Funds Should Invest Farther Afield," *Boston Globe*, 5 May 2011, citing a study by Yael Hochbert and Joshua Rauh, two Northwestern economists who found that in-state investments generated 8.62 percent less annually than out-of-state investments (available at www.kellogg.northwestern.edu/faculty/hochberg/htm/HR.pdf). All the "in-state" investments, however, turn out to be "in-state" hedge and venture funds that then invest in global companies.

7. Not every state follows the SEC on this. To check out how your state securities regulations apply to investment clubs, you can follow these links and resources provided by the SEC: www.sec.gov/investor/pubs/invclub.htm.

Chapter 10. Investing in Yourself

1. ABC News' *Good Morning America*, "Warren Buffett's Tips for How You Can Make Money Now," 10 July 2009.

2. "Take Control of Your Credit Cards," *Consumer Reports* 72:11 (November 2009), pp. 16–19.

3. For this and other examples in this chapter, we will focus on traditional tax-deferred IRA and 401(k) options. The calculations would change a bit for Roth IRAs, where the taxes are paid up front, but not the conclusion. The traditional retirement accounts are far more common than the Roths.

4. Another quibble might be with my assumption that a given mortgage payment will buy as much house as an identical rent payment. The relationship between rent and mortgage is a complex one and varies over time and over markets. Robert Shiller argues that one sign that housing is in a bubble is whether mortgage rates grow faster than rent rates. The assumption here is that mindful housing shoppers decide in advance how much they can afford, and then look at the two scenarios accordingly. Shiller, *Irrational Exuberance*.

5. Shiller, p. 22: "People are living in larger homes than they were decades ago and are spread out over more properties, more people are living in a house by themselves, more children are moving out and starting their own homes rather than living with their parents until marriage. How could they afford this if home prices were rising steeply? This suggests that in the United States real home price growth must have been less than real per capital person income growth, which was 2% a year from 1929 to 2003."

6. See chapter 1, note 11, infra.

7. U.S. Environmental Protection Agency, "Energy Efficiency: Reduce Energy Bills, Protect the Environment" (http://www.epa.gov/cleanenergy/documents/suca/consumer_fact_sheet.pdf).

8. Ibid.

9. Personal communication, 20 July 2011.

10. At the core of this contradiction are different, and inconsistent, views about discount rates. For years, economists discounted the costs and benefits for a given infrastructure project, like a highway or an airport, at 5 percent per year. No one knew exactly where the 5 percent number came from, but economists nevertheless happily applied it. The result was that long-term costs and risks were essentially discounted away, which meant that it didn't matter if

the bridge you were building collapsed in forty years. The world clearly doesn't work this way, and the discount obsession has been quietly discarded. But it's worth pointing out that putting utility savings in terms of years of payback, rather than on the same rate of return basis as all other investment decisions, is essentially a remnant of an obsolete economic practice.

11. The 5 percent rate of return of the stock market is the appropriate rate for this comparison, not 7 percent, because we're talking about a onetime investment over a ten-year period (rather than annual investment over forty-four years). The relative value of tax deferral here is very small.

12. Diana Farrell and Jaana K. Remes, "How the World Should Invest in Energy Efficiency," *McKinsey Quarterly*, July 2008.

13. For the U.S. Department of Energy's comprehensive database of state incentive programs for energy efficiency and other renewable energy initiatives, see www.dsireusa.org.

14. Travis Madsen, et al., "Energy Saved, Dollars Earned: Real World Examples of How Energy Efficiency Can Benefit Maryland Consumers," monograph (Baltimore: Maryland PIRG, February 2008), p. 1.

15. If you invested $38,750 in enough energy efficiency and household energy production to avoid the need for any outside purchases of electricity and fuel, a 16 percent rate of return would exactly equal your annual expenditures on energy today. You can justify spending more, of course, if you do not insist on the 16 percent annual rate of return.

16. *Good Morning America*, "Warren Buffett's Tips."

17. Jessica Jean Martin, "Time to Put the I Back in Investing," *Toronto Star*, 12 February 2009.

18. Thanks to Philippa Rappoport for sharing this wonderful book.

INDEX

ABOUT THE AUTHOR

Michael Shuman is director of research for Cutting Edge Capital, director of research and economic development at the Business Alliance for Local Living Economies (BALLE), and a fellow of the Post Carbon Institute. He holds an AB with distinction in economics and international relations from Stanford University and a JD from Stanford Law School. He has led community-based economic-development efforts across the country and has authored or edited seven previous books, including *The Small-Mart Revolution: How Local Businesses Are Beating the Global Competition* (2006) and *Going Local* (1998). His articles have appeared in *The New York Times*, *The Washington Post*, *The Nation*, *The Weekly Standard*, *Foreign Policy*, *Parade*, and *The Chronicle of Philanthropy*. He lives in Silver Spring, Maryland.

ABOUT POST CARBON INSTITUTE

Post Carbon Institute provides individuals, communities, businesses, and governments with the resources needed to understand and respond to the interrelated economic, energy, environmental, and equity crises that define the twenty-first century.

ABOUT THE FOREWORD AUTHOR

Peter Buffett is an Emmy Award–winning musician as well as a composer, philanthropist, and author of *Life Is What You Make It*, a *New York Times* best seller.

Get excerpts, resources, and more from the

Community Resilience Guides series at

resilience.org

 post carbon institute

"This logo identifies paper that meets the standards of the Forest Stewardship Council®. FSC® is widely regarded as the best practice in forest management, ensuring the highest protections for forests and indigenous peoples."

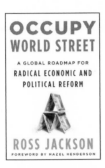

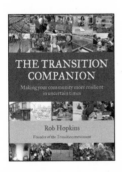

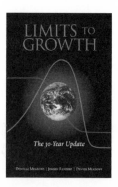
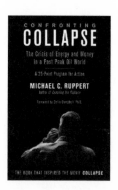